Library of
Davidson College

MIMESIS
From Mirror to Method

Edited and with an introduction
by John D. Lyons
and Stephen G. Nichols, Jr.

MIMESIS
From Mirror to Method,
Augustine to Descartes

Published for Dartmouth College
by the University Press of New England
Hanover and London, 1982

University Press of New England
Brandeis University
Brown University
Clark University
Dartmouth College
University of New Hampshire
University of Rhode Island
Tufts University
University of Vermont

Copyright © 1982 Trustees of Dartmouth College

All rights reserved. Except for brief quotation in critical articles or reviews, this book, or parts thereof, must not be reproduced in any form without permission in writing from the publisher. For further information contact University Press of New England, Hanover, NH 03755.

Printed in the United States of America.

LIBRARY OF CONGRESS CATALOGING IN PUBLICATION DATA

Main entry under title:
Mimesis, from mirror to method, Augustine to Descartes.

"This series of essays grows out of contributions to the first colloquium, held in September 1981, by the Dartmouth Study Group in Medieval and Early Modern Romance Literatures"—Pref.

Includes bibliographical references and index.

1. Mimesis in literature—Addresses, essays, lectures.   I. Lyons, John D., 1946–   II. Nichols, Stephen G.   III. Dartmouth Study Group in Medieval and Early Modern Romance Literatures.
PN47.M55   1982   809   82-40340
ISBN 0-87451-224-1

Contents

Preface	vii
Introduction	1
Eugene Vance Saint Augustine: Language as Temporality	20
Stephen G. Nichols, Jr. Romanesque Imitation or Imitating the Romans?	36
Kevin Brownlee Reflections in the Miroër aus Amoreus: The Inscribed Reader in Jean de Meun's Roman de la Rose	60
Marina Scordilis Brownlee. Autobiography as Self-(Re)presentation: The Augustinian Paradigm and Juan Ruiz's Theory of Reading	71
Robert Hollander Imitative Distance: Boccaccio and Dante	83
Nancy J. Vickers The Body Re-membered: Petrarchan Lyric and the Strategies of Description	100
Murray Krieger Presentation and Representation in the Renaissance Lyric: The Net of Words and the Escape of the Gods	110

Thomas M. Greene   132
Erasmus's "Festina lente": Vulnerabilities of the Humanist Text

Terence Cave   149
The Mimesis of Reading in the Renaissance

John D. Lyons   166
Speaking in Pictures, Speaking of Pictures: Problems of Representation in the Seventeenth Century

Michel Beaujour   188
Speculum, Method, and Self-Portrayal: Some Epistemological Problems

Juan Bautista Avalle-Arce   197
Novelas ejemplares: Reality, Realism, Literary Tradition

Timothy J. Reiss   215
Power, Poetry, and the Resemblance of Nature

Contributors   249

Notes   251

Index   275

Preface

This series of essays grows out of contributions to the first colloquium, held in September 1981, by the Dartmouth Study Group in Medieval and Early Modern Romance Literatures. In calling for a meeting of specialists in historical fields usually studied in isolation from one another, the group intended to remedy the lack of a forum for the sustained examination of romance literatures in their continuity and gradual evolution from the Middle Ages to the early modern period. We hope that in their published form these studies will advance two methodological goals. The first is the growth of historical literary studies across the boundaries that have obscured continuities in form and concept while at the same time rendering difficult the appreciation of real change. At the colloquium, participants demonstrated that a major adjustment is required when the historical territory is so radically redefined. It is stimulating, though not always easy, for Augustinians to work with Cartesians and for specialists in the Renaissance period to answer the questions of scholars in the "renaissance" of the Middle Ages. We are more convinced than ever that the restoration of such dialogue among scholars in this era is not only desirable but very urgent.

Our second goal is the healing of another fracture, one that has appeared more recently between specialists in literary theory or in the theory of criticism and those who work intensively in textual literary history. Our belief is that no theory can be properly grounded without constant reexamination of a broad spectrum of texts and that literary history, for its part, can become aimless unless it formulates its assumptions and justifies its procedures.

In choosing to devote this first colloquium to the concept of *mimesis*, we pay homage to the memory of one of the greatest individual efforts to span the totality of romance literature, Erich Auerbach's *Mimesis*. Yet we recognize that in recent years new approaches to the question of reality represented in language have expanded the significance of the term mimesis. The activities of the production and recognition of likeness by the author/reader appear to us through an intense preoccupation with the human subject performing these actions. Our intention is to profit from this refinement and expansion of the concept in order to reexamine the problems of representation in medieval and early modern literature. From the late antique attempts to read the world as a mirror of a more perfect order, Western thought moved to a time when the mirror was deliberately darkened. A new concept replaced the mirror: the increasingly rigid prescription of the human model for imitation, a concept we know as method.

The present volume is the result of generous collaboration. The response of the distinguished scholars who participated in the colloquium has been heartening. We are confident that this fruitful exchange will affect both scholarship and teaching of literature in the medieval and early modern period. We wish to thank the other members of the study group, Kevin Brownlee, Marina Brownlee, and Nancy Vickers, for their contributions to this project. The organizational work of Suzanne Coonley, of the Comparative Literature program at Dartmouth, has been invaluable both for the colloquium and for the completion of this volume. Dean Hans H. Penner, by his presence at our gathering and by his encouragement of scholarly initiative, has established a climate for our continued work at the college. The Ramon Guthrie Fund provided the material support for the early stages of this venture.

Hanover, New Hampshire JOHN D. LYONS
STEPHEN G. NICHOLS, JR.

MIMESIS
From Mirror to Method

Introduction

Since antiquity, mimesis—imitation—has played a fundamental role in most theories of fine arts and literature. Yet, during this same period, people have argued about the exact definition of mimesis: does it guarantee the objective nature of the work of art, its truth value, or is it also a powerful means for portraying the role of subjectivity in art? Does it help to fix an image of objective reality in the mind of the viewer, to show how the world in sheer actually *really* is? or does it rather demonstrate the performative role of artist and viewer, speaker and reader, in determining reality as idea, as a subjective experience of the world?

For those who see objectivity as its prime function, mimesis constitutes that aspect of the work of art that represents whatever is thought to possess the most concrete reality prior to the activity that brings the work of art into existence: the gesture of painting, of speaking, or of carving. Literature, like the other arts, is therefore an imitation of some reality outside itself. In Western culture, judgments of its values and theories of its production have been largely concerned with the difference between the representing and the represented objects.

The other view of mimesis does not emphasize the independent existence of the object represented, but rather focuses on the gesture of the person or subject who undertakes to displace our attention from the world of pre-existent objects to the work itself. This kind of mimesis, more akin to performance than to representation as traditionally understood, will be judged by a comparison of performances, juxtaposing successive gestures. It will flourish in theater, in the Christian artistic tradition where the *imitatio Christi*, the imitation of Christ, served as a mimetic paradigm, in that branch of the study of human acts that we call methodology, and in the literary concern with reperforming (or with refusing to reperform) the acts of an earlier author.

In light of contemporary concerns with representation and

method, it would be worthwhile to study the interplay of these two polar concepts of mimesis. The task becomes even more compelling, however, because of the frequent neglect of the historical and conceptual link between these concepts. Consider the case of Erich Auerbach, for example, who gave wide currency to the term with his book *Mimesis: The Representation of Reality in Western Literature.* Auerbach, and his contemporary E. R. Curtius, devoted much of their intellectual energies to exploring the nature of representation in the late antique, medieval, and early modern periods; each conceived of mimesis primarily as a formal function of the literary work. Auerbach, for example, thought of literature as a kind of representation that actualized phenomenal reality by means of language. Thus he could argue that the basic impulse of Homeric style sought "to represent phenomena in a fully externalized form, visible and palpable in all their parts, and completely fixed in their spatial and temporal relations."[1]

In this mode, mimesis constituted, for Auerbach, a tight bond between the literary work and its historical context, providing "a concrete insight into social and political reality."[2] At other times, it might take on existential and, consequently, ahistorical overtones, conveying "a sense of existence understood tragically as a man in solitude facing moral decisions."[3] This mode emphasizes the lyrico-descriptive role of the critic-as-interpreter: "Roland loves danger and seeks it; he cannot be frightened. Furthermore, he sets great value upon his prestige. He refuses to grant Ganelon the briefest moment of triumph. And so his first consideration is to point out emphatically, for all to hear, that he, unlike Ganelon in a comparable situation, has not lost composure."[4]

In either case, the locus of critical inquiry and justification for the analysis lay in the study of the formal characteristics of the work of art, particularly style and structure perceived as products of historical consciousness. So E. R. Curtius conceived of the study of literature as working in the "garden of literary forms—the genres or metrical and stanzaic forms; the set formulas or narrative motifs or linguistic devices."[5] One tilled this garden organically and methodically:

Historical investigation has to unravel and penetrate literature. It has to develop analytic methods . . . which will "decompose" the material (after the fashion of chemistry with its reagents) and make its structures visible. . . . Only a literary discipline which proceeds historically and philologically can do justice to the task.[6]

Representation, then, amounted to a certainty that could be exposed unproblematically, almost as a universal law of nature, a scientific fact, provided one took the proper vantage point and employed the correct methodology. In such a scheme, the work of art and its constituent elements served primarily the perceived function of culture: to transmit one stage of human consciousness to another. Literature would thus appear as a reflector in the fullest sense of the term.

Critics viewed the work, in short, as a product of representation, a methodological exemplum. What we miss in these theories might be summed up as the concept of represent*ing*, taken as the active participation of the reader/viewer in the cognition and definition of the work of art. In recent years, mimesis has come to imply not simply depiction of phenomenal reality, but also the incorporation into the figurative act of the problematics of portrayal; that is, how the sheer fact of reproducing the world as sign, the world as language, may expose and call into question precisely those conventions meant to systematize and objectify representation. In other words, we now stress the subjective and intellective role of the reader/viewer in mimetic theory.

We also pay close attention, when studying a text, to the strategies present in it that tend to solicit certain kinds of intellectual cognition while inhibiting others. We think of the work, to paraphrase Michel Foucault, as a representation of representation, and as a definition of the space, both phenomenal and notional, that such representation opens up to us. We see in works of art or literature not simply the *concentration* of ideas that constitute a cultural identity, but also the potential (or real) *dispersion*, the evasions implicit in those same concepts.

In consequence, we do not simply look for and perceive identity, the persons and events that constitute the subjects of mimesis; we also observe dissimilarity, the disappearance of such persons and events, or what amounts to the same thing—their resistance to the identities assigned by such cognitive sciences as history and literary criticism. Textual analysis, then, shows not only the strengths of art, but also—to use the felicitous term highlighted by Thomas Greene's essay here—the vulnerability of the text, a vulnerability arising from the agonistic and conflictual dynamics that occur as language, convention, intention, tradition, and desire all converge in one space.

And so, if we continue to study the products of representation from historical periods, we do not claim to do so—as did Auerbach, Curtius, Spitzer, Vossler, Croce, and others—in order to recover as fully as possible the historical subjects within the consciousness of another age. Without refusing the arduous task of recovering meanings, linguistic nuances, contextual relations, or identifying the layers of cultural and intellectual knowledge within a given work, we also study medieval, Renaissance, or seventeenth-century texts to discover how the works continue to perform the act of representing for us by eliding their own original subjects, thus making us simultaneously conscious of their presence and absence. In other words, if *representation* makes us conscious of the proximity of historical works and cultures, *representing*, paradoxically, stresses their distance. While exposing the ties of convention, knowledge, expertise, cultural assumptions, and ideologies linking past and present, the latter focuses less on the inevitability of such bonds than on their vulnerability.

Representation and representing—not only of reality, but *a fortiori* of the relations between past and present realities—very much correspond, as the papers here gathered will demonstrate, to the preoccupations of philosophers, writers, and artists from Augustine to Descartes. Whether viewed from the Neoplatonic concept of human consciousness as a *minor mundus* reflecting the cognitive and creative processes of a Prime Mover, or from Aristotelian/Cartesian methodological approaches to cognition and representation, mimesis constitutes a crucial and complex problem in medieval and early modern texts just as surely, and often for the same reasons, as it does in texts of later periods.

Eugene Vance, for example, dealing with Saint Augustine as

the thinker who "inaugurated the semiological consciousness of the Christian West," shows how "all of Augustine's endeavors in metaphysics, epistemology, and exegesis coincide with a relentless effort to define the functions and limits of human language." To this end, Vance explores the ways by which Augustine conceived of language's capacity to represent the temporal world, or, more precisely, temporality itself.

He discusses Augustine's conception of how language, by inscribing temporality within discourse, might be seen as differentiating speech in the phenomenal world from its divine counterpart. Language itself, particularly formal discourse, might be seen as providing an image of the creation story. From this perspective, the divine world would be conceived as perfect, without ambiguity or temporal limitation; that is, an unambiguous speech, simultaneous rather than sequential, and without sense.

Human speech, in contrast, incorporated a disjunction between past and present—the past of origins, of conception—and the present of execution; the past of writing, and the present of reading. This disjunction could be conceived as reproducing in the paradigm of human communication a continual image of the distance separating man from the original conception of the species articulated by the divinity in creation, particularly Genesis 1:26. Since thought precedes speech, speech represents the futurity of thought, and thought itself constitutes the past of discourse. In this way, postlapsarian humans might be seen as constantly in motion between the past of conception and the future of execution, for example, "I am going to do this, now." An atemporal present, motionless and enduring, disappeared from human experience as a consequence of the Fall. All these conditions of temporality, including the past/future dichotomy that separates a writer from his audience, contribute to the arbitrariness of the verbal sign, Augustine holds, and thus render problematic anything approaching unambiguous understanding among humans. Polysemia and complexity in discourse reflect the distance separating the world from its creator.

Stephen G. Nichols's article, as its title indicates, challenges the assumption that imitation in Romanesque art and architecture is merely the unsuccessful recreation of the monuments of Roman antiquity. This assumption, from which the very terms *roman* and *romanesque* are derived, cannot account for the quantity and the specific forms of invention during the eleventh and twelfth centuries. In Nichols's view the Romanesque does not function by implicit intertextual reference—as it does, for instance, in Renaissance or neoclassical texts—but by explicit incorporation of earlier texts or artistic objects in order to create an intratextual dialogue between model and imitation. A detailed analysis of the Cross of Lothar, a processional cross of the early eleventh century, shows the incorporation of concrete symbols from earlier reigns, those of Augustus and of Lothar II, and the careful arrangement of both sides of the cross to provide an ethical and philosophical subtext—in a quite literal sense—for the historical face. The relationship between history and religion through the symbolism of the trinity on the back of the cross is accounted for by the philosophical trinitarianism of the Irish Neoplatonist Eriugena. This doctrine, based on the passage from essence through power to operation, provides a means of understanding human intelligence and creativity as these mirror, in their process, the much greater and anterior divine being. Of capital importance to Eriugena is a *cogito* by which man becomes aware of the power and the limits of that power that characterize us after the Fall. Mankind, by participating intersubjectively and collectively in an attempt to conceive some of the knowledge lost to us in the Fall, could discover the powers of creation and of the subject's inability to create *ex nihilo*. Such reflection thus forces a reassessment of the project of creating as an independent subject. The two successive movements require self-awareness within history. Thus romanesque imitation is not a failed imitation of the classical model but a system of symbols based on the understanding of human imitation of the divine.

Kevin Brownlee also speaks of the way in which medieval literature appropriates paradigms of the Roman cultural heritage in order to represent them in a transformed context. In Jean de Meung's *Roman de la Rose*, literature may be seen as providing a paradigm of the means by which the medieval present demonstrated its continuity with, and control of, the past. The concept involved reinforcing the authority of the myths of the past as originary constructs that established the power of the word to manage reality; present authors inherited that power. At the same time, they needed to demonstrate that their fabulatory skill equaled, or even surpassed in certain ways, that of their predecessors.

In the case of Jean de Meung, a late thirteenth-century writer, Brownlee shows how skillfully he inscribes representative portions from Roman authors, such as Sallust and Ovid, into his own text as a means of demonstrating how the vernacular language—the *present* form of discourse as opposed to the Latin *past*—could incorporate and extend the insights provided by the older, authoritative works. In his "Mirror of/for Lovers," as he calls his work, Jean de Meung anticipates Dante by appropriating an authoritative status for his work—by showing how it could internalize, through a system of reflectors, classical authorities—in a manner hitherto reserved for Latin authors. Representation, for Jean de Meung, includes representing Latin *poetae*, so that one reads them through the optic of the new work. Jean de Meung thus teaches that reading, like writing, privileges a mimetic process of re-presenting. When he claims, in the course of the work, to be a *poeta*, he may do so justifiably, having raised the status of the vernacular *poète* to the same rank attained by his Latin predecessors.

Within the context of the Spanish literary tradition, Marina Brownlee shows how the Archpriest of Hita, Juan Ruiz, in his *Libro de Buen Amor* (Book of Good Love), focuses on the problems of reading and interpretation by simultaneously appealing to and questioning the paradigm of spiritual autobiography given by Saint Augustine in his *Confessions*. Augustine offered an imitative model that a hypothetical ideal reader might follow to achieve an eventual conversion, thus replicating Augustine's own spiritual trajectory. Juan Ruiz transposes this model into a polysemous and ironic one in which we read in the subject's exploits, not the compelling clarity and dignity of divine purpose, but the arbitrariness and opacity whereby events in the world are resistant to the kind of interpretation proposed by Augustine.

In this way, the *Libro* maintains a bifocal tension between the pious postulation of an ideal reader à la Augustine and the recognition that he does not and cannot exist. Representation in the *Libro* thus sets up the paradigm of an ideal reader that the reading act, the representing, forces the reader to reject and reformulate.

In dramatizing the Augustinian paradox, the *Libro* distinguishes between autobiography as an imitative model for salvation and autobiography as a mimetic parable of the human condition that poetically corrects Augustine by offering a confession without conversion.

Robert Hollander, too, demonstrates the insights to be gained by examining the way in which mastertexts "read" one another in the Middle Ages. Like Juan Ruiz's reading of Augustine, Boccaccio's specular confrontation with Dante's *Commedia*, in the *Decameron*, offers another example of the reprocessing of an earlier text, in which the earlier is seen as a venerated but not infallible authority by the later text.

Taking two of the *novelle* in the *Decameron*, I,1 and VI,10, Hollander demonstrates hitherto unremarked inscriptions or citations of Dante's *Commedia* that place the two works in a sharply specular relationship. In outlining his oxymoronic notion of "imitative *distance*," Hollander asks precisely why Boccaccio should choose to reprocess Dante's work in the way he does. To pursue this question, Hollander argues, is to gain a clearer sense of the nature of representation in each work, independent of one another, while at the same time increasing our awareness of the continual effort in the Middle Ages to define and practice a form of representation that would provide the most accurate depiction of reality.

Hollander shows quite perceptively that the *Decameron* utilizes what we would see as process-oriented mimesis to reperform Dante's text in order to expose its lack of objectivity: its failure to represent the world with sufficient verisimilitude. The *Decam-*

eron, itself, then attempts to correct the perceived failing. Hollander thus argues, at least implicitly, that specular confrontation of texts within texts provided the means by which medieval authors evaluated and refined the representative process. This in turn shows that the exemplum or imitative model still flourished as the principal critical tool in the Middle Ages, not yet replaced, as it would be in a subsequent age, by the analytic criticism we associate with Cartesian methodology.

Nancy Vickers studies mimesis in the work of Boccaccio's contemporary Petrarch. In addition to its apparent roots in the epideictic tradition of ceremonial praise, Petrarch's description of Laura appears, in Vickers's account, rooted in a strategy of defense against the threatening appearance of the woman-deity. The description of Laura in a series of comparisons to precious objects and substances is shown to be produced by the interplay of two descriptive metaphors for the speaker himself, whose myths of predilection, clearly and textually located in Ovid's *Metamorphosis*, are those of Narcissus and of Actaeon. One mythic figure is destroyed by the discovery of sameness while the other encounters a fatal otherness. Like Actaeon, the Petrarchan speaker-protagonist finds himself transformed by the vision of Diana/Laura into a stag, the object of the hunt and no longer a hunter. Central to this transformation, and to Vickers's reading, is the act of sprinkling, or scattering *spargere*, as it appears both in the narrative and in the poet's description of his song. The description of Laura does not coalesce into a unitary vision of a physically whole person. Object, song, and singer are all scattered. The fragmentation imposed upon the mythic Actaeon is therefore applied by the more self-conscious or forewarned Petrarchan speaker to both figures in the couple. His own sacrifice of his substance (*me ne scarno*) is the necessary counterpart to his activity of incarnating Laura in words, but he parries her power as a forbidden vision by dismembering her as well. Representation is thus, in Petrarch, insistently presented as a process, one that cannot be successfully completed or closed, cannot cohere into a smooth mirroring of an external reality. Instead, the making present, the re-presenting of the vision of Laura, depends on the constant activity of a subject, either the speaker-poet or the reader, presented with the pieces of a voyeuristic puzzle.

With Vickers's account of Petrarch's description we move into a conception of mimesis that stresses the nonobjective aspect of representation, even in cases where the object represented belongs in some way to an external, visible reality. The "outside" is conceived as being the ongoing and often dangerous product of the writing and reading of texts. The increasingly independent and subjective aspect of mimesis is further generalized in the late Renaissance and up to the seventeenth century. More and more, in other words, the mimetic balance tilts toward the performing or methodic subject, whose own account of this imitative activity and whose own responsibility for that activity are increasingly pronounced.

Murray Krieger shows how this performing mimetic subject works in the English Renaissance lyric to control the linguistic dynamics in poems by Raleigh, Campion, Shakespeare, Ben Jonson, and Sir Philip Sidney. This performing subject calls into question the system of conventionally accepted meanings it inherits. On the one hand, it destabilizes meanings by collapsing differences into apparent identity, while on the other it elides independent identities, "so that there is no single, undifferentiated verbal self."

Krieger sees such "duplicitous manipulations of words" as an attempt by the poet to achieve a representational power in language hitherto unattained. And yet this very straining to achieve new representational goals anticipates failure. Poets like Sidney conjure the love object only to discover the impossibility of objective re-presentation. "Words," their poems show, "are empty and belated counters because it is their nature to seek to refer to what is elsewhere and has occurred earlier."

Still, the very power of the name of a beloved, like Sidney's Stella, shows how the performative power of language may overcome this belatedness. It may make language not a secondary representer, but a primary celebrant of a presence, the linguistic and poetic force of the beloved's name in all its polysemous potential. In this sense, language recuperates its mimetic power and becomes truly presentational. And so the poet weaves his verbal network, with the shuttlecock incessantly darting to and fro between failed representation and satisfying presentation.

Returning to the continent, we find a slightly different aspect of the concept of representation through reenactment and through the assumption of personal authorial responsibility in the text of Erasmus discussed by Thomas Greene. Greene undertakes a quest for an organizational principle for Erasmus's vast, meandering, and constantly expanding—in successive editions—collection of essays on ancient epigrammatic expressions, the *Adagia* (first edition, 1500). Here mimesis is not the representation of the material world but the attempt to reproduce the history of a phrase.

By taking as the basis of this textual analysis the adage that Erasmus himself called "royal," *Festina lente* ("Make haste slowly"), Greene sets forth an emblem of his own enterprise as well as that of Erasmus. Carefully and slowly Green circles the text, expositing now one and now another of the accounts Erasmus gives of the origin and meaning of this adage. Then Greene sets forth his fundamental challenge to Terence Cave's position in the *Cornucopian Text* (1979) a position that Greene associates with "Derridian dissemination, with its deteriorating dispersal, diaspora, metempsychosis, oriented toward a destructuring future." The Humanist dissemination, actively undertaken by Erasmus as the expositor of a hidden textual knowledge and advanced materially by his printer Aldus, is on the contrary a dissemination that attempts tirelessly to respect an origin. The paradox of the Humanist mission is therefore fully displayed in the *Adagia* as a tension between expansion and contraction. The jewellike, impenetrable, timeless visual symbol, the hieroglyphic, protected by the Egyptian priest, is admired by Erasmus. The adage itself, difficult and compact, is collected into the treasury that constitutes the body of the *Adagia*. Yet the adage, already more open than the hieroglyphic to general comprehension, already removed by its linguistic quality from a direct possession of its referent, and more dependent on circumstance and adaptation for its meaning, is expanded still more and rendered more historically contingent by the creation of the adage-essay. Erasmus as a Humanist works to open the kernel of meaning, expanding what had been condensed, and gives mysteries to the vulgar. The Humanist thereby accepts history, for he works to bring the secrets of the past to the present, despite the dangers of such divulgation. The central principle of the adage-essay, in Greene's view, is an "*etiology* . . . a retrospective explanation of textual coming-into-being." The Humanist here performs a mimesis of textual history through the shaping of his own text, stylizing, says Greene, the course of history much as a novel stylizes the world of a real society. Greene directs this description against the perpetual deferral of meaning found by Cave in Erasmian texts, a deferral in which Greene finds the projection of a twentieth-century demand for ultimate closure. The vulnerability here ascribed to the Humanist text is the acceptance of contingency, the acceptance of the knowledge that its own detection or construction of an origin may be surpassed by subsequent historical interpretations and constructions.

Cave, in his contribution to the present volume, prefers to describe this contingency in terms of a specific role assigned to the reader during a period that runs roughly from Erasmus through Pascal. During the sixteenth and early seventeenth centuries a generative, open-ended practice of reading and a particular insistence on the representation of the reader himself come into prominence. This paradigm contrasts with an earlier imitative and a later representational paradigm. In the earlier period, Cave finds that both Scholastic and Humanist studies of discourse give low priority to the reader. They subordinate the reader either by giving rules for recovering the original meaning allegorically or by Humanist philological and contextual commentary. The permanence of the ancient text takes clear precedence over the local and transient figure of the reader. Secular rhetoric in Humanist practice was directed at the formation of writers and speakers, not of readers. And in Neoplatonist theory the listener is merely filled with a supernatural enthusiasm communicated by the poet. Hence, argues Cave, "reading is a mimetic act which seeks to restore the totality and integrity of the original discursive performance."

In the sixteenth century, however, the act of reading (or more broadly speaking, of reception) is itself more frequently represented and given greater weight in relation to the original text. In Marguerite de Navarre's *Heptaméron* the stories are less important than the discussion among the members of the audience. Similarly in Erasmus's *Convivium religiosum* a dialogue of readers takes on a life that goes considerably beyond the texts discussed. These Renaissance readers differ from the reader as he appears in the *Ovide moralisé*, where the allegorization performed by the narrator seems an external accretion. They also differ from the incorporation of the lover as a personification of the reader in the *Roman de la Rose*, where this personification clearly guides the reader by linear progression through the text. By contrast, the first meeting between Pantagruel and Panurge in Rabelais's *Pantagruel* does not provide the reader with a specific model of interpretation and obliges us to take the initiative by inserting the episode into its tacit historical relationship with a recurrent motif in the *Odyssey*. The Erasmian or anti-Ciceronian position shifts the emphasis from universal nature to the individual nature of the reader, who is the agent of assemblage of texts into meaningful patterns.

Erasmus is still more constrained by respect for the original text, transformed not in the moment of reading but in the moment of rewriting, than is Montaigne. With the latter's *Essais* free quotation, a practice that gives the modern author a wholly new status in regard to the ancient text, replaces the glossing of the Scholastics. Montaigne objects to glossing, not because it deviates from the original text, but because it does not avow its deviation and instead claims to be simply a perfect restatement. Montaigne not only recognizes his deviation from the intention of the texts from which he takes his quotations but insists on the particular kind of reading that his own example will require. Addressing the reader directly and representing the intended audience of his text as a member of his family or as a friend, Montaigne emphasizes the need for a correspondence between the possibilities offered by the text and the needs or desires of the reader. By quoting without acknowledgment, rephrasing an author, and giving an entirely new context to what he has taken from an ancient text, Montaigne gives the reader a model of how to read the *Essais*. In order to be properly read, argues Cave, the *Essais* must be "misread, contested, dismantled, deformed and reformed in the name of a new subject." This is what Pascal does, imitating the gesture of Montaigne in a way that fulfills the latter's practice by a total modification of intention and content.

After Pascal, Cave sees two complementary but opposing positions on representation in the text. One, the avatar of the generative text of the Renaissance, but without the Renaissance insistence on the moral or practical function, draws attention to the discursive performance itself but admits an inability to move outside the text to show anything else. The other position, which is the neoclassical paradigm analyzed by Reiss, suppresses reference to its own functioning, its own performance, and pretends to be a transparent representation of the world at large.

This transition between the Renaissance emphasis on the role of the interpreter and the neoclassical "transparency" of representation is the subject of John Lyons's essay. Dealing specifically with the way in which seventeenth-century French authors use painting as an episode in fiction or as a metaphor in philosophical texts, Lyons argues that the viewers of paintings—like the readers described by Cave—are emphasized far more than the objective or concrete scene depicted on the canvas. But in Madame de Lafayette's novels (1670 and 1678) and in the contemporaneous writings of Jansenist philosophers Nicole and Arnauld, the freedom of the viewer to interpret what he or she sees is limited both by inherent psychological and intellectual weakness and by the corrective method that can be applied to overcome or mitigate that defect. Lafayette evokes a world in which the difficulty of direct verbal communication leads to the use of a complex series of painted images through which the principal characters attempt to bridge the gap between minds. But the representational act fails, for no visual sign can convey what is internal and abstract.

Parallels appear between this failure and the Jansenist denunciation of the habit of defining ideas as "images painted in our brain," together with the artistic vogue of anamorphic paintings in the sixteenth and seventeenth centuries. Anamorphoses are images that appear distorted or completely abstract unless they are seen from a narrowly defined and unusually situated standpoint. Lyons argues that both Jansenist logic and anamorphic paintings stress concurrently the subjective aspect of knowledge and the necessity of finding a proper method for looking at and defining things. Lafayette's work appears therefore as the negative indication of the need for a positive method as it appears in logic and perspective. The novel, Jansenist logic, and anamorphosis support Lyons's contention that representation is subordinated to the execution of certain acts by the painter and, especially, by the viewer. Hence the importance of assuming the proper stance toward images in a specific method of viewing.

Michel Beaujour's article on the Renaissance self-portrait describes this movement from rhetoric to methodology in the modern scientific sense. Like Cave, Lyons, and Reiss, Beaujour describes the dismemberment of an epistemological continuum or compromise which had permitted ethics, epistemology, rhetoric, political theory, and natural history to enjoy considerable discursive cohesion.

This change appears in the "perversion"—as Beaujour calls it—of rhetoric into a tool of discovery, where previously it had been a form of "storage-retrieval" system with which to find the proper topics or commonplaces to fill one's discourse. Despite early views of Montaigne's *Essais* as a mere accumulation of commonplaces or as a *speculum*, Beaujour argues that its emphasis on the gesture (all Montaigne's doubt, he notes, is *doubting*) makes the essay a complex heuristic device, but one that is caught between two poles: the representation of a pre-existing entity on one hand and the creation or invention (in the modern sense) of an entity in the course of the writing itself. The self-portrait is thus the kind of text that, from Montaigne through Descartes and Bacon, confers upon the author a kind of generative authority based on a self-reflection that becomes progressively more acute and disruptive until, as we see in Reiss's article, the seventeenth century imposes authority to the exclusion of self-reflection. The violence of this emphasis on the authoritative transparency of representation through "correct" method sunders much of ethical and religious thought from the currents that lead toward the dominant aspects of the Enlightenment.

While Beaujour examines the Renaissance rejection of dialectic form in favor of the experience of the cognitive process itself, Juan Bautista Avalle-Arce's essay on the *Novelas ejemplares* (1613) treats Cervantes's exploitation of dialogue (dialectic) form as a means of exploring the cognitive process in terms of fiction.

The major contribution of Cervantes to the concept and practice of literary mimesis is represented here by a discussion of the several Cervantine novellas which constitute ironic permutations of the canonical construction of the picaresque novel. The principal variations on this form are, first, the liberation of the characters from the determinism that accounts for all aspects of the picaro's existence and, second, the institution of a dual viewpoint. This latter development is cast in terms of a dialogic form, as reflected by the very titles of individual novellas, for example, *The Two Damsels*, *Rinconete and Cortadillo*, and, most explicitly, the *Dialogue of the Dogs*.

It is this last and most problematic ("baroque") of the *Novelas ejemplares* that Avalle-Arce singles out, devoting to it his most extended analysis. Within the entire collection of novellas this concluding tale constitutes, on the one hand, Cervantes's boldest exploration into the representation of reality in literature—its parameters. At the same time, however, it constitutes a skeptical commentary on the problematic nature of reality itself.

A balance of skepticism about representation and faith in method apparent in the texts studied by Beaujour and Lyons yields to a situation described by Timothy Reiss as a monolithic, universal rationality of representation. Method—in Reiss's view—has become so entrenched by the mid-seventeenth century that discussion of the distance separating writer and reader, model and imitation, are no longer current. Political insistence on the foundation of a single, universal order as expressed in the codification of a single, acceptable usage in language (the king's language, the language of the Académie, or of the Royal Society) unites author and reader in the assumption of a single view of reality. The "cornucopian" textuality analyzed by Cave and the sense of the historical contingency in description of origin that appears in the Humanists are no longer conceivable in a society in which responsibility and intention pass from the reader into a monolithic social definition of universal reason.

Reiss traces the evolution of a sixteenth-century commonplace of political writing—the idea that corruption of language is concomitant with, and perhaps responsible for, the decay of civil society—into a major assumption of philosophers, aestheticians, and poets. Both Bacon and Descartes claim that general laws of reason and human nature can be discovered and that such laws can be assumed into a method through which we represent reality in language. The syntax of such a language, which would show the agreement between the reasoning process of the human mind and the reality of the world around us, corresponds to the claims of the neoclassical poet to present a *verisimilar* fiction. Such verisimilitude, Reiss argues, does not consist of the presentation of recognizable events from the world of everyday reality but in the connections among the events within the theatrical world. Tragedians in the seventeenth century aim at the performance or mimesis of the ideal universal reason to which the poet, the audience, and the theoretician assented.

Such a fictive embodiment of the claim of universal reason is a performance of an ideal model, just as the method proposed by Bacon and Descartes is the performance, in science, engineering, and metaphysical enquiry, of an ideal universal reason. This universal model replaces the mimesis of individual figures of authority (for example, the figure of an *auctor* or classical author) as transmitted by literary or scriptural tradition. By positing that nature and reason are one, the literature of the seventeenth century can pretend, not only to expound nature or to refer to it, but to function like nature. Poets should defer to Aristotle, not because of his historical status, but because he had described the universal, atemporal rules of reason and nature. In this vision, totally opposed to the historical contingency of the Humanists as described by Greene, Reiss finds that the concepts of justice and beauty are fused in an atemporal emergence of the underlying rationality of the world.

Reiss proposes the view that with certain relatively minor qualifications the conception of representation in Western literature has remained the same from the seventeenth century until the present. Certainly the main current of literary fiction has assumed a political and moral framework sufficiently widespread to justify claims to proper representation of the "real" and to distinguish the category "literature," with its claims to unite general and particular truth, from other discourses that represent either abstract conceptions or fragmentary experience. Meanwhile, the means and effects of such representation have gone largely ignored in criticism and literary history.

The conflation of what we have called the two aspects of mimesis, the representational and imitational or methodic, during the classical and romantic periods, may explain the twentieth century's rediscovery of the problematic nature both of representation and of method. Because representation seemed for so long to be a concept based on a natural and commonsense activity, one that did not call into question the act or responsibility of a person, the discovery that representation is an act that imposes determinacy and closure has come with almost explosive force. The discovery of the deferral of meaning may be, as Greene points out, the corollary of a modern need for closure, something that is therefore located within readers and not in the nature of some atemporal logic of representation. The rediscovery of intertextual creativity in the twentieth century can be considered a return to the earlier acceptance of the imitative function in writing, the relationship between one author and another or between text and text. The recrudescence of debate in the realm of methods of reading can also be considered in some way a realization, similar to that of Molière's bourgeois gentleman, that our "natural" activity of reading can be described in terms of our imitation of (or rejection of) the model provided by other readers.

All of these contemporary concerns have in common an awareness that literature cannot be considered simply or even primarily as representation of a common, external reality. They point to an understanding that the active relationship to the prior activities of others, a domain that is the object of the theory of imitation, has to be taken into account as we study the ways in which literature represents. These twin faces of mimesis are probably best epitomized by the Petrarchan myth of Actaeon, as Vickers describes it: the discovery of the world around us (the represented world) within our own struggle to represent it (our own performance). In the Petrarchan moment of fragile equilibrium between the act of representing—never completed—and the object represented—never fully actualized—mimesis is most irritatingly and intriguingly set forth as central to the project and tradition of the romance literatures.

Eugene Vance

Saint Augustine
Language as Temporality

Surely it is not an exaggeration to claim that Saint Augustine inaugurated what we may call the semiological consciousness of the Christian West.¹ All of Augustine's endeavors in metaphysics, epistemology, and exegesis coincide with a relentless effort to define the functions and limits of human language. Many empirical features of verbal signs, whether pronounced, written, or merely thought, gave rise to analogies that nourished Augustine's speculations about man's relationship to himself, to people and things, and to God. My specific concern here is to explore Augustine's thoughts about the manner in which language may be said to reflect the temporal world, or, more precisely, temporality itself. I should like to expose a bundle of ideas that subsisted in medieval culture, with varying degrees of prominence and explicitness, until the rise of Humanism.²

To begin, let us recall some of Augustine's thoughts about the nature of time itself. Such thoughts are expressed most succinctly in a famous passage in Book 11 of the *Confessions*, and I shall summarize these thoughts briefly and uncritically.³ Augustine says that even though God created the temporal world, God remains eternally present to himself as pure Being beyond time. The creation exists in time, but what we call the past and future of that creation cannot properly be said to "exist": only the indivisible present exists, and the past and future may be apprehended only in and through that present. Thus, if we commonly speak of past and future times, these are not really objectively extant times; rather, they are experienced subjectively or intramentally, that is,

Saint Augustine: Language as Temporality 21

as moments of presence *in* the mind and *of* the mind to itself. For the mind has the special power both to make the past "present" through the faculty of memory and to make the future "present" as expectation. Time is apprehended and measured subjectively when the mind "distends" itself in the present toward the past, which is made present by means of the memory, and toward the future, which is made present to the mind as expectation. The mind apprehends time as a synthesis of these three presences within itself. Therefore, if beings may be said to move in time, their movement is not time itself; nor is time measured by their actual movement. The measuring of time is an act of synthesis that occurs wholly within the mind.

We shall see that it is strikingly characteristic that Augustine's physical theories of time and movement in Book 11 of the *Confessions* rest on concrete observations, not of bodies moving in space, but rather of speech (in this instance, poetic speech) unfolding as a sequence of measurable, vocal sounds. When we recite a verse of poetry, he says, we measure the length of its syllables by comparing the long syllables to the short ones. But how, he asks, can we measure a sound except by hearing it in the present? Yet, once the whole sound has been heard, it no longer exists. How, then, can it be compared to a *second* sound that, again, will no longer exist in the present when *it* is complete?

> In so far as sense perception is clear, I measure the long syllable by the short one, and I perceive that it is exactly twice as long. But when one syllable sounds after another, and if the first is short and the second long, how will I retain the short syllable and how will I apply it to the long syllable while measuring it, so as to find that the latter is twice as long? For the long syllable does not begin to sound until the short syllable itself has ceased to sound. Do I measure the long syllable itself while it is present, since I do not measure it until it is completed? Yet its completion is its passing away. Therefore, what is it that I measure? Where is the long syllable that I measure? Both of them have sounded, have flown off, have passed away, and now they are not.[4]

Although it may seem surprising that Augustine elects language as the empirical foundation for his physics of movement and time, we should recall that Augustine considered verbal signifiers—*voces*—to be corporeal things, even though what they signify is not corporeal but mental.[5] Moreover, Augustine's attitudes toward things and words (as things) are identical. Since the knowledge of a thing is different from (and preferable to) the thing itself, things are to be treated as signs. Things themselves cannot be known directly by the mind, and knowledge of things must pass through signs: "All doctrine concerns either things or signs, but things are learned through signs" (*DDC.* 1.i.2). Augustine's tendency to treat things, not for themselves, but as signs, remained a habit of medieval culture during the centuries that followed.[6]

In Book 11 of the *Confessions*, Augustine illustrates his analysis of the soul's apprehension of time by describing what happens when we recite a psalm:

I am about to recite a psalm that I know. Before I begin, my expectation extends over the entire psalm. Once I have begun, my memory extends over as much of it as I shall separate off and assign to the past. The life of this action of mine is distended into memory by reason of the part I am about to speak. But attention is actually present and that which was to be is borne along by it so as to become past. The more this is done and done again, so much the more is memory lengthened by a shortening of expectation, until the entire expectation is exhausted. When this is done, the whole action is completed and passes into memory. What takes place in the whole psalm takes place also in each of its parts and each of its syllables. (*Conf.* 11. xxviii. 38)

Augustine's analysis here may be a bit plodding, but what follows is a stunning leap by analogy beyond the knowledge of corporeal things to that of the divine:

The same thing holds for a longer action, of which perhaps the psalm is a small part. The same thing holds for man's entire life, the parts of which are all the man's action. The same thing holds throughout the whole age of the sons of man, the parts of which are the lives of all men. (*Conf.* 11. xxviii. 38)

And, just as Augustine's mind is capable of holding present within itself the whole psalm that he will recite as a temporal sequence, so too the mind of God knows the totality of time as pure presence to itself. God's knowledge occurs without divisions in the divine mind, without any process of differentiation, and this power distinguishes God's mind from man's:

> Far be it that in such [mortal] wise you should know future and past. Far, far more wonderfully; far more deeply do you know them! It is not as emotions are changed or senses filled up by expectations of words to come and memory of those past in one who sings well-known psalms or hears a familiar psalm. Not so does it befall you who are unchangeably eternal, that is, truly eternal, the creator of minds. Therefore, just as in the beginning you have known heaven and earth without change in your knowledge, so too "in the beginning you made heaven and earth" without any difference in your activity. (*Conf.* 11. xxxi. 41)

If divine knowledge of temporality occurs, unlike man's, without division or difference within the knowing mind, so, too, God's eternal Word, unlike human speech, produces itself without any succession of syllables unfolding in time:

> So you call us to understand the Word, God, with you, O God, which is spoken eternally, and in which all things are spoken eternally. Nor is it the case that what was spoken is ended and that another thing is said, so that all things may at length be said: all things are spoken once and forever. . . . Therefore no part of your Word gives place to another or takes the place of another, since it is truly eternal and immortal. (*Conf.* 11. vii. 7)

It is the corporeal nature of the creation that necessitates our knowledge of God as three separate persons with three separate names that must be pronounced in three separate utterances:

> But I would like to affirm plainly that the Father and the Son and the Holy Spirit, being of one and the same substance—God the Creator, the omnipotent Trinity—are inseparable in their works, but it is the creation, so greatly dissimilar and corporeal, which constrains them to become separate in their manifestation, just as, with our words, which are of course corporeal sonorities, the Father and the Son and the Holy Spirit cannot be named except by fractions of duration proper to each, and clearly separated and occupied by the syllables of each word. Indeed, in the substance in which they subsist, the three are one, Father

and Son and Holy Spirit, . . . free of all temporal movement and of all intervals in space and time. But in my words, "Father," "Son" and "Holy Spirit" are separated, and it is impossible to name them together, and in writing they occupy different spaces.[7]

Augustine's metaphysics of the Word stood in opposition to Epicurean and Lucretian materialism, which was purely stochastic. Lucretius believed that the universe was a cataract of falling seeds or atoms. Existing things arise when a *clinamen* occurs, that is, when atoms bump each other because of their difference in mass and suddenly diverge from their vertical axis of fall and form temporary configurations, like eddies or whirlpools: these are the forms of created things.[8] Since atoms are also letters, these configurations also produce words or meanings. However, such things, like their meanings, convey no divine intentionality, no ultimate *telos*, and they disperse forever when the eddy caused by their clinamen expends itself and its atoms resume their fall in the cataract.

As opposed to the divine Word, which is always without difference with regard to itself, human speech unfolds as a succession of different sounds, and the capacity of these sounds to signify is dependent solely on social convention (*DDC*. 2. i. 1–2). This inherent arbitrariness of the verbal sign is a result of God's punishment of man's pride in the catastrophe of Babel. Moreover, this same arbitrariness applies to the relationship between letters and the sounds that they signify:

But because vibrations in the air soon pass away and remain no longer than they sound, signs of words have been constructed by means of letters. Thus words are shown to the eyes, not in themselves, through certain signs which stand for them. These signs could not be common to all peoples because of the sin of human dissension which arises when one people seizes the leadership for itself. A sign of this pride is that tower erected in the heavens where impious men deserved that not only their minds but also their voices should be dissonant. (*DDC*. 1. ii. 1)

It is only by common consent among societies after Babel that a given sound may signify something, and Augustine considers the verbal sign to be a basic social contract: a "pact," to use his term (*Conf.* 1. xiii. 22). The laws of this pact should not be allowed to become a tyrannical force. Thus, Augustine decries the readiness of a Roman crowd to go into an uproar if an orator drops his "h" when he utters the word *homo* in a discourse before them (*Conf.* 1. xviii. 29).

Clearly, Augustine's insistence upon the arbitrary nature of the bond between signifier and signified went against the grain of that tradition that is commonly called "Cratylism," after the opinion of one of Socrates' interlocutors, who held that words are in some obscure way replicas of the substances that they name.[9] Such doctrines had persisted in movements distinct from Platonism—for example, in Stoic theories of language.[10]

Augustine's belief in the conventional nature of the sign also set him apart from tendencies in Jewish thought to stress the necessity of relationships between Hebrew words and the things they name. The Hebrew root (*dabher*) gives rise not only to the infinitive "to speak" (*ledabher*) but also to the substantive "word" (*davaar*) and to the identical substantive, "thing" (*davaar*). Jewish midrashic tradition situates the origin of the world, in the words of the Torah, "conceived as a textual object of pure anteriority and pure genetic power. As such, it signifies in two ways, as a discourse, and by its visible shape; its letters, words, and layout operating as an iconic and symbolic sign system."[11] If, in the beginning, God spoke the Creation through the Torah, it is only through the subsequent words (*dvaarim*) of the Law and the Prophets that the history of Israel will materialize as events.

As we might expect, Augustine himself was intrigued by the problem of explaining how God, whose Word is eternal and without difference, is said in Genesis to have created the temporal world by his verbal commands. Did God say "Let there be light" in the eternity of his Word, or did he say it in time?[12] Augustine resolves this enigma by suggesting that the Creation occurred in four phases. First, there was the creation in God's Word (in *Verbo Dei*), where all things were not fully created but were spiritual and eternal; second, there was the creation in the elements of the world, where all things to come in time were created simultaneously; third, all things were created in time, each thing in its own time, and no longer simultaneously (*De Gen.* 9. x. 17); fourth, all things were created in seeds (in *semenibus*), by which Augustine apparently means the process of material causality and engendering. At the same time that God first created the light, which was a purely spiritual light, he created the angels, and God continues to illuminate these as he speaks. To lesser, temporal beings such as man, God speaks through the mediation of the creation, whether spiritually (as in dreams) or corporeally, as in forms and voices (*De Gen.* 8. xxvii. 49). After the fall, God walked in the garden in the evening, leaving his light behind him, and henceforth spoke to men by things of the creation (*De Gen.* 11. xxxiii. 43).

Hence, Augustine believed that the meaning of the language of the Scripture is strictly autonomous from the temporal, verbal signs by which it is expressed, and such atemporal meaning must be grasped by the reader in a direct process of illumination from within. For this reason, the Scripture may be translated from one historical language to another. Thus, if Moses first wrote the words of Genesis in Hebrew,

he wrote them and he passed away. He passed away from this world from you [God] to you, and he is not now here before me. If he were, I would catch hold of him, and I would ask him, and through you I would beseech him to make these things plain to me. I would lay my body's ears to the sounds breaking forth from his mouth. If he spoke Hebrew, in vain would his voice strike upon my senses, and none of it would touch my mind. But if he spoke in Latin, I would know what he said.

Yet how would I know whether he spoke the truth? Even if I knew this, would I know it from him? Truly, within me, within the dwelling place of thought, Truth, neither Hebrew nor Greek nor Latin nor barbaric speech, without mouth or tongue as organ, and without the noise of syllables, would say to me, "He speaks the truth." (*Conf.* 11. iii. 5)

If Augustine dwells on the transiency of spoken sounds in order to speak dialectically of a transcendental Word where the bondages of time and space do not pertain, his search for this Word was born of immense personal suffering and loss in his relationships with people—whether as friend, lover, son, and, finally, as the father himself of a son whom he loved but outlived. Since biographical events in the *Confessions* are often construed as events of Augustine's life in language, it is entirely in character with Augustine that he should first ponder the transiency of verbal signifiers through the despair caused by the death of a close childhood friend shortly after Augustine's first appointment as a teacher of rhetoric—that most vain of sciences—in Thagaste. This was Augustine's first experience of mortality and the effects of losing his soul's other half were overwhelming: "Wretched was I, and wretched is the very soul that is bound fast by friendship for mortal things, that is torn asunder when it loses them, and then first feels the misery by which it is wretched even before it loses those things" (*Conf.* 4. vi. 11). Augustine extrapolates from this loss a comprehensive vision of the destruction of all things in time. All created things

> rise and they set, and by rising, as it were, they begin to be. They increase, so as to become perfect, and when once made perfect, they grow old and die, and even though all things do not grow old, yet all die. . . . this is the law of their being. (*Conf.* 4. x. 15)

Once again the example of spoken language is privileged by Augustine. Created things that succeed each other in time are parts of a whole, just as words in an utterance are multiple parts of a sentence whose meaning is integral: "See, too, how our speech is accomplished by significant sounds. There would be no complete sentence unless each word departs, when all its parts have been uttered so that it may be followed by another" (*Conf.* 4. x. 15).

Man's understanding is necessarily fragmentary and sequential because of his original sin. Were it not for that, God would wish for man to enjoy total, unmediated knowledge:

> But if fleshly sense had been capable of comprehending the whole, and had not, for your punishment, been restricted to but a part of the universe, you would wish that whatever exists at present would pass away, so that all things might bring you the greater pleasure. (*Conf.* 4. xi. 17)

Augustine is vexed not only by the incommensurability between conventional language and an ineffable God, but also by the paradox of even attempting to utter in temporal, vocal signs a notion such as that of eternity. In his commentary upon Psalm 76, which takes the form of a sermon, Augustine gives rhetorical emphasis to this paradox by performing, so to speak, a discursive *via negativa*. Commenting upon the verse "I meditated upon days past, and I held in my mind eternal years," Augustine calls into question his own license to speak:

> Consider whether this does not demand, rather, great silence. Let all external sound be far from me, all clatter of human things, when I wish to meditate within me upon the eternal years. . . . In conversation, we say "This year." But what do we possess of this year, except the day in which we exist? For those days which have preceded are past, and nothing remains of them; the days to come are not yet in existence.[13]

But how can we presume, Augustine continues, to speak even of today? Or even of this hour? Or even of this very moment?

> What moment? Even as I utter syllables, if I must utter two of them, the second does not sound until the other is no longer. And even within this syllable, if there are two letters, the second does not sound until the first is no longer. What, then, is our place in those years? (*Comm.*, p. 214)

Augustine denounces, then, the whole attempt to speak in time about eternity in a language which is itself a perfect reflection of the temporal. Instead, we may only speak truly of time and of eternity by speaking with God from within: "For you remain the same, and your years do not disappear. Such are the years that the man who progresses meditates in silence, and not in exterior babbling" (*Comm.*, p. 214).

One may imagine how Augustine's discursive strategies in this sermon must have stirred his audience. Nevertheless, consummate rhetorician that he was, Augustine held his art in contempt. In a treatise entitled *De catechizandis rudibus*, which is devoted to methods of instructing newcomers to the Church, Augustine describes what occurs in the mind of an orator who struggles to enlighten his speakers with spiritual truth.[14] An intellection of the truth originates in the soul as a lightninglike flash that is always hidden in its secret place. This timeless flash in some marvellous way leaves prints (*impressiones*) in the memory, a kind of mental language that is distinct from historical or conventional language. These prints subsist during that brief interval of time when we assign to them syllables of historical language (Latin, Greek, Hebrew), which are phonetic signs (*signa sonantia*) directed at our audience. But "how remote," Augustine says, "is the sound of the voice from the intellectual flash when it does not even resemble the imprint on the memory!" (*De cat.* ii. 4). This inadequacy of exterior language to primary intuition is vexing to the orator: "I become sad that my tongue cannot suffice to my heart" (*De cat.* ii. 3), and "my discourse is slow, long, and dissimilar to it" (*De cat.* ii. 3). Furthermore, "the tedium that we feel with our language when we begin to speak only makes our language even more languid and obtuse than it was before we spoke" (*De cat.* ii. 3).

Although Augustine holds that the sequentiality of verbal signs is a necessity of man's status as a fleshly and mortal inmate of the temporal creation, he nevertheless considers that verbal signs may manifest an order that is rational and that, though it is manifested in words as material things, transcends their materiality and becomes, thereby, pleasing to the soul. Such is the case with poetic language. Poetry as form is the art of the muses, or music, and music is the art that teaches how to measure sounds well (*musica est scientia bene modulandi*).[15] Just as a beautiful building pleases us by the harmony of its proportions, which architects call ratio (a term that translates the Greek *logos*), so too poetic language displays movements that are properly measured and have a similar capacity to delight us.[16] However, the truth of poetry is in its form, not its content: "Our praise of the meter is one thing, our praise of the meaning (*sententiam*) is something else" (*De ord.* 2. xi. 34). The art of poets is therefore that of giving order to speech, and hence is the "power of lying reasonably" (*rationabilim mendaciorum potestas*) (*De ord.* 2. xiv. 40). The capacity of music to integrate several voices into a harmonic whole is the very model of civic order, as well, and on this point Augustine cites Cicero's *De republica* 2, pp. 42–43:

As, among the different sounds which proceed from lyres, flutes, and the human voice, there must be maintained a certain harmony which a cultivated ear cannot endure to hear disturbed or jarring, but which may be elicited in full and absolute concord by the modulation even of voices very unlike one another; so when reason is allowed to modulate the diverse elements of the state, there is obtained a perfect concord from the upper, lower, and middle classes as from various sounds; and what musicians call harmony in singing, is concord in matters of state, which is the strictest bond and best security of any republic, and which by no ingenuity can be retained where justice has become extinct.[17]

Poetic form originates in the foot, which is the basis of meter, and which is composed of short and long syllables. These have a ratio of 1:2, and this ratio not only corresponds to the relationship between God and the creation, but is the basis of "what the Greeks call 'harmony'" (*De trin.* 4. ii. 4). This dimension of poetic language is distinct from the terrain proper to the grammarian. For the rules of the grammarian that determine the lengths of syllables are tied up with the history of the language, and they rest strictly upon authority (*De mus.* 2. i. 1). The metrical proportions of the poetic line are universal, and hence beyond all temporal authority. Though poetry, as language, is corporeal movement and is among the lowest of beauties because "its parts cannot all exist simultaneously,"[18] yet poetry is capable of manifesting, in time, an order that is not itself temporal:

A line of poetry is beautiful in its own way though no two syllables can be spoken at the same time. The second cannot be spoken until the first is finished. So in due order the end of the line is reached. When the last syllable is spoken the previous ones are not heard at the same time, and yet along with the preceding ones it makes the form and metrical arrangement complete. (*De vera rel.* xxii. 42)

Thus, the art of poetry is an ideal that is distinct from the actual succession of sounds in the uttered poetic line. The art of poetry derives from a spiritual competence, but such ideal art is compromised by the actual performance in language:

The art of versifying is not subject to change with time as if its beauty was made up of measured quantities. It possesses, at one and the same time, all the rules for making the verse which consists of successive syllables of which later ones follow those which had come earlier. In spite of this the verse is beautiful as exhibiting the faint traces of the beauty which the art of poetry keeps steadfastly and unchangeably. (*De vera rel.* xxii. 42)

Augustine scorns as "perverse" those who prefer the materiality of poetry itself over the unperformed rules of art by which poetry is made:

Some perverse persons prefer a verse to the art of versifying, because they set more store by their ears than by their intelligence. So many love temporal things and do not look for divine providence which is the maker and governor of time. Loving temporal things they do not want the things they love to pass away. They are just as absurd as anyone would be who, when a famous poem was being recited, wanted to hear one single syllable all the time. (*De vera rel.* xxii. 43)

Augustine's extremism here may seem a bit fanciful, but it is a springboard for a daring analogy between the temporal process of the recited poem and the temporality of history. It is easy for us, he says, to grasp and judge the totality of a poem, because we are not *part* of that poem. However, because of original sin, we labor as *part* of history; hence we are not able to stand apart from it and grasp its totality:

There is no one who cannot easily hear a whole verse or even a whole poem; but there is no one who can grasp the whole order of the ages. Besides, we are not involved as parts in a poem, but for our sins we are made to be parts of the secular order. The course of history is made up of our labors. (*De vera rel.* xxii. 43)

Man labors, then, in a poem of history that he cannot read as a whole. Nevertheless, God has disposed the poem of history as a set of rhetorical oppositions based on the opposition of good and evil,

thus embellishing the course of the ages, as if it were an exquisite poem set off with antitheses. For what are called antitheses are among the most elegant of the ornaments of speech. . . . As, then, the oppositions of contraries lend beauty to the language, so the beauty of the course of this world is achieved by the opposition of contraries, arranged, as it were, by an eloquence not of words, but of things. (*C.D.* 11. xxiii)

The Creation, then, is a region of difference (*regio dissimilitudinis*) in more than one sense: not only is it absolutely different from a God who may not be known except through Christ and by the *via negativa*, but the temporal creation is always different from itself. Angels, by contrast, inhabit a spiritual realm where there is no difference and where they understand God's *logos* as a discourse proffered without syllables, without syntax, and without enigma: "They always behold your face, and, without any syllables of time, they read upon it what your eternal will decrees" (*Conf.* 13. xv. 18).

How can man presume to pass from the lower beauties of poetry and music (or of things) to the highest? This question preoccupied Augustine in the final book of *De musica*. Having given an exhaustive (and exhausting) inventory of metrical combinations, both actual and possible, in Latin, Augustine suddenly turns to epistemological dimensions of poetic beauty. The harmony (*numeri*) produced by the movement of corporeal things is the lowest manifestation in a hierarchy of harmonies. First, then, there is the harmony (*numeri*) of sounds (*sonantes*) produced by physical bodies; second, there is the harmony that is heard by the ear (*occursores*); third, there is the harmony that is proffered (*progressores*), which is actually produced by an activity of the soul from within; fourth, there is the harmony of memory (*recordabiles*), which is either imprinted *à priori* on the memory or retained by it. Finally, there is the harmony of judgment (*iudicales*), which is that ultimate, innate capacity for man to admire or to reject what is beautiful or ugly (*De mus.* 6. x. 28). Although this latter harmony is superior to all the others, it is activated by corporeal harmony. This enjoyment by the soul of rhythms manifested through and in the body is a consequence of man's original sin, after which the soul became subject to bodily passions (*De mus.* 6. xi. 33). Degrading though this may seem to the soul, the rhythm and harmony in the body is not in itself bad, even if the body itself is the soul's prison. To the contrary, all harmonies, within the soul or without, are only manifestations of a universal harmony called reason (*ratio*), and this harmony transcends all others (*De mus.* 6. xi. 33). All other harmonies derive from this harmony of reason:

> There, there is no time, for there is no mutability; from there come all times which are formed (*fabricantur*), ordered, and regulated (*modificantur*), like an imitation of eternity, as the revolution of the sky returns to the same point and brings back to the same point the celestial bodies, obeying, by means of days, months, years, and lights, and other astral movements, the laws of equivalence, unity and order. Thus, the things of the earth are subjected to those of the heavens, and by the harmonious succession of their times they associate their movements with a kind of poem of the universe. (*De mus.* 6. xi. 29)

Though Augustine's treatise on music soars into a truly magnificent Neoplatonic vision of the "One," and of "He who, alone, proceeded from the One and who is united to the One in Charity," Augustine's vision is heavily indebted to his Neoplatonic forebears. It would be wrong of us, though, to assume that this metaphysical flight is a mere emulation of Augustine's "sources." To the contrary, as a theoretician of language, Augustine listened first to the Scripture and to his own suffering and passions as his informants, and he labored in the laboratory of his own soul to produce a doctrine of peace and salvation in which he could believe. However, such a peace implies a transcendence of mediations of any kind, including those of people and language. At the same time as Augustine was completing the *Confessions*, he was writing the *De doctrina christiana*, which is a treatise about signs and exegesis, and his attitude toward signs parallels his attitude toward people. Some things, he says, are to be enjoyed, and some are to be used. Signs are to be used, not enjoyed. But what about people? Bear in mind that the following passage is written by a man whose last barriers to faith were his chair in rhetoric and his attachment to his mistresses:

> There is a profound question as to whether men should enjoy themselves, use themselves, or do both. For it is commanded to us that we

should love one another, but it is to be asked whether man is to be loved by man for his own sake or for something else. If for his own sake, we enjoy him; if for the sake of something else, we use him. But I think that man is to be loved for the sake of something else. In that which is to be loved for its own sake the blessed life resides; and if we do not have it in the present, the hope for it now consoles us. But "cursed be the man that trusteth in man." (*DDC*. 1. xxii. 20)

If there are hints in this somewhat sad passage that Augustine is still laboring with this question, we may find in Book 11 of the *Confessions* a more concrete expression of the tension between human love, or love of mediations, and divine love that is immediate. Augustine has now been converted; hence he has fulfilled his mother's dominant (and dominating) desire, which is to see her son reborn as a Christian in the Mother of the Church. Augustine, on his side, is soon to be free of his mother's tireless procurations in his behalf, since Monica is impatient to die. Monica and her son have undertaken the voyage to their native Africa, but it is a journey that she will not live to complete. Shortly before her death, Augustine and Monica are resting in Ostia, and they contemplate a garden from their window. This garden is the last of a series of archetypal gardens in the *Confessions*, and the sight of it instigates what is in my opinion one of the great moments in the metalanguage of the West. Together, Augustine and his mother experience a Neoplatonic ecstasy during which they abandon ordinary language, in favor of "inward thought and discourse," which is the language of the "heart's mouth" (*Conf.* 11. x. 23), and they strive for spiritual wisdom that lies beyond all representation. After a momentary union with this wisdom, they return to the "noise of our mouths, where a word both begins and ends" (*Conf.* 11. x. 24). Then, in a mighty sentence that is dialogue become monologue, a sentence formed of "if" clauses and conditionals yet interlaced with declaratives and imperatives drawn from the Scriptures, Augustine and Monica speculate about salvation as the entry into a life where understanding is at once immediate and eternal. Here, language is employed once more to perpetrate a peculiar paradox, which is that of declaring in mortal words the silence of ineffable wisdom. Since such a sentence does not bear either excerpting or summary, I conclude by citing it in its entirety:

Therefore we said: If for any man the tumult of the flesh fell silent, silent the images of earth, and of the waters, and of the air; silent the heavens; silent for him the very soul itself, and he should pass beyond himself by not thinking upon himself; silent his dreams and all imagined appearances, and every tongue, and every sign; and if all things that come to be through change should become wholly silent to him—for if any man can hear, then all these things say to him, "We did not make ourselves," but he who endures forever made us—if when they have said these words, they then become silent, for they have raised up his ear to him who made them, and God alone speaks, not through such things but through himself, so that we hear his Word, not uttered by a tongue of flesh, nor by an angel's voice, "nor by sound of thunder," nor by the riddle of a similitude, but by himself whom we love in these things, himself we hear without their aid,—even as we then reached out and in swift thought attained to that eternal Wisdom which abides over all things—if this could be prolonged, and other visions of a far inferior kind could be withdrawn, and this one alone ravish, and absorb, and hide away its beholder within its deepest joys, so that sempiternal life might be such as was that moment of understanding for which we sighed, would it not be this: "Enter into the joy of your Lord?" When shall this be? When "we shall all rise again, but we shall not all be changed." (*Conf.* 11. x. 25)

Stephen G. Nichols, Jr.

Romanesque Imitation or Imitating the Romans?

"A name is an uncertain thing, you can't count on it." Bertholt Brecht's aphorism might well be applied to the term *Romanesque*, by which we designate the art and letters of the period from the beginning of the eleventh century to roughly the end of the twelfth. Although we tend to use it more than we think about it today, the term can be seen as an image inscribing within itself a misconception about the nature of imitation in the period that constitutes a serious potential for misreading its texts and artifacts. And this has been so since the term was created almost two hundred years ago.

On December 18, 1818, a Norman botanist and antiquarian named Charles de Gerville wrote to a friend:

> I have sometimes spoken to you of "Romanesque architecture" [*architecture romane*]. This term of my own making strikes me as happily invented to replace the meaningless terms "Saxon" and "Norman." Everyone agrees that this heavy and vulgar architecture is the *opus romanorum*, deformed and successively degraded by our primitive ancestors. Thus did this Romance Language—whose origin and degradation are so analogous to the origin and development of the architecture—evolve from a similarly mangled Latin Language.[1]

What Gerville identifies as characteristic of the architecture—and what consequently determines his choice of name—is the absence of an enunciating subject within the work capable of imparting a clear intentionality, or at least the failure of such a subject to make itself conspicuous in the works by comparison with the well-defined and articulated subject of the presumed classical model. As a result, he saw in the Romanesque monuments only an inadequate, inferior imitation of their Roman antecedents.

In consequence, he imputes to these monuments a theory of imitation, as opposed to representation, based on the role of the subject inscribed within the text. My colleague, John Lyons, has defined purely imitative processes, such as Gerville perceives, in terms of a passive or emulative enunciating subject. "Imitation," Lyons observes, "may be seen as the performance of actions already performed by another."[2] It presupposes a mimetic subject that adopts the viewpoint and expressions of others as exemplary. In short, "the subject has become a *performer* of examples rather than a creator of examples."[3]

The mimetic subject, so conceived, appears as an image of a subject alienated from its own enunciation, a self incapable of independent, original thought or expression. As we shall find, this conception could hardly be wider of the mark! Going back to Gerville's letter, we can only construe his references to "*nos rudes ancêtres*"—with its connotations of "uncouth," "vulgar," and "uneducated"—as the historical equivalent of the alienated subject. This alienation remained problematically inscribed in Gerville's term "*architecture romane*," literally "Romance architecture," as a linguistic analogy, conveying the imprecise outlines of a model speech imperfectly learned and articulated over a long period of time.

The implications of social, as well as mental, deficiency existed in Gerville's formulation, but it remained for an Anglican clergyman, William Gunn, to make such social and class considerations explicit in his independent and almost simultaneous invention of the term in 1819.

Gunn, too, took as a given that Romanesque architecture developed from an inability of its authors to imitate properly the Roman model. Unlike Gerville, however, Gunn does perceive an enunciating subject within the monuments, but a debased one, weary of the discipline of classical imitation:

Architects became at length disdainful of imitation. They seemed to have become weary of making columns by prescribed proportions and of decorating them with leaves and volutes. *They wished to become original authors and to invent new fashions.* An opinion seemed to prevail that merit consists only in variety and invention.[4]

Gunn recognizes an incipient assertion of subjectivity here, but views it in social terms, as the vulgar pretension of the lower class trying to ape a style and sophistication of its betters whom it could not understand. He imparted this sociological judgment into the term Romanesque, which he coined:

> From the utter impossibility to adopt a term sufficiently expressive, I feel myself under the necessity of modifying one for my purpose. The Italian term *–esco*, the English and French *–esque* is occasionally allowable; thus we say *pittoresco, picturesque,* and *picotresque,* as partaking of the quality to which it refers. A modern Roman, for instance, of whatever degree, calls himself *Romano*, a distinction he disallows to an inhabitant of his native city, whom, though long domiciled, yet from dubious origin, foreign extraction or alliance, he *stigmatizes* by the term *Romanesco*. I consider the architecture under discussion from the same point of view.[5]

In Gunn's eyes, Romanesque architecture was "a vicious deviation" from the classical model, arising from a clumsy attempt to modify it.[6] This abortive attempt at representation of a new kind could be seen in the tendency of early medieval architecture to reuse elements of Roman buildings in new constructions. Gunn termed this process "secondary adaptation" and took it to be part of a principle of construction that he called "minute combination"—that is, construction by simple rearrangement of existing architectural elements in appropriate contexts.[7]

"Secondary adaptation" and "minute combination" were, for Gunn, ipso facto proof of an impoverished or alienated enunciating subject. He appealed to the Longinian concept of sublimity as proof that an inferior artistic product naturally mirrored a deficient inner being: "A celebrated critic of antiquity has defined sublimity—'an image reflected from the inward greatness of the soul.' And we are compelled to acknowledge that grandeur and perfection can never result from minute combination."[8] In short, there can be no plenitude of being inscribed in such texts or monuments.

Now one would not bother to disinter these long-forgotten texts if the terms roman/Romanesque did not elicit a misleading assumption about the nature of Romanesque representation that continues to trigger misreadings. Two recent examples may serve to illustrate the point.

In her authoritative book, *Initiation à la symbolique romane* (1977), M. M. Davy describes the twelfth century as a coherent era "*whose creative initiative far exceeds its taste for imitation.*" Yet, in a startling proof of the seductive power of the term and concept *roman*, she restates—with no apparent knowledge of Gerville's work—the linguistic analogy that led him to coin the term in the first place. Davy's comment leaves no doubt but that the term *roman* is meant to provide, not only an image of its origins, but also of its presumed mimetic mode of symboling: "ce terme *roman* donné principalement à l'art manifeste son lien avec l'art romain. Il désigne aussi la langue romane qui succède au latin, c'est-à-dire à la langue romaine."[9] Here the formula has been stripped of its pejorative connotations, but *not* its mimetic assumptions.

Still more recently, M. F. Hearn, in his book *Romanesque Architecture*, speaks of the Romanesque revival of monumental stone sculpture as imitating the form and function of its Roman model:

All the advances of the sculptural revival which emerged in the work of the regional schools . . . successively increased the striking parallels between Romanesque sculpture and the architectural sculpture of ancient Rome. In view of these correlations, it is clear that Romanesque sculpture has been very aptly named.[10]

The name Romanesque may indeed be appropriate, as Hearn suggests, but we do not seem, in over one hundred and sixty years, to have come to grips with the nature of "the intertextual dialogue or conflict" that Terence Cave so aptly identifies as "the essential character of imitation."[11] In other words, we have yet to come to grips with the nature of the presence of the Roman in the Romanesque, or even with the quality of its absence.

In labeling Romanesque as bad imitation, both Gerville and Gunn raised the question of presence and absence, if only implicitly. Presence and absence constitute fundamental components in imitation, as Cave once again reminds us when he compares mimesis to metaphor. For, "like metaphor, which displaces the proper term, mimesis necessarily entails the absence of that which it purports to represent: the word representation itself implies a secondary or feigned presence."[12]

That is precisely what differentiates early medieval works from classical, Renaissance, or neoclassical texts and has led, over the years, to so much misunderstanding of the symboling activity of the period. In Romanesque works, the feigned or secondary presence that would be immanent or implicit in the texts of other periods often appears as a manifest image. It is as though the subtext were incorporated as an element of the surface structure. In consequence, the intertextual dialogue or conflict between the model and the text that we find implied in the works of many other periods here becomes internalized as part of the narrative. The dynamics of the text thus include the confrontation between text and model, as well as the transformations resulting from this conflict. These factors all point to the importance of the enunciating subject in the Romanesque text, or precisely that element supposedly so deficient.

Let us consider, for example, a prominent but relatively little-studied Romanesque masterpiece, a processional cross, known as the Cross of Lothar, dating from around the year 1000, and most probably made for the emperor Otto III (Figure 1).[13] Preserved in the cathedral treasury at Aachen, the cross offers a fertile field for our inquiry, since it introduces, to the best of our knowledge, a number of new symbolic elements. By studying the cross, we may not only better understand the existence of a Romanesque theory of representation but just how innovative and philosophically grounded a theory it was.

The cross consists, first of all, of two starkly contrasted sides: the obverse, with its richly jeweled and ornamented raised surface, and the reverse, a starkly simple engraved space (Figure 2). From the viewpoint of narrative, the contrast between front and back is reversed: the front offers no manifest story, at least nothing that leaps to the eye; its narrative potential is clearly symbolic.

Romanesque Imitation or Imitating the Romans? 41

FIGURE 1. *Cross of Lothar, Rhenish, c. 1000 C.E. (recto), Aachen, Cathedral Treasure.*

FIGURE 2. *Cross of Lothar, Rhenish, c. 1000 C.E. (verso) Aachen, Cathedral Treasure.*

The back, on the contrary, presents an immediately recognizable account of the crucifixion.

Looking more closely at the obverse (Figure 3), we see that it utilizes in a most self-conscious manner the principle of "secondary adaptation" and "minute combination" that Gunn found so unsatisfactory a characteristic of Romanesque. The jewels might be a neutral kind of decoration, but the cameo sculpture placed so obviously in the center of the cross (Figure 4)—the pictures show how salient it is—conveys a definite connotation of a past historical period and style. It is, in fact, an authentic cameo sculpture of the emperor Augustus, dating from the first century. The smaller intaglio portrait of a ruler lower down on the front of the cross, below the portrait of Augustus, also dates from an earlier time. From its inscription, we can identify it as a signet or seal from the reign of Charlemagne's grandson, Lothar II, who ruled from 855–69.[14]

The cross itself, dating from around the year 1000, thus mani-

FIGURE 3. *Cross of Lothar, Rhenish, c. 1000 C.E. Detail of Augustan cameo.*

FIGURE 4. *Cross of Lothar, Rhenish, c. 1000 C.E. Detail of Augustan cameo showing salience of jewel.*

fests a dynamic of historical continuity and change: an image of, and metonymic reference to, earlier and successive periods. By implication, the present contains the past, but, more important, it re-presents it diagenetically.

In this way, the cross becomes a composite text, inscribing on its surface the dialectical connection between the past orders to which the portraits testify and the present Ottonian regime responsible for the masterwork.

The Augustan cameo plays a fundamental role in establishing the textual value of the cross. It introduces a perspectival image of the model that Otto's imperium sought at once to imitate and transform. From the medieval viewpoint, the Augustan age connoted above all the historical moment of Christ's birth. The fifth-century historian, Orosius, breaking with Saint Augustine's hostile attitude toward the Roman Empire, saw the age of Augustus as a moment divinely selected and prepared by the creative trinity for Christ's advent.

As Dante would later remind his readers in *De Monarchia*, "the world was never so peaceful as at the time of the rule of Augustus, called by Saint Paul, 'the fullness of time.' This was the time awaited or produced by the Son of God for his incarnation, and it was a time of perfect monarchy."[15]

Luke 2:1 was taken as evidence that Christ had chosen to be born under Augustus, thereby sanctioning the Imperial Roman World. On the basis of such facts, Orosius declared a relation of commutivity between the terms *populus Christianus* and *populus Romanus*.[16]

The Augustan cameo must serve as the point of departure for reading the text because its iconography *and* iconology establish a "vocabulary" that will be repeated and transformed throughout the rest of the text in various ways.

The bust of the emperor—to take the most obvious detail—provides the first model of transformation, repeated in the intaglio of Lothar below, only to be contrasted, reversed, and finally extended by its relationship with the crucifixion scene on the back. This disembodied portrait bust, with its rigid pose, contrasts strikingly with the contorted, full-bodied Christ figure, but in this text it is the imperial portrait, not the Christ figure, that initiates the rhetoric of transformation from human to divine state. We'll see why shortly.

First, let's recall that the impassive, stonelike immobility of the visage expressed the quality that distinguished an emperor from other humans. Ammianus Marcellinus, writing in the fourth century, states that "rigidity, fixity, and stonelike inflexibility of men were indispensable for reproductions of the emperor who thus expressed the superhuman impassibility of the man filled with divine grace."[17]

The Reichenau Apotheosis of the emperor Otto III (Figure 5), executed in the 990s, the crowning of the emperor Henry II (Otto's successor) from the Bamberg Apocalypse (Figure 6), and other imperial portraits available from this period, demonstrate the continuity in Romanesque art of the rigid, immobile pose as a signifier of divinity in the human. By the early eleventh century, the work of the Carolingian philosopher John Scottus Eriugena

FIGURE 5. *Gospel Book of Otto, Reichenau, c. 990–1000 C.E. Apotheosis of the emperor Otto. Aachen, Cathedral Treasure.*

FIGURE 6. *Bamberg Apocalypse. The crowning of Otto III or Henry II by Peter and Paul, c. 1002–1014 C.E. Municipal Library, Bamberg, Bibl. 140 (A. II 42), f° 59v.*

had gained sufficient currency to show why and how immobility evoked divinity. In consequence, when the great Romanesque theophanic portals were executed at Moissac, Autun, Vézelay, and elsewhere (Figures 7 and 8), immobility was the *only* posture considered appropriate for portraying divinity in the midst of a perpetually moving world.[18]

The iconographic details attributed to the emperor, the laurel wreath and the eagle, also linked the imperial office to divinity. The eagle symbolized Jupiter, who bestowed the laurel wreath of triumph on the winners in Roman victory ceremonies. The evergreen laurel itself thereby signified divine recognition of human achievement.

By situating the cameo in this context, the original Augustan iconography could be troped sylleptically as Christian symbol with no alteration to the image itself. Consequently, what occurs in this text is rather more sophisticated than the simple substitution of Christian meaning for formerly pagan symbols, such as had occurred in early Christian art when the laurel wreath was shown being given to Christ—sometimes by an eagle—to symbolize his triumph over death.

The textual problem begins with the intratextual dialogue created by incorporating the Augustan cameo in the center of the *Ottonian* cross. The cameo thereby participates both literally and figuratively in a sylleptic process of textual exchange and reversal. It literally displaces the usual text of the cross face, the crucifix, and consequently calls attention to what is absent. In Cave's terms, the imposition of the cameo is a mimesis—that is, a performance—of the metaphoric and ironic mode that differentiated Christian discourse from ordinary, historical narrative. The *presence* of the crucifixion image, of course, is reasserted on the back of the cross, where it literally serves as a subtext to the Augustan cameo.

Obviously, the crucifixion scene on the reverse authorizes the sylleptic repredication of meaning in the cameo; but, conversely, the cameo itself serves as an emblem or blazon for the rhetorical processes that control the strategy of the text as a whole. It is

FIGURE 7. *Saint-Pierre, Moissac. Christ-Ruler-of-the-Universe. Tympanum and portal, c. 1110 C.E.*

FIGURE 8. *Saint-Lazare, Autun. Tympanum, west façade. Last Judgment, 12th century.*

thus the presence of the Romanesque that permits the dialogue of contrast and transformation.

Without the Augustan presence on the front, for example, we would not understand the innovative nature of the iconography of the crucifixion scene on the back. The sun and moon on the arms of the cross continue the victory symbolism begun in the cameo: "*sol* and *luna* were the triumphal symbols of the victory and glory of the empire in Roman art."[19] Here they appear with the triumphal laurel wreath held by the hand of God (*dextera domini*) to make an unproblematic assertion of the crucifixion as a symbol of the victory and glory of a transformed empire—an empire whose meaning has profoundly altered with very little change in imperial symbolism: again the sylleptic process at work.

Still, such a statement could have been made without displacing the crucifixion from the front of the cross. A more complex rhetorical significance must be posited here, something we may understand by looking at the most spectacular innovation: the placing of the dove within the wreath held by the *dextera domini*.

The triumph of the crucifixion was held to be a triumph of the Logos, the second person of the Trinity, symbolized by the dove, but beyond that, of the Creative Trinity as a whole. The latter represented the rhetorical power responsible, not only for the descent of the divinity on earth, but also for the creation of the earth, of history, and consequently of the Augustan order on earth and within history. The triumph of the Logos was a triumph of the Word, of the rewriting of the world.

By incorporating the dove within the wreath, the text inscribes within the crucifixion scene—for the first time so far as we know[20]—an image of the Trinity responsible (1) for the creation which encompassed both the Augustan and the Christian *historia*, (2) for the image itself, and (3) for the viewer's understanding of it. In other words, this trinitarian image imitates the manifest and immanent forms assumed by the Creative Trinity.

Accordingly, it presents in manifest form the Father (as the *Dextera Domini*), Son, and Holy Ghost represented by the dove; then it moves from the literal to a more figurative but still concrete mode with the dove as the sign of the Logos or second person of the Trinity, and by a common metonymy, of the entire Trinity.[21] Finally, we find the completely immanent manifestation of the Trinity in the abstract symbolism of the three circles on the arms and upright of the cross.

This progression from manifest sign to immanent symbol constitutes another level of intertextuality. If the earlier reading revealed the historical intertext provided by Orosius and his successors, this configuration of symbols points to a metaphysical and ethical intertext. It situates within the text a reminder of the way in which—according to the Neoplatonic philosophical systems then current—the Trinity created History and the World by a three-fold process that moved from pure idea or essence (*ousia*), to potential or power (*dynamis*), and finally to the act of giving differentiated form to matter by means of operation (*energeia*)—in short, the same kind of circular movement from abstract symbol to concrete manifestation used to portray the images of the Trinity on the Cross of Lothar.

In reminding the viewer of the trinitarian principles of creation, the cross illustrates a basic principle of Romanesque imitation theory, namely, the self-referentiality of the divine creative process as conceived by the Greek fathers and vigorously promulgated in the West by Scottus Eriugena. In other words, the innovative emphasis on the Trinity in the cross may be seen as a kind of "signature" or image of a theory of representation and participatory perception for which Eriugena's philosophical anthropology provides one of the clearest explanations.

Eriugena—whose work stood at the center of the development and dissemination of ideas regarding essence and universals in the tenth and eleventh centuries, according to John Marenbon's new book[22]—stressed the importance of the Trinity as a key to understanding human intelligence and creativity. The "little trinity" in humans mirrored the creative Trinity of the Godhead and helped to demonstrate how, and in what manner, man could be a secondary creator, or *officina omnium*, "workshop of everything."[23]

First, Eriugena demonstrated the presence of the Trinity in divine creation. He argued that creation itself constituted a theophany, for "God himself was both the Maker of all things and made in all things."[24] This did not mean that the Godhead as a whole was literally present in each object, but rather that what was revealed in the thing was the creative power and existence of the Godhead. The object did not thus call attention to itself as an accidental, materially substantive, or formal thing, but rather to its status as representative of a universal.[25] Accordingly, it solicited the viewer to contemplate the process by which it had moved from undifferentiated idea—essence—to realized manifestation, or act. Consciousness of the creative process and awareness of perceptual activity thus took precedence over the accidental or material nature of the object.

As God is One in Three, so each creature manifests in its ontological structure a triadic character reflecting Father, Son, and Holy Spirit. . . . As God is both Beginning and End, or in Aristotelian terminology, both an efficient and final cause of the universe, so each real being is both an efficient and final cause, a center of creativity mirroring that of its Creator.[26]

Creationist activity, in Eriugena's system, involved a procession away from the Unitary One, the Prime Mover, a procession from unity to multiplicity, from sameness to difference. That aspect of the Godhead responsible for the creative procession was the Trinity, and three stages defined its descent toward the sensible world: the abstract stage of essence, the sensible but still undifferentiated stage of power, and the final, formal incorporation into matter by operation.

Each stage in this descent corresponded to a specific person of the Trinity. The Holy Spirit, symbolized by the dove, was the agent responsible for making manifest in the world the power of the Creative Trinity. On the Cross of Lothar, this Person appears for the first time juxtaposed between the First and Third, the images of Father and Son, thereby suggesting yet another dimension to the triumphal imagery of the crucifixion. That explains perhaps why the *Dextera Domini* confers the victory wreath on the dove in this image. In this case, however, the triumph refers, not simply to the historical and eternal victory over death, but also to the triumph of human knowledge foretold in Christ, since "the foretaste of future grace may be found in the imprint of the Trinity left in the human mind."[27]

The trinitarian view of divine creation activity provided Eriugena and his followers with a model for human symboling activity. For the basis of all true contemplation of things, says Eriugena, is dialectic. Dialectic enables humans to analyze, describe, categorize, and reproduce "every one of those things which can be understood."[28] Now the basis of dialectic "in every rational and intellectual nature," Eriugena says, is the human equivalent of the same three elements found in the Creative Trinity: *ousia, dynamis,* and *energeia.*

In other words, humans manifest in their ontological structure a triadic character mirroring that of the Trinity: "a being is, it is capable of something, and it is effective in what it does."[29] Eriugena follows Augustine (*De Civitate Dei* 11.16, for example) in arguing that "we recognize in ourselves an image of God, that is, an image of the Trinity."[30] But for Eriugena, this "little trinity in man" turns out to be the sign of a very active intelligence—"conceived as the tripartite structure of the rational soul"—and interested less in overcoming doubt than in playing a central role in "the cosmic mediation between essence and existence."[31]

Consequently, there can be no such thing as passive perception in the Romanesque aesthetic. All contemplation involves performance, a dialectical participation in the object contemplated that moves in two directions: toward differentiating the role of self in the object—the enunciating self and the perceiving self—and, ultimately, toward a recognition of the same, universal creative principle in all things—namely, the divinity.

Eriugena casts this performative perception in terms very close to the Cartesian *cogito*:

There is no nature, whether rational or intellectual, which does not know that it is, although it may not know what it is. . . . Thus, when I say, "I understand that I am" do I not imply in this single verb "understand" three meanings which cannot be separated from each other? For I show (1) *that I am,* and (2) *that I can understand that I am,* and (3) *that I do understand that I am.* Do you not see that by the one verb are denoted my *ousia* and my power and my act? For I would not understand if

I were not, nor would I understand if I lacked the power of understanding, nor does that power remain latent in me, but breaks forth in the operation of understanding.[32]

As Brian Stock has pointed out, this *cogito* emphasizes the *active role* of understanding: "the activity of thinking is more significant in the overall cognitive process than the objects thought about. Man, to anticipate Descartes, is a *res cogitans* . . . and consequently, the active intelligence—conceived as the tripartite structure of the rational soul—occupies a central place in the cosmic mediation between essence and existence."[33]

Turning these concepts back onto the problem of representation, we see that the viewer was not simply supposed to apprehend an object, *but to create a place of definition for it in the mind.* The mind then became the locus where the object existed as definition, that is, as understood. But understanding had ontological implications in Eriugena's theory of the *cogito*.

In understanding, the individual showed a capability for intelligent interaction with objects—that is, of establishing a dual awareness regarding the nature of the observed phenomenon, on the one hand, and, on the other, of drawing conclusions about the self and the world based upon metacritical consideration of the processes of observation, methodically if not methodologically examined. The second kind of knowledge, the self-consciousness, concerns us here. For this knowledge enabled individuals to discover the "little trinity" within, the creative mechanism that made humans the *officinae omnium*, and demonstrated the way in which the self could resemble higher forms:

The act of defining is the act of a reasoning and understanding nature. . . . For no nature that does not understand that it itself *exists* can define either a nature that is equal to itself or one that is inferior. For as to that which is its superior, how can it get to know that when it cannot rise above the knowledge of itself? Therefore the intellectual nature alone, which is constituted in man and angel, possesses the skill of definition.[34]

But this knowledge of the resemblance of self to higher forms engendered a second level of consciousness: an awareness of the limits of human knowledge, as opposed to divine comprehension, and thus of the consequent difference between the human situated in time and place as opposed to superior beings who exist eternally.[35] Discovery of the fact of existence did not entail knowledge of the quality of existence: one could know *that* one was without knowing *what*.

The second stage of the Eriugenean *cogito*, then, moves on from the fact of existence, from *esse tout court*, to consider the implications of being. In this movement, the real implications for a theory of representation unfold, helping us to understand the full significance of the reiterated images of the Trinity on the Cross of Lothar. The Trinity, in this stage of the Eriugenean *cogito*, becomes the key to intersubjective knowledge, to explaining how one mind may apprehend the knowledge contained in another. This *cogito* thus conjoins the concept of perception as definition in the mind of the perceiving subject with the concept of communication of knowledge. Taken together, they authorize a notion of artistic representation as a propaedeutic of being, a way to guide the rational intelligence back to God.

As Brian Stock reminds us, Eriugena held that Genesis 1:26 (*Faciamus hominem ad imaginem et similitudinem nostram*) utilizes two terms, *image* and *likeness*, which authorize a dual conception of human nature: an essential nature (image) and an accidental nature (likeness).[36] These correspond to two kinds of knowledge about humans in the postlapsarian world: God's own and man's. From the former perspective, man may be defined essentially as "a certain intellectual notion eternally produced in the divine mind";[37] this essential concept cannot be known by humans in their present state. At the same time, humans may be conceived from a different viewpoint: "in their sexual generation in the existing world."[38] Human knowledge about the self, so conceived, necessarily remained partial and incomplete: a signature of man's condition, and an imprint on the mind of what had been lost in the Fall.

Initially, humans were created—still according to Genesis 1:26—with complete knowledge: only in the Fall, along with sexual differentiation, did the distinction between essential and accidental being develop: "The penalty of man's transgression against nature is revealed [by his ignorance of his true self]. If man had not sinned, he surely would not have suffered ignominious generation from the two sexes like irrational animals."[39]

Christ provided the link between man's originary state and his mundane, divided self. Of all humans, says Eriugena, Christ alone embodied the essential and accidental knowledge in unitary being, as he embodied other forms of *un*differentiation, such as sex. Significantly, Eriugena speaks of the differentiated condition of humans as their "wound." Christ thus exemplifies the whole or sound body and mind—the image and likeness of God conceived at the creation in which resemblance would be absolute and difference nil:

> That man who alone was born in the world without sin—namely the redeemer of the world—nowhere and never endured such ignorance, but as soon as he was conceived and born, he understood himself and all things. And he was able to speak and teach, not only because he was his father's Wisdom, which nothing eludes, but also because he had received undefiled humanity in order to cleanse the defiled. Not that he received a humanity different from that which he restored, but he alone remained undefiled in it, preserved in the innermost reasons of violated nature for the purpose of healing its wound.[40]

Again the concept of the active understanding comes into play. To conceive of Christ in this way, the individual had to view him not simply as an *exemplum*, or didactic model, but rather as metaphor, a figurative trope, the image of man conceived in the mind of God and spoken by the divinity; in short, as a historical representation of the divine concept of human essence. So conceived, Christ confirmed the possibility of conceptualizing the circularity of history, not only in human terms generally, but specifically in terms of the intellectual odyssey each person was required to perform in order to imitate the procession from the divine mind and return to it exemplified in Christ's own story.

Christ's example demonstrated both the original and future human condition: "the foretaste of future grace may be found in the imprint of the Trinity left in the human mind."[41] The mind discovered this imprint through the contemplation of Christ's story by turning back upon itself and recognizing that its own intellectual processes constituted an analogical procession and return that linked it to Christ. But if this were so, then it must also be linked to other minds that performed the same intellectual process. Intersubjective communication thereby became, not only possible, but necessary for conceiving the unitary knowledge lost in the Fall.

Postlapsarian humans lived, not only separated from complete knowledge of themselves, but separated from one another. Recognition of the trinitarian mental process common to all humans, however, made it possible to reproduce, through intersubjective understanding, a momentary mimesis of the originary unity in which they once lived.

In what Stock terms "the final stage of Eriugena's *cogito*,"[42] we see how the triadic understanding—*essentia, virtus,* and *operatio*—was thought to guarantee the possibility of uniting consciousness, by reproducing in one's own mind the understanding of another.

When I understand what you understand, I am brought into your understanding, and in a certain manner I am made into you. Similarly, when you clearly understand what I clearly understand, you bring about my understanding, and from two intellects, from that which both of us understands sincerely and without hesitation, one is made. For instance, let us introduce an example from numbers. You understand a number consisting of six to be equal to its parts; and I not only understand that, but also understand that you understand, just as you understand that I understand. Both of our intellects are made one by the number six; through it, I, for my part, am made into you, and you are also made into me.[43]

We cannot fail to note how this example predicates its assumptions on a hierarchy of knowledge and representation. It does not simply reveal a means of knowing but a natural order in which the reader/viewer will assume a preordained place. Accordingly, while both minds move in the same direction, one of them, the author's, precedes the other, not only in providing the examples, but also in interpreting them. In consequence, we readily see how the vaunted unity of consciousness could be teleologically directed, a fact of no little significance for the development of Romanesque art and letters.

Inevitably, the insistence on the intellectual participation of the reader/viewer inherent in the concept of the active understanding renders the Eriugenean *cogito* of crucial importance for the development of an art based upon the concept of directed vision. For the reader need not passively "consume" a didactic text, but might perform his own "proof"; the circularity of the process assured the desired confirmation.

We saw how, for example, that when properly cued, contemplation of the Trinity made the individual aware of the trinitarian nature of his own thought processes, and, consequently, of the inner self as a mimetic re-presentation of the universal Creative Trinity. Communication of such insights, via an aesthetic construct like the Cross of Lothar, permitted other individuals to make the same observations qua individuals, while at the same time discovering their affinity with another mind, the artist's, and hence to realize their dual status as individual and member of a collectivity. This discovery of dual identity represents the transition from the knowledge of self as genus to self as species recounted in Eriugena's commentary on the parable of the Ten Virgins; like the imprint of the Trinity itself on the mind, it foretold "the return of all mankind to its pristine natural state . . . [for] the species is the number of the elect of the human race."[44]

In this system, the interpretation of biblical parables, the making of images, or the retelling of history all lie on a continuum of creative activity shared by maker and by thoughtful perceiver, each of whom, in performing or defining the work in the mind, demonstrated that he was an *officina omnium*. Mind and image could thereby exist in a specular confrontation aimed at overcoming difference by means of incessant mental activity. The stakes were high in this game of salvation in which players used, not dice, but books and images:

> To the number of the Wise Virgins none is admitted unless he is resplendent with the light of wisdom and glowing with the flames of divine love, the wisdom and love nourished by richness of knowledge and action.

To this marriage [with the Bridegroom] no one lacking in knowledge and action . . . is permitted to ascend, but he is wholly excluded from it. Not nature but grace raises the human mind to that height; and the merit of obedience to the commands of God and of the purest knowledge of God afforded in this life by books and by creation lifts one up.[45]

We can now perceive the basis of a Romanesque theory of representation predicated upon a mimetic subject, an "I" that intellects itself in and through texts. Two reciprocal movements of differentiation and identification define the nature of subjectivity in this theory.

First comes the affirmative movement, a dialectic whereby the subject participates in the text and thus transforms it into an awareness, an assertion of self as an independent being capable of effective act. This movement culminates in the discovery of responsibility for one's own discourse.

The Eriugenean *cogito* makes clear that understanding is, not simply an imitative act, but rather an agonistic hermeneutic, probing the limits of human creative power. For, paradoxically, this affirmative movement of self-discovery leads directly to a recognition of the limits of human discourse, and thus to an ultimate negation of the human subject as creator.

This second motion of the mind begins with the recognition that the triad of powers that constitute understanding were insufficient to create *ex nihilo*. Rather, they mirrored a still more powerful creative triad, that of the Trinity.[46] Human discourse, Eriugena pointed out, could neither be wholly subjective nor literal. For, as Matthew 10:20 attested, "It is not you who speak, but the spirit of your father who speaks in you." Logically, then, the discovery of the self would lead beyond the stage of differentiation to a return towards the source of being and *energeia*: in other words, towards a spiritual reunion with the primary enunciating subject.

What Eriugena envisaged was an epiphany: a meshing of the triad of human powers with the Trinity in a conjoined discourse. Such a union of the mimetic "I" with the originary subject would produce a theophany or revelation of the divinity in the human, a process known as theosis. Theosis was an enactment of the divinity in the human subject and thus a transformation of the mimetic "I" into a metaphoric "we" signifying a plenitude of being and meaning.[47]

Humans could not produce theosis, since it was a state of grace, but they could ascend to the level of being where it became possible by a radical shift in their manner of intellecting the world, and thus by a shift in discourse or representation. They had to abandon the literal language of historical time and place, the univocal language of phenomenal reality, in favor of the triune dialectic described above. The model for this more difficult and veiled language was, of course, scripture.[48]

We are now in a position to draw some conclusions about the aesthetic implications of such a theory of representation. The ideal art work would be a relatively complex one capable of providing a paradigm, preferably manifested within the work, of the two movements by which understanding of self and self-transcendence could be achieved. A work, in other words, that would represent the reciprocal affirmation and negation of the enunciating subject that the viewer would, in turn, perform.

Historical representation necessarily would occupy a prominent role in the text, since the first movement of understanding performed by the viewer required that he situate himself in terms of the flux and the continuity of history. Moment and place, like time and self, were also represented dialectically, as at once continuous and mutable,[49] for the accidentals of history had to be confirmed in this way if the work were to achieve the first goal—the understanding of the self as a differentiated being literally situated in history and speaking the language of an historical time and place.

The second movement required a metaleptic discourse—indirect and symbolic—capable of undermining the historical language, now perceived as too literal, as incapable of performing the triune dialectic. In its place, one would find the hierarchical and figurative language that could enact the ascent toward theosis.

Returning at last to the Cross of Lothar, we can now see not only that this masterwork of Romanesque art does possess the characteristics outlined above, but why. First, from the point of view of *techne*, or fabrication, the elaborately extruded, luxurious obverse (which contrasts so strikingly with the delicately even reticently incised reverse) signifies the two complementary but successive movements of spiritual assertion: the affirmative and the negative. These two movements correlate historically and ethically to the worldly and spiritual forms assumed by the Church in the transformed Roman Imperium, figured on the front of the cross, and the oxymoronic counterstatement of that glittering splendor by the faintly incised Verbum on the back. One literally had to traverse the affirmative stage to understand how its negation could lead to a greater synthesis and unity than could ever be contemplated by the historical imperium, no matter how all-embracing. Taken together, the two constitute the kind of transcendent *translatio* of historical place and time expressed in the concept of the heavenly and messianic Jerusalem of Revelation 21.[50]

Second, from the viewpoint of reader response/viewer participation, we now understand that in performing the stations of this cross, so to speak, the viewer, in a first movement of understanding, could situate himself historically, politically, and ethically, thereby discovering his own accidental and historical being. This first step in the mimetic project, initiated by contemplating the Augustan cameo, would result in an awareness of self in relation to a divinely ordained, hierarchical order, that of the continuous, but transformed, Roman Empire.

Within the text, the viewer would also discover a model *cogito* in the compelling images of the Trinity. These images, and the *cogito* inscribed in them, undermine at the most profound level, even as they support at a more mundane stage, the historical images of empire and the whole notion of historical being. And so the second act would produce a gradual displacement of the differentiated self toward the universal, Christian *cogito* of the text. The viewer would literally fall into line in the procession and return enacted by the cross in the state rituals for which it was intended.

Representation in Romanesque texts, then, when properly understood, leads not to a discovery of the absence of an enunciating subject or of an alienated subject. We find, rather, a rigorously intellectual *cogito* ascending from history and differentiation toward a metaphysical epiphany. It is less a question of imitating *the* Romans, finally, than of imitating Romans, and particularly Romans 16:25.

Kevin Brownlee

Reflections in the *Miroër aus Amoreus*
The Inscribed Reader in Jean de Meun's *Roman de la Rose*

In Jean de Meun's continuation of Guillaume de Lorris's *Roman de la Rose*, the inscribed reader is invested with special significance. Jean gives a clear signal of this at the midpoint of the conjoined *Rose* text. Here the God of Love describes—and renames—Jean's part of the poem in terms of its effect on its readers: Love will sing to Jean "such airs that, after he is out of his infancy, he will, indoctrinated with [Love's] knowledge, so flute [Love's] words through crossroads and through schools, in the language of France, before audiences throughout the kingdom, that those who hear these words will never die from the sweet pains of love, provided that they believe only him [Jean]. For he will read so fittingly that all those alive should call this book *The Mirror for Lovers*, so much good will they see there for them . . ." (". . . notes teles / que, puis qu'il sera hors d'enfance, / endoctrinez de ma sciance, / si fleütera noz paroles / par carrefors et par escoles / selonc le langage de France, / par tout le regne, en audiance, / que ja mes cil qui les orront / des douz mauz d'amer ne morront, / por qu'il le croient seulement: / car tant en lira proprement / que tretuit cil qui ont a vivre / devroient apeler ce livre / le *Miroër aus Amoreus*, / tant i verront de bien por eu" [10,608–22]).[1] Jean's future readers, then, will rename his poem by virtue of the accuracy and utility of its reflected image of themselves. Jean's *Rose* is thus explicitly presented as mimetic with respect to its readers. How and to what effect can only be determined by considering the image (or images) of his public that Jean incorporates into the very substance of his text.

Before going on to examine in detail the *Rose*'s single most important treatment of Jean's literary public, a few preliminary remarks are in order.

Firstly, as has been remarked with great intelligence by Patricia Eberle,[2] the title *Miroër aus Amoreus* is quite deliberately polysemous. It is a "mirror *for* lovers" in the sense of effectively teaching the art of love (that is, for the use of, for the advancement of, lovers). It is a "mirror *of* lovers" in the sense of accurately reflecting lovers as they are. For the purposes of the present analysis I shall use the term "didactic" to designate the mimetic status of the text as determined by the first meaning of the title. ("This is how lovers must behave if what they want is amorous success.") Didactic efficacy is not necessarily linked to exemplarity, to the imperative, to "should."[3] I shall use the term "representational" to designate the mimetic status of the text as determined by the second meaning of the title (again, without any component of exemplarity: "This is how lovers *do* behave"). The term "imitative" will be used to indicate that the text is presenting to the reader a model to be imitated, that *should* be imitated.[4]

Roughly two thirds of the way through the conjoined *Rose* text occurs Jean de Meun's most elaborate direct address to his readers. Indeed, Pierre Col, one of the principals in the *Querelle du "Roman de la Rose,"* considered this passage to be unique in the poem in that "la seulement parle il [Jean] comme aucteur."[5] The speech takes the form of a detailed apologia: the author defends himself against possible critics of his diction and his subject matter. At the same time, Jean utilizes the format of the apologia to inscribe an image of his public into the text of his poem. This is done by means of a consecutive presentation: four different "categories" of Jean's audience are addressed in sequence, each category being linked to a different presentation of Jean's subject matter and to a different aspect of his identity as author figure. In order to consider the nature and poetic function of Jean's inscribed audience, it is not only necessary to examine each of these four categories individually but also (and more important) to see how only at the level of their interaction may the "image" of Jean's public be said to exist within the poetic economy of the *Rose*.

First of all, in what is a kind of prelude to Jean's apologia, there is a direct address to the reader that serves to introduce the elaborate allegorical battle between the troops of the God of Love and the uncourtly guardians of the Rose. In this introductory passage (15,105–23), Jean adopts an author/subject matter/audience configuration that is a reproduction in miniature of that employed by Guillaume de Lorris. The inscribed public is one of "loyal lovers" ("leal amant" [15,105]), who are told to "pay attention now" ("or antandez"), which clearly echoes Guillaume's "let him who wishes to love now pay attention" ("qui amer veut, or . . . entende" [2059]). Further, Jean explicitly presents the *Romance* as an "adequate art of love" ("art soufisant . . . d'amors" [15,114]), recalling the description in Guillaume's prologue: "this is the *Romance of the Rose* in which the art of love is entirely contained" ("ce est li *Romanz de la Rose* / ou l'art d'Amors est tote enclose" [37–38]). Jean's self-presentation as author figure is thus here carefully modeled on Guillaume's: that of an Ovidian authority on love who teaches his reader how to achieve amorous success. The status of the text thus appears to be didactic (even calling attention to its efficacy in this domain) without necessarily being imitative. This presentation of text and author are, however, almost immediately rendered problematic as Jean foregrounds what seem to be inescapable hermeneutic difficulties in a direct address to the reader qua interpreter:

> Et se vos i trovez riens trouble,
> g'esclarcirai ce qui vos trouble
> quant le songe m'orrez espondre.
> Bien savrez lors d'amors respondre,
> s'il est qui an sache opposer,
> quant le texte m'orrez gloser;
> et savrez lors par cel escrit

> quant que j'avrai devant escrit
> et quant que je bé a escrire. (15,115–23)

> And if you have any difficulty, I will clarify what confuses you when you have heard me explain the dream. Then, if someone creates opposition, you will know how to reply about love, when you have heard me gloss the text. And then, by this text, you will understand whatever I have written before and whatever I intend to write.

This promise to gloss the dream that is the story line of the *Rose* explicitly harks back to a similar promise in Guillaume de Lorris (2065–74). But even as Jean's authorial stance seems to be linked more closely to Guillaume's, a crucial difference between the two *Rose* poets is being established. That Guillaume's promise to gloss his text is never fulfilled can be "explained" by the fact that his part of the *Rose* is "unfinished." This is, of course, not the case with Jean, in the context of whose continuation the equally unfulfilled promise to gloss the dream must be viewed as signifying a model of reading in which the opposition text/gloss ceases to operate, in which these two opposing categories of discourse are, as it were, "conflated" to produce a narrative functioning as its own gloss.[6] Jean is thus simultaneously establishing Guillaume as authority for his own inscribed author/reader configuration and suggesting that Guillaume's model is of necessity only partially adequate.

This suggestion is greatly elaborated in the "digression" that constitutes Jean's apologia properly speaking, which is introduced as follows:

> Mes ainz que plus m'an oëz dire,
> ailleurs veill un petit antandre
> por moi de males genz deffandre,
> non pas por vos fere muser,
> mes por moi contre eus escuser. (15,124–28)

> But before you hear me say anything more, I want to move aside a little to defend myself against wicked people, not so much to delay you as to excuse myself to them.

The opposition established between the second person *vos* (presumably the "loyal lovers" of 15,105) and the third person *eus* (that is, the "wicked people" of 15,126) involves a significant and explicit expansion of the inscribed courtly audience (derived from Guillaume) with which the passage had started. By the very act of identifying the "males genz," Jean incorporates them into *his* (as opposed to Guillaume's) public, at the same time as he refuses to address them directly.

In the first segment of the apologia proper (15,129–64), this initial "leal amant"/"males genz" opposition is strictly maintained and carefully exploited as Jean names and responds to the charge that he has used improper, uncourtly language—"words [or speeches] that seem too bawdy or too foolish" ("paroles/ semblanz trop baudes ou trop foles" [15,131–32]). This charge is (hypothetically) brought against Jean by "the slanderers" ("li medisant" [15,133]), but it is only the second-person "amorous lords" ("seigneur amoreus" [15,129]) who are addressed directly. These latter are requested to act as intermediary between the author and his critics, to "courteously [courtaisemant] oppose them" (15,136). This construct is highly significant on several counts. First, it involves a reversal of the conventional courtly lyric opposition between *amant* and *médisant*. Jean depicts the (conventionally *un*courtly) *médisant* as reproving him for uncourtly diction, while the *amants* are to defend this diction in (and this is the final irony) a *courtly* manner. This reversal involves nothing less than a subversion of Guillaume's entire system of (courtly) poetic diction.

At the same time, Jean qua author figure is commenting on the important debate on poetic language between Raison and Amant that had occurred earlier in the poem (6898–7174). Amant's position in this debate is (in effect) now associated with that of the *médisants*, while that of Raison (paradoxically?) appears linked to the courtly lovers in Jean's audience. A radical differentiation between author and protagonist, between poet and lover, is thus effected. Furthermore, this differentiation is accentuated when one realizes that Jean has exploited the conventional courtly situation of the slandered lover in order to present himself qua poet—qua *author*—slandered for his *words about love*, not for his loving.

Jean's final defense against the charge of using bawdy language involves a further link between his self-presentation as author figure and the inscribed public in the *Rose*. One component of Jean's public (the *seigneur amoreus*) is instructed to reply on behalf of the author to another component (the *médisants*) that Jean's poetic language is determined by the requirements of his subject matter ("la matire" [15,143]), which "draws [him] toward such words [or speeches] by its own properties" ("qui ver tex paroles me tire / par les proprietés de sai" [15,144–45]). In going on to cite Sallust as *the* classical authority who supports his position, Jean implicitly makes several important statements about the mimetic status of his text and thus about its author/reader configuration. Jean utilizes a direct quotation from the *Bellum Catilinae* (III,2) to present the poetic discourse of the *Rose* as being (in some sense) as *true* as historical discourse (as *historia*): Sallust defines a writer (*escrivein*) as "he who wants to set down [deeds] accurately in a book, the better to describe the truth" ("qui le fet / veust metre propremant en livre, / por mieuz la verité descrivre" [15,152–54]). Furthermore:

> . . . quiconques la chose escrit,
> se du voir ne nous velt ambler,
> li diz doit le fet resambler;
> car les voiz aus choses voisines
> doivent estre a leur fez cousines. (15,158–62)

> . . . if anyone writes something without wishing to rob us of its truth, then what he says must resemble the deed. Words that are neighbors with things must be cousins to their deeds.

By utilizing Sallust as the model for his own self-presentation as author figure at this point, Jean claims a representational status for the *Rose*. Indeed, he holds up "accurate," "truthful" representation as an imperative, which should determine (and can be used to justify) poetico-linguistic practice. This explicit expansion of Guillaume de Lorris's exclusively courtly discourse is closely linked with Jean's expansion of Guillaume's inscribed courtly public to include both *amants* and *médisants*, each reading in a different way.

The second segment of the apologia proper (15,165–212) involves yet a further expansion of Guillaume's courtly public as Jean turns to address "all you worthy women, whether girls or ladies, in love or without lovers" ("vos . . . toutes, vaillanz fames, / soiez damoiseles ou dames, / amoureuses ou sanz amis" [15,165–67]). This category of Jean's inscribed (feminine) audience transcends both the opposition married / unmarried and the opposition lover / nonlover,[7] leaving us with a potentially universal female figure who, I would like to suggest, is qualified as "worthy" (*vaillanz*) precisely in her capacity as reader of Jean's text.[8] This generalized female reader figure is appealed to as Jean defends himself against possible charges of antifeminism:

> . . . se moz i trouvez ja mis
> qui samblent mordant et chenins
> ancontre les meurs femenins,
> . . . ne m'an voilliez pas blamer
> ne m'escriture diffamer,
> qui toute est por anseignement (15,168–72)

> . . . if you ever find set down here any words that seem critical and abusive of feminine ways, then please do not blame me for them nor abuse my writing which is all for instruction.

The key word here is "seem" ("samblent"), for Jean qua author flatly denies ever having said anything "against any woman alive" ("contre fame qui soit en vie" [15,178]). Further, he justifies the treatment of women in the *Rose* by valorizing the representational status of the text in terms of a generalized, didactic authorial stance (that is, one that transcends the limitations of a mere *art d'Amors*):

> Mes por ç'an escrit les meïsmes
> que nous et vos de vos meïsmes
> poïssons connoissance avoir,
> car il fet bon de tout savoir. (15,181–84)

> But we have set these things down in writing so that we can gain knowledge, and that you too may do so by yourselves. It is good to know everything.

The obvious implication of this stance is that Jean's female readers can learn about *themselves* by reading his text, in which they will see themsleves truthfully reflected (not simply as lovers but as women).

The final element in Jean's self-defense against the charge of antifeminism is directly related to the authorial claim to write for instruction ("anseignement" [15,173]). Jean guarantees the truth of his own text by means of a striking (and somewhat playful) conflation of bookish and experiential authority:

> ne ja de riens n'an mentirai,
> se li preudome n'en mentirent
> qui les anciens livres firent.
> Et tuit a ma reson s'acordent
> quant les meurs femenins recordent . . .
>
> Cist les meurs femenins savoient,
> car touz esprovez les avoient,
> et tex es fames les troverent
> que par divers tans esproverent;
> par quoi mieuz m'an devez quiter:
> je n'i faz riens fors reciter,
> se par mon geu, qui po vos coute,
> quelque parole n'i ajoute,
> si con font antr'eus li poete,
> quant chascuns la matire trete
> don il li plest a antremetre;
> car si con tesmoigne la letre,
> profiz et delectacion,
> c'est toute leur entencion. (15,192–96; 15,199–212)

I shall never lie in anything as long as the worthy men who wrote the old books did not lie. And in my judgment they all agreed when they told about feminine ways . . .

They knew about the ways of women, for they had tested them all and had found such ways in women by testing at various times. For this reason you should the sooner absolve me; I do nothing but retell just what the poets have written between them, when each of them treats the subject matter that he is pleased to undertake, except that my treatment, which costs you little, may add a few speeches. For, as the text witnesses, the whole intent of the poets is profit and delight.

Not only is the textual substance of the *Rose* thus authorized by the Latin *poetae*, but Jean presents himself as engaged in the same activity as the *auctores*, as continuing, as adding to their corpus.[9] Indeed, Jean emerges as nothing less than a vernacular *poeta*, claiming for his vernacular poetic enterprise all the authority associated with the canonical Latin poetic texts. It is in this context that any apparent casuistry with regard to writing and lying must be understood: Jean is appropriating to the *Rose* nothing more (but also nothing less) than the "poetic truthfulness" of the *auctores* (which, however, he further valorizes by linking it directly to empirical truth).

The specific model underlying Jean's stance as vernacular *poeta* is Horace, for Jean implicitly includes himself in the plural subject of the famous Horatian formulation concerning the fundamental intention of poets: "poets want either to profit or to delight or to say things at once pleasing and helpful to life" ("Aut prodesse volunt aut delectare poetae / aut simil et iucunda et idonea dicere vitae" [*Ars poetica*, 333–34]).

In the third and final segment of the apologia (15,213–72), Jean answers criticism from people (*gent* [15,213]) who "feel that I reprove them in the chapter where I record False Seeming's words" ("santent que je les remorde / par ce chapistre ou je recorde / les paroles de Faus Samblant" [15,215–17]). A whole new category of Jean's public is here being addressed: the religious in general and the mendicant friars in particular. The *Rose* is presented as so accurately representational that its (highly critical) depiction of the hypocrite will immediately be recognized as a self-portrait by all hypocritical readers, who will feel themselves attacked and wounded. Significantly, this procedure is described by means of the image of Jean as a (metaphorical) archer: "I take my bow and bend it, sinner that I may be, and let fly my arrow to wound at random. To wound, yes; but to recognize, in the world or in the cloister, the unlawful people, the cursed ones whom Jesus calls hypocrites. . . . I never aimed to hit any other target; it is there that I wanted, and want, to place my arrows" ("ainz pris mon arc et l'antesoie, / quex que pechierres que je soie, / si fis ma saiete voler / generaument por affoler. / Por affoler? Mes por connoistre, / fussent seculier ou de cloistre, / les desloiaus genz, les maudites, / que Jhesus apele ypocrites, / . . . Onc d'autre saign ne fis bersaut, / la vols et veill que mi fers aut" [15,227–34; 15,243–44]).

The act of reading here becomes an assault on the (hypocritical) reader. Further, this metaphor of assault involves Jean portraying himself in terms highly reminiscent of the God of Love shooting his arrows straight into the heart of Amant the protagonist (see 1681ff.). In yet another transformation of Guillaume's initial configuration, then, Jean qua narrator seems to assume vis-à-vis the reader of the Rose the authoritative role of the God of Love vis-à-vis the work's protagonist. (There is perhaps the further suggestion that in Jean's part of the Rose the reader in some sense replaces the protagonist as focal point.) At the same time Jean's didactic authorial stance is expanded. In the context of religious practices (in which a potentially universal public is at issue) the text of the Rose calls for negative imitation: "I can strike no one who wants to protect himself as long as he knows how to see where he stands. Even he who feels himself wounded by my arrow may take care to be a hypocrite no longer and will be rid of his wound" ("car je ne puis nullui ferir / qui du cop se veille garder, / s'il set son estat regarder. / Neïs cil qui navré se sant / par le fer que je li presant, / gart que plus ne soit ypocrites, / si sera de la plaie quites" [15,254–60]).

Jean's explicit authorization for this stance involves a widening of the scope of his self-presentation as author figure: clerkly bookish authority is conflated with experiential authority, on the one hand, and "philosophical" authority, on the other: "I never said anything that may not be found in writing, and proved by experience or at least is capable of being proved by reason" ("onc riens n'en dis, mien esciant, / conmant qu'il m'aut contrariant, / qui ne soit en escrit trové / et par experimant prové / ou par reson au mains provable" [15,263–67]). The suggested distinction here between experience and reason recalls the distinctive authorities of la Vieille and Raison, which exist in a kind of complementary distribution—but are both "contained" by Jean's authorial voice.

The full import of the final expanded authorial stance in the apologia only becomes clear when the model for Jean's attack on the mendicant orders in the "chapter" of False Seeming is recognized as Guillaume de Saint-Amour, especially his *Tractatus de periculis novissimorum temporum ex Scripturis sumptis* (*On the Perils of the Last Times, Taken from Scriptures*).[10] Jean's claim of written authority is thus quite literally true.

Further, this claim itself has as its visible subtext a specific passage in *De periculis*[11] in which Saint-Amour affirms that his arguments come "not from [his] own invention but from the truth of Holy Scripture" ("non ex inventione nostra, sed ex veritate sacre scripturae," edition of 1632 as cited by Lecoy). Jean thus appears to be using Saint-Amour as an intermediary in order to claim a link with the ultimate written authority, the Bible.

The overall image of Jean's public that emerges from his apologia thus involves an expansion of Guillaume de Lorris's courtly public into a potentially universal audience. Jean's text functions as a mirror for this necessarily heterogeneous public by simultaneously reflecting different segments of it in different ways. It is in the simultaneous existence of these segments as reflected in Jean's poem—the level on which the various categories of Jean's inscribed audience "interact" as part of the text of the *Rose*—that indicates the work's (purposely heterogeneous) mimetic status.

Similarly, Jean's configuration of model authors in the apologia presents (and authorizes) a purposely heterogeneous poetic discourse. Again, Guillaume serves as the point of departure: his courtly diction is incorporated into the global linguistico-poetic system of Jean's *Rose*, which simultaneously claims to use vernacular verse *as if it were* Latin prose historiography (Sallust), Latin poetry and versified "literary theory" (Horace), and Latin theological polemic linked to Scripture (Guillaume de Saint-Amour). What emerges is thus a new kind of vernacular poetic discourse that is potentially universal.

Marina Scordilis Brownlee

Autobiography as Self-(Re)presentation
The Augustinian Paradigm and Juan Ruiz's Theory of Reading

The *Book of Good Love* (hereafter referred to as the *Libro*) continues to perplex its readers. The four prevailing (and mutually exclusive) interpretations of this enigmatic fourteenth-century text explain it either as: (1) an *ars amandi*;[1] a didactic treatise;[2] an affirmation of the "poetic truth" of a minstrel's songbook (of goliardic inspiration), including its function as *ars poetica*;[3] or a hagiographic parody.[4]

This lack of critical consensus would no doubt have gratified Juan Ruiz, the Archpriest of Hita, for it attests to his stated objective in writing the *Libro*—namely, to produce a (necessarily) polysemous text:

> . . . this book of mine, to every man or woman, to the wise and the unwise, to whomsoever may understand the good and choose salvation and do good works loving God, and likewise to whomsoever may desire mad and heedless love on the road which he walks along, to each one it can truly say: I will give you understanding.[5]

The object of this study is to demonstrate that the *Libro* is profoundly concerned with the problem of interpretation, that it in fact thematizes the problem of interpretation, functioning as a logical extension of Augustinian hermeneutics. More precisely, Augustine's *Confessions* may be seen to function as an important heuristic tool in the elucidation of the Archpriest's problematic text.

In a suggestive analysis of the Archpriest's dialogue, Pierre Ullman underscores its filiation with Augustine's principle of voluntarism, that "evil is in the eye of the beholder," so to speak, that what is revealed to a given individual (his particular interpretation) is determined by his moral state, his good or bad will.[6] Ullman convincingly traces this argument in the prologue. However, despite the initial presence of this Augustinian resonance, he casts doubt on its function as an informing principle for the Archpriest's text as a whole: "The prologue is not an integral part of the book. It was not initiatory; on the contrary, it was probably added in the second redaction as justification" [for the bawdy material contained therein] (p. 154).

Contrary to Ullman's reading, I would like to suggest that Augustine's notion of voluntarism—rather than serving merely as camouflage—functions in fact as an "opening signal," an informing element that determines the narrative strategies of the entire work to follow. It is Augustine's idea of voluntarism and its bearing on exegesis that Juan Ruiz exploits in his re-writing of the *Confessions*—thereby revealing his own theory of reading. (This paradigmatic function of the Augustinian autobiography is what is meant by my title, "Autobiography as Self-(Re)presentation.")

In his own text, the Archpriest responds both formally and thematically to the *Confessions*, taking as his point of departure a paradox that is inherent in the Augustinian text—the discrepancy between, on the one hand, Augustine's reiterated belief that what one comprehends in a work depends on his moral state[7] (hence that any text will be subject to many different interpretations) and, on the other hand, that it is possible to write his *Confessions*, not only to achieve his own salvation, but that of his "universal reader" as well. The *Confessions* is presented simultaneously as a record of Augustine's conversion and as a paradigm for his universal reader of a "conversion mechanism," as it were. However, since by Augustine's own admission no universal reader exists, his text cannot logically function as a conversion mechanism to persuade those readers who are not already thus inclined or predisposed. While this logical discrepancy is not problematic for Augustine, for Juan Ruiz it is. It is precisely this paradox (positing the existence of a universal reader but realizing that he does not exist) that generates the bifocal tension found within the *Libro*.[8]

Memory is the key that determines both the form and content of the *Confessions*. Memory serves as a form of mimesis for Augustine both as representation of "things that actually happened" and of "things as they are in general." The *Confessions* is a narrative of memories in which Augustine tells us: "I am investigating myself, my memory, my mind."[9] From the perspective of the time of writing he is analyzing his past life—the "now" of the believing Christian versus the "then" of the reprobate. For example, he examines his motivation in stealing the pears from the pear tree, which (as he now realizes) he stole, not because he was hungry, but simply because he delighted in committing sin.[10]

Like Augustine, Juan Ruiz also ponders the power of human memory at the beginning of his book, but he arrives at the opposite conclusion:

The psalmist says: "the thoughts of men are vain." . . . And I further say that this comes from poorness of memory, which is not instructed by the good understanding, so that it cannot love the good, nor remember it in order to do it. . . . Man's memory is feeble; . . . to keep all things in the memory and not to forget, is more divine than human. (P. 8)

For Juan Ruiz, then, memory lacks the corrective power that it has for Augustine. As a result, the Archpriest is writing his book from the perspective of a sinner, whose poor memory allows him to be continually susceptible to earthly temptation: "I am a man like any other sinner," he tells us in stanza seventy-six. At the time of writing he is as unresistant to sin as he was during the time of narration.

Indeed, the prologue to the *Libro* constitutes an inversion in miniature of the narrative strategies employed by Augustine in the elucidation of his epistemology in the *Confessions*. That is, Augustine recounts his wayward past and subsequent conversion as a necessary means of attaining the moral excellence that is the essential starting point for proper scriptural exegesis, which the last three books of the *Confessions* treat in detail. Significantly, Juan Ruiz inverts this procedure, beginning his prologue with the words "Intellectum tibi dabo" ("I will give you understanding"), taken from Psalm 31. What follows in the remainder of the prologue is a lengthy exegesis that illustrates, not only his exegetical mastery, but at the same time his profound skepticism regarding the didactic efficacy of exemplary literature:

> God knows that my intention was not to compose the book in order to provide ways to commit sin or speak evil, but was to guide everyone back to good memory of good deeds, and to give examples of good conduct, and admonitions for salvation. . . . However, since to sin is a human thing, if any should choose—which I do not advise them to do—they will find here some ways for it. (P. 10)

This epistemological discrepancy between the two authors is clearly illustrated by the Archpriest's re-writing of Augustine's famous pear tree incident:

> Many ladies have I done much service to, yet nothing have I accomplished. Although I have proven that my natal destiny was this: to put my efforts into serving the ladies and into nothing else [and never to succeed in possessing them]; nevertheless, although one may not taste the pear of the pear tree, just being in its shade is a pleasure for everyone. (Sts. 153–54)

Two important transformations of the Augustinian text are at issue here. First, unlike Augustine, the Archpriest does not engage in persuasive Christian rhetoric; he is not explicitly trying to convert his readers, because for him reading cannot logically perform this function.[11] Rather than offering a model for salvation, he offers a parable of the human condition—a specular text, not an imitative one. This first transformation is concretized by the symbolic function of the trees. For while Augustine rejected the pear tree for the shade of the fig tree at the moment of his conversion, Juan Ruiz—as he tells us—remains perpetually in the shade of the pear tree. John Freccero notes that

The fig tree in the garden of Milan in the eighth book of the *Confessions*, for all of its historicity, is at the same time meant to represent the broader pattern of salvation history for all Christians. The moment represents the revelation of God's word at a particular time and place, recapitulating the Christ event in an individual soul. Behind that fig tree stands a whole series of anterior images pointing backward to Genesis.[12]

On the other hand, as Marcia Colish explains, the pear tree for Augustine signifies the "love of sin," functioning as "an inverted reflection of the perfect love of God."[13] Hence, in the Augustinian system, the pear tree represents the Tree of the Knowledge of Good and Evil, and by opting for it the Archpriest presents himself as a postlapsarian Adam. (This is, moreover, why he adopts the pseudonym "Juan Ruiz," which is akin to the English "John Doe.")

The second transformation in question has to do with the Archpriest's self-presentation as a failed lover (quite unlike Augustine)—a persistently blundering, comical, would-be lover (implicitly exemplifying human folly). While an amorous failure, however, he is at the same time a poet who makes poetry out of failed love experience in praise of God. (It is of paramount importance to note that each episode of the *Libro*, while an amorous failure, explicitly leads to the writing of poetry.) Hence, the Archpriest valorizes "poetic truth" as a means of reflecting "religious truth"—a sharp contrast to Augustine, for whom poetic fiction is a moral vacuum, as he explains in the *Confessions*.[14]

Genre and narrative structure further reinforce the reading-theory put forth by each author. Both texts are inscribed prayers containing a narration of the protagonist's exploits. Both texts involve a program of quotations from Psalms that are glossed by the narrative itself. Both authors plead for intercession by means of their writings. Finally, Juan Ruiz and Augustine alike draw upon the poetic resources of romance.[15] In their respective works each author juxtaposes secular romance (love quest) with "sacred romance" (religious quest).[16]

In the case of Augustine, the love quest—his obsessive carnal desire—leads him ultimately to religious quest (by means of the all-important faculty of memory). He undergoes a linear (explicitly chronological) progression, beginning in a state of moral impoverishment that leads to a period of psychomaquia during which he seeks (and ultimately attains) Christian truth. The linearity of this quest is repeatedly emphasized by the author, who traces the progression from infancy to adulthood, designating each stage in his spiritual development according to his chronological age at that particular moment.[17]

For the Archpriest, on the other hand, since man is not aided by his avowedly imperfect memory, he must necessarily remain in a perpetual state of alternation between the values of secular and sacred romance, so to speak. This claim is borne out by the fact that the protagonist does not undergo any chronological development or have any indication whatsoever of age attached to him. While not knowing his age, we similarly do not know how much time elapses between the beginning and end of the narration. Indeed, rather than being linear, the temporal designations of this autobiography are clearly (and surprisingly) cyclical in nature (suggesting, I would argue, the limitations of human memory).[18] The protagonist pursues thirteen different women—a recurring pattern in which his love is frustrated each time. These multiple scenes of (comically exaggerated) failed love serve an emblematic function. They simultaneously underscore the comicality of such relentless fleshly pursuits, while stressing the universality of their impulse.

The midpoint sequence in each of the two texts further illuminates the reading-theory advanced by each author. Both protagonists are plagued by lust, which serves as the central theme of their respective midpoints. Both texts focus on the transformation of the protagonist in the context of religious experience.[19] In each case, the particular treatment accorded to this structurally significant moment in the texts mirrors the reading-theory projected by Augustine and Juan Ruiz respectively.

The Augustinian midpoint (discussed above in terms of the emblematic significance of the fig tree) is the point at which the *Confessions* moves from being a specular text to an imitative one. That is to say, it is the particular moment of Augustine's conversion—as well as being a parable of Christian salvation in general.

The Archpriest also conveys the parabolic function of his Everyman figure at the midpoint of his text; he does not, however, offer a model to be imitated—the text remains specular, mimetic.

The midpoint of the *Libro* narrates the love affair of Lady Sloe with the male protagonist. This narrative is of crucial importance, for within it a highly significant narrative shift occurs. Namely, the identity of the hero who is revealed to us at the tale's conclusion is not (as we have been led to expect) that of the Archpriest himself but rather of Sir Badger. The narrator concludes this tale of seduction by glossing it as follows: "I told it in order to give you a parable and not because it really happened to me" (st. 909).

What the Archpriest does at this point (the structural midpoint of his text) is to transform the narrator-protagonist configuration of the *Libro* in such a way as to redefine the text's status as (fictional) autobiography. The fact that this transformation takes place at the structurally significant midpoint of the poem underscores the fact that it cannot be read simply as fictive autobiography, but must be viewed as the work of a "devious" author figure who exploits a whole repertoire of narrative perspectives, who is capable of shifting from one to another without forewarning his reader (in this case from a first- to a third-person protagonist), yet who maintains a first-person structure throughout.[20]

What follows directly after this unanticipated narrative shift is a group of four narrative episodes in which the protagonist is confronted by savage mountain women. These four episodes constitute a closed system of sorts, in that they do not refer to any other part of the *Libro*. Indeed, this fact has traditionally puzzled critics, leading them to judge this narrative sequence as extraneous to the *Libro*—as works that the Archpriest, in his capacity as minstrel, very likely composed prior to the writing of the *Libro* and that probably formed part of his songbook.[21] Nonetheless, they may be seen to conform to the narrative strategy adapted by the Archpriest to his rewriting of Augustine, a strategy established at the beginning of the *Libro* and elaborated throughout.

These four narratives involve a series of permutations of the narrator-protagonist's identity—a series of variations, as it were, on the theme of the mutable narrator-protagonist configuration, which has just been articulated in the tale of Lady Sloe. These permutations result from the fact that the male protagonist in each of these four lyrico-narrative units has a strikingly different identity (although, as in the Sloe/Badger sequence, here too we have a first-person structure sustained throughout all of the rustic encounters). In the first of these episodes he is identified as a squire (st. 961b); in the second (sts. 991i; 992c) as an anonymous man (not an archpriest); in the third he is a shepherd (st. 994a); in the fourth he is an *hidalgo* (st. 1031b). The protean nature of this narrator-protagonist represents, on the one hand, a remarkable innovation in autobiographical discourse. In addition to its generic implications, however, it fortifies the Archpriest's presentation of himself as a common man, as an Everyman figure—a fundamentally un-self-reflexive individual whose thoughts and impulses tend to be more earthbound than divine. Hence, in contradistinction to Augustine, what occurs at the center of the Archpriest's text is, not individual conversion, but rather an affirmation of human pluralism, which accords with his reading-theory.[22]

In a very interesting study exploring the *Libro* in terms of hagiographic parody, André Michalski finds characterological reminiscences (parodic inversions) of the principal characters in the *Confessions* and concludes that the *Libro* is a coherent parody of the *Confessions*, an "anti-Augustine," as he terms it.[23] Michalski interprets Juan Ruiz as a parody of Augustine, his procuress (Trotaconventos) as a parody of Monica, Venus as a parody of the Virgin, and Sir Love as a parody of St. Ambrose.[24]

Suggestive though these parallels are, they oversimplify the Archpriest's text. Rather than constituting an inversion of the Augustinian model, these characters serve to underscore the complexities that the *Libro* generates and the particular way in which it re-presents the *Confessions*. While Augustine was profoundly saddened by the death of Monica, his fervent religious belief prevailed in assuaging his grief. By contrast, the *planctus* delivered by Juan Ruiz at the death of Trotaconventos is the mordant lament of a secular man who is tied to his earthly existence. By generating this analogy for his reader, the Archpriest is being implicitly didactic, offering an *exemplum ex negativo*. Similarly, Michalski's conception of St. Ambrose and the Virgin in the *Confessions* as inversions of Sir Love and Lady Venus further underscores the subtlety of the Archpriest's poem. For at its midpoint Juan Ruiz is not converted to the religion of Sir Love.

Instead, the collective protagonist who is revealed to us in the parable of Lady Sloe and the four rustic encounters that follow is—as before—poor of memory, corruptible, comical, yet also religious. As soon as the protagonist (who now appears to regain his identity as archpriest) escapes from the very uncourtly mountain wenches, he prays to the Virgin, offering in her honor two poetic compositions on the theme of Christ's Passion. The contrast between this devotional poetry and the rustic encounters could not be greater. But, I would argue, it is intended as an implicit commentary on human nature—on the duality of man, on the one hand, the desires of the flesh; on the other, the desire to serve God. Significantly, this bivalence of human impulses is clearly articulated by Augustine in the opening lines of the *Confessions*:

Man is one of your creatures, Lord, and his instinct is to praise you. He bears about him the mark of death, the sign of his own sin, to remind him that you thwart the proud. But still, since he is part of your creation, he wishes to praise you (P. 21)

In contradistinction to Augustine, Juan Ruiz exemplifies this human duality by composing his book according to cyclical structures, which become increasingly evident in the second half of his text.

The meaning produced by this cyclical framework is, in effect, that human history (on the individual level) repeats itself. Our memory is short and imperfect, as the Archpriest emphatically reminds us at the outset of his narrative. Therefore, one person cannot profit from the experience or admonitions of another. We know that earthly love, like earthly life, is transitory. Nonetheless, the flesh is weak—so that once the epic battle of Lady Lent and Lord Meatseason culminates on Easter Sunday, it is not Christ but rather Sir Love who (along with Lord Meatseason) emerges as the ruler of Earth, and whose victory is celebrated in a triumphal procession (palm branches and all). Next year, we realize, the scene and its outcome will be precisely the same.[25]

The riddle of the seasons functions similarly. Sir Love offers four closely related versions of the same riddle that, as he later explains, represents the four seasons of the year:

Three knights were eating at a single table, seated by the fire, each one by himself; they could not have reached one another with a long pole, and between them the edge of a coin could not have fitted (St. 1271)

In glossing this enigma along with the other three, Sir Love reveals that these are "the four seasons of the year of the celestial sphere; the men are the months. . . . They advance but they do not overtake each other, they meet at their borders" (st. 1300). The seasons, then, like human time and like human history, repeat themselves.[26] Such time is cyclical, not linear.

The structural oscillation of the *Libro* (like the protagonist's oscillation between the poles of sacred and secular romance) is intended to mirror the cyclical (oscillating) nature of the human psyche in general. And it is for this reason that the Archpriest's book lacks "poetic closure," as he explicitly tells us:

Because the Holy Virgin is, as I have said, the beginning and end of all good, so I do believe, I composed four songs for her, and thereupon I shall put an end to my book, but I shall not close it. . . . Whoever hears it, if he knows how to compose poetry, may add more and emend whatever he wishes to. (Sts. 1626, 1629)

The only thing that breaks the cyclical rhythm of man's oscillating human nature—as happens with Trotaconventos—is death. The passing of Trotaconventos occasions a bitter diatribe against Death itself by the otherwise mischievous and light-hearted Archpriest (sts. 1520–75). This is the only truly somber moment in the entire work, and it is a very eloquent one.

In sum, for the Archpriest it is our feeble memory that prevents us from being educable, susceptible to the kind of persuasive Christian rhetoric designed by Augustine in order to lead us to good conduct. Rather than writing an overtly exemplary work, therefore, Juan Ruiz chooses instead to expose our human foibles, to represent man as he really is, implicitly (yet unmistakably) criticizing him, but realizing that one cannot convert others through reading (the premise of the Augustinian model) because no universal reader with a univocal interpretation exists. It is for this reason that he literally personifies his book, allowing it to address its readers as follows:

> I, this book, am akin to all instruments of music: according as you play music well or badly, so, most assuredly, will I speak; if you know how to pluck my strings, you will always hold me in mind. (St. 70)

With this first-person intervention by the book itself, Juan Ruiz emphasizes (by extreme example) the fact that one cannot prescribe interpretation for another reader. The dispute between the Greeks and Romans (sts. 44–69) and the conflicting interpretations of the astrologers (sts. 123–42) further elaborate this fundamental belief in the problem of interpretation.[27]

The text remains necessarily polysemous—as does the very term *buen amor* (simultaneously denoting the *fin'amor* of courtly love and the Christian love of God).[28] The task of interpretation thus remains each reader's problem, as Augustine himself acknowledged but from a very different perspective.

Hence, the *Libro* functions, among other things, as a dramatization of the Augustinian paradox. It is a mimetic (specular) text that poetically "corrects" Augustine's imitative text—it is a confession without conversion. Moreover, it is in the Archpriest's re-presentation of Augustine that the *Libro*'s unity resides.

One final remark. As we have seen, the Archpriest presents us with a mimetic text (not with an exemplary, imitative one) that is a logical corollary to his particular reading-theory—his belief in the limits of imitative literature in terms of reader response. For, while imitative literature presupposes that its readers will be ultimately illuminated by its didacticism, the ending of the *Libro* explicitly acknowledges that it can, and (of necessity) will, be read according to a multiplicity of interpretations.[29]

Viewed as an illustration and thematization of the limits of imitative literature, the *Libro* constitutes a real tour de force in medieval narrative. And, I would suggest, this is what the Archpriest implies when he claims in his prologue to be offering us a "new Book."[30] As such, the *Libro* creates a radically new type of exemplary discourse.

Robert Hollander

Imitative Distance
Boccaccio and Dante

That Boccaccio, as he composed the *Decameron*, was keenly aware of Dante's *Commedia* is not a matter in dispute.[1] However, it is fair to say that in large part the actual interchange between the two most favored works of the Italian fourteenth century has not been closely examined. Almost all who have studied Boccaccio's Dante have concerned themselves primarily with the *Trattatello in laude di Dante* and the *Esposizioni sopra la Comedia*. A possible reason for such concentration on the overtly Dantean writings at the expense of Boccaccio's fictions is that these fictions—and especially the *Decameron*—conceal more than they reveal of their dependence on the *Commedia*. Thus the general understanding would seem to be that, if the *Decameron* does in fact reflect the *Commedia*, we are left largely to our own labors and experiences in determining where and in what manner. At the same time—and now that Pier Giorgio Ricci has shown that the *Trattatello* itself was almost certainly composed between the summers of 1351 and 1355—we should be increasingly aware of the close relationship between Boccaccio's public profession of his admiration for Dante and his own work in fiction. For if the strategies that inform his treatment of Dante in the *Decameron*, the *Corbaccio*, and the *Trattatello* are perhaps different, the three works are contiguous vernacular enterprises; they probably contain more common concerns and interests that reflect a renewed involvement with the text of the *Commedia* than is generally suspected.

Whatever his eventual purpose in doing so, Boccaccio seems intent on reminding readers of his *Decameron* that they should keep Dante's great poem near at hand. We need read no further than the subtitle, "Prencipe Galeotto," to understand that the *Commedia* is to be taken as analogous to the *Decameron* in some respect. And if the subtitle's citation of *Inferno* V is not urgent enough a signal, the following announcement that the work will contain "cento novelle" is surely meant to remind us of its most recent precursor, also divided into one hundred compositional units. While the *Proemio*, if we leave to one side a possible echo or two, shows little sign of attention to the *Commedia*, the *Introduzione* clearly asks us to remember the grand design of Dante's poem: "This dreadful beginning will be for you [readers] not unlike a rugged and steep mountain to those who climb it" (*Introduzione*, 4). Branca's note to this passage suggests both a textual and an existential connection between our two writers; in his view the *Decameron* exists as a counterpart to the *Commedia*, each thirty-five-year-old protagonist/author thus further linked by the dates of his so different visions, 1300 and 1348. And whatever we choose to make of the innate but clear comparison suggested by Boccaccio's text, it does ask that we entertain (without necessarily accepting) the notion that the *Decameron*, like the *Commedia*, is the record of a spiritual voyage that moves from hell, if not to heaven, at least to the Earthly Paradise.

In his second and penultimate presentation of his own attitudes as author of the work, the *Introduzione* to Day Four, Boccaccio's reminiscences of Dante are unmistakable. Complaining that his tales should have been spared the anger that they have generated in some readers, he describes their wrath as "the violent and scorching wind [vento] of envy," which "should have struck only high towers or the very tops of the trees" [*non dovesse percuotere se non l'alte torri o le più levate cime degli alberi*]; further, his *novellette* (one notes the self-deprecating diminutive), written in the vernacular (and not Latin), in prose (and not verse), and offered "senza titolo," and thus either incomplete or composed of various subjects (as opposed to being completed or polished and unitary), are also to be seen as being composed in "the lowest and most humble style possible" [*in istilo umilissimo e rimesso quanto si possono*] (IV, *Introduzione*, 2–3). The citations of

Paradiso XVII, 133–34 ("Questo tuo grido farà come *vento*, / che *le più alte cime* più *percuote*") and of the *Epistola a Cangrande* ("Nam si ad materiam respiciamus, a principio horribilis et fetida est . . .; ad modum loquendi, *remissus* est modus et *humilis*" [*Epistole*, XIII, 31]) are evident, even obvious. Envy (the word will appear twice again in Boccaccio's next sentence) is not only the true motivation of his detractors but is presented as being utterly out of place as a response to the ultimately "low" *Decameron*, if it might more reasonably be allowed as a response to the "high," or at least "higher," *Commedia*. Every verbal gesture made toward Dante's poem is so flagrantly humble as to invite our delight and suspicious laughter. The "outdoing topos" is rearranged so as to become a claim for having been utterly outdone. If Cacciaguida foretells Dante's huge success in reaching the heights ("le più alte cime"), Boccaccio's poor fictive thing is situated in "profondissime valli"; and if Dante wrote in the vernacular, he at least did so in the noble vehicle of verse, while Boccaccio has limited himself to mere prose. Further, if Dante has claimed, disingenuously or not, a style "remissus . . . et humilis," Boccaccio will go still deeper in self-abasement: "in istilo umilissimo e rimesso quanto il più si possono." It is a richly self-conscious moment. And once again, whatever our interpretation of Boccaccio's desire to remind us of the role of Dante's great poem in defining his own greatest work, we must admit that the *Commedia* is summoned up as the single most significant vernacular antecedent to the *Decameron*. That is, in my opinion, an unchallengeable perception. The task confronting those who study Boccaccio's work closely is first to give over an understandable but dangerous assumption, that two such tonally different masterpieces can have but little in common. Then, once we begin to allow ourselves to perceive how much of Dante's work is in fact reprocessed in Boccaccio's *cento novelle*, we may also begin to understand what those texts are doing there in the first place. In what follows I will offer some possible evidence on the first point and some hypothetical exploration of the second, confining myself to two of the *novelle*, I, 1, and VI, 10.

1. CEPPARELLO AND BRUNETTO: "HOW MAN MAKES HIMSELF IMMORTAL"

The first tale of the *Decameron* had many claims to come first, all of which Boccaccio honored. Of these, I think one (and it is the only one to which I here even advert) is its setting in the very events of 1301 that led to Dante's exile: Boniface's summoning of Charles of Valois into Tuscany to humble the White Guelphs in Florence. We probably ought to consider the possibility that in Boccaccio's mind the narrated action that initiates the metamorphosis of Cepparello into a saint intersects historically with the very moment that began the terrible series of events that led to the exile and, not coincidentally, to the completion of the *Commedia*. That papal summons brings Musciatto Franzesi back to Italy in Charles's entourage and requires him to find a stand-in usurer to do his dirty work in Burgundy. "Perhaps the worst man ever born" (I, 1, 15), Ser Cepparello da Prato is lent two attributes by Boccaccio that should probably draw more enlightened attention than they have: He was a notary ("egli, essendo notaio" [I, 1, 10]), as his title ("ser") would have already indicated; he was a homosexual ("He was as fond of women as are dogs of sticks; but he took more delight in the other sex than any other wicked fellow" [I, 1, 14]). If we were to ask ourselves whether there exist any noteworthy literary representations of homosexual notaries in previous medieval texts, we do not have far to seek: "Siete voi qui, ser Brunetto?" (*Inferno* XV, 30). I suggest that ser Cepparello da Prato is Boccaccio's parodic version of Dante's Brunetto Latini.

It is perhaps surprising that no one has heretofore offered this hypothesis. For instance, we have for some time recognized that ser Cepparello is modeled on a historical figure, one Cepperello or Ciapperello Dietaiuti (how Boccaccio must have enjoyed that surname!) da Prato. As Branca's notes make clear, all but two of Boccaccio's particulars are fitting: "he was not a notary; he was a married man who had children." Why should Boccaccio have chosen a historical figure as the basis for his literary character and then lent him two peculiarities of which we have no record, unless he meant them to serve as iconographic indications that point to a figure whom we might thereby recognize? Without further evidence or any justifying hypothesis, it nonetheless seems to me a likely interpretation, one that makes a certain immediate sense. Yet I believe that a justifying hypothesis does exist and that there is further evidence.

Boccaccio's Cepparello, like Dante's Brunetto, is portrayed as a homosexual only upon his author's word or, perhaps more accurately, invention. Another similarity is apparent when we consider that each of them has left Tuscany to live in France. Here is a brief portion of Panfilo's account of Cepparello's behavior as *notaio*:

This Ciappelletto's life was as follows: being a notary, he was terribly ashamed when one of his documents—and he drew many—was found to be anything but an imposture [*altro che falso trovato*]. . . . He bore false witness with the greatest delight, whether bidden to do so or not.

And here is Boccaccio in the role of *chiosatore* of Brunetto's life and work in his *esposizione* of *Inferno* XV:

This ser Brunetto Latino was a Florentine; he was most accomplished in various of the liberal arts as well as in philosophy; his foremost professional capacity was practicing the notarial art [*notarìa*], in which he excelled. He took such great pride in himself and in this profession that, having made a mistake in drawing a contract and as a result having been accused of imposture [*falsità*], he desired, before being condemned for imposture, to confess his error. He then in disdain departed from Florence, where he left behind in memory of himself a book that he had written called the *Tesoretto*, and went to Paris, where he lived many years and wrote . . . in the vernacular of France . . . the *Tresor*. Some years ago he died, in Paris, I believe.

Since Boccaccio, in his *Esposizioni*, never refers overtly to his own fictions, we can only imagine what he felt as he wrote this passage. It is inconceivable that he did not think of his own homosexual notary, ser Cepparello da Prato, Florentine exile, confessor of his faults, dying in France, leaving his "tesoro" behind him in that foreign land. (Cepparello's entombment as a saint in

Burgundy [I, 1, 87] is perhaps remembered obliquely in a passage of the *Trattatello* [I, 108] that may have served as a bridge between the conclusion of the first tale and *Esposizioni* XV, 18. Describing Ravenna's rich reliquary tradition [tombs of martyrs and emperors], he sees the city as also being the "perpetual guardian of so great a treasure [*tesoro*] as the remains of [Dante], whose works the entire world beholds with wonder." The veneration of Dante's corpse in Ravenna, described in a passage that Boccaccio may have composed within a year of completing the *Decameron*, is thus a glorious counterpart to the foolish veneration of the body of Cepparello in France.) These two notarial literary figures are closely related by antithesis, if they share the sin against nature; Brunetto is an honest notary, the very opposite of Cepparello. While more than twenty years intervene between Boccaccio's description of Cepparello and his later encomium of Dante's Brunetto, and while caution urges us against easy assurance that the view of Brunetto found in the *Esposizioni* was operative in the first tale of the *Decameron*, it is nonetheless at the very least possible that Boccaccio's close knowledge of the *Commedia* would have revealed exactly such responses as these in 1348–50.

On the evidence, we may say with some certainty that in 1373 Boccaccio thought of Brunetto as a counter-Cepparello; that in 1348–50 he very likely had exactly this Brunettian lore in mind and thought of Cepparello as a counter-Brunetto. With or without the possible confirmation offered by the *Esposizioni*, the essential context of Boccaccio's first novella is so richly suggestive of Brunetto and his mission—teaching Dante "come l'uom s'etterna"—that it seems likely that he built his fictional version of Cepparello Dietaiuti out of an inverse representation of the virtues of Brunetto Latini. Once again Boccaccio's later thoughts about Brunetto may be instructive. Near the end of his commentary on *Inferno* XV he explodes into praise of the true immortality gained in fame by poets or any other "componitore in qualunque altra scienza o facoltà" (99). Brunetto's claim that he lives on still in his *Tesoro* (XV, 119–20) offers Boccaccio a final occasion on which to sing the praises of poetry. Yet it also must have reminded its author of his own Cepparello, perverse achiever of another kind of immortality. Boccaccio's gloss may thus be seen to be pertinent both to Dante's poem and to his own *Decameron*.

Panfilo's concluding reflections upon the tale which he has told rehearse dutifully the dual possibilities that Christians, as a matter of doctrine (and on the authority of Dante as well), must entertain: Cepparello may have been taken up into heaven or down into hell. It is not a matter that we in this life may know. And no matter how much more likely the second alternative seems, it is significant that Panfilo, despite his own opinion that the false saint has most likely been damned, insists on presenting the issue as an open question. As we reflect on this most dubious of possibilities, considering whether or not Cepparello has won immortality in heaven as he has won it in the credulous minds of the Burgundians, do we hear a distanced reformulation of Dante's final vision of ser Brunetto ("e parve di coloro / quelli che vince, non colui che perde")? If so, the resonance serves as a mild rebuke to the poet who claimed to know the denizens of hell and heaven. For surely, in Boccaccio's sense of Brunetto's work in *Esposizioni* XV, there is better ground to think of Brunetto as saved than as damned. A damned Brunetto (on Dante's authority) and a potentially saved Cepparello (on Dante's own formulation of what we foolish and curious mortals explicitly cannot know) tend to call into question Dante's poetic stance as *vates*, while at the same time making his Brunetto a figure of the poet worthy of emulation. Boccaccio's Cepparello thus serves to remind the attentive reader that the way in which man may make himself immortal has been debased in a leaden age.

If Boccaccio has rooted prolusory passages of his *Decameron* in Dante's *Commedia* by means of a continuing series of allusions that most readers will readily accept as being immediately evident, he has in his first novella, in the formulation offered here, raised an at once more general and more delicate series of allusions to a specific Dantean text: *Inferno* XV. He has done so without once directly quoting the text in question, relying instead on his reader to be reminded by several rather vivid, if general, likenesses and parallels to appreciate first the overall appositeness of Dante's Brunetto to his Cepparello, then the antithetic nature of the resemblance. If we conclude by considering Cepparello a "false Brunetto" (and I am aware that the evidence for doing so is not so much conclusive as suggestive), we must also consider that such a delicate art of citation, of summoning up the presence of an earlier text, leaves us wondering at Boccaccio's intent. I suggest that in the *Decameron* the *Commedia* is not only a revered text, one that authorizes Boccaccio's choice of words, characters, and events, but is also a text that is being gingerly scrutinized for its possible failings on two main grounds, its poetic truthfulness and its moral applicability. It is my growing sense that Boccaccio's Dante is seen first of all as a maker of fictions, no matter how strongly he wishes to be taken as veridical reporter, and second as an incurable optimist in his insistence that his moral vision is applicable to a Boccaccian world populated by scoundrels, from Cepparello to Gualtieri, Griselda's pitiless husband. If such an appreciation is at all correct, Boccaccio's Dante becomes a different figure from the one that he is generally perceived as being, a precursor who is always poetically relevant yet not finally to be trusted. On Dante's home ground Boccaccio is usually content to be the dutiful commentator whose disputes with his *auctor* are unintentional, the result of an early humanist's misperceptions of Dante's poetic first principles. On his own turf, however, Boccaccio's gentle attacks on Dante are wholly intentional, deriving from the position of a man of the world who respects but cannot accept the idealistic zeal of the *Commedia*. This is not the place for me to advance a ground theory of interpretation of the *Decameron* based in its reception of Dante's poem. All I would suggest now is that Boccaccio's great work is far more bitter than it is generally perceived to be, that it presents us as we are, interested primarily in our personal *utilità* (the perverse version of Horatian and Augustinian usefulness), our motto present in this first novella as a description of Cepparello himself, a man "who cared for nothing if not for himself" (I, 1, 25).

2. FRATE CIPOLLA IN CERTALDO: THE FRIAR AS POET

Only two of Dioneo's ten tales are not concerned primarily with sexual license, those that conclude the sixth and tenth days of the *Decameron*. And while my own discussion of I, 1 and VI, 10, as tales that contain hitherto unremarked presences of Dante, is but a result of my recent readings and is put forward without prejudice to eventual, more wide-ranging investigations, there is some likelihood that Boccaccio thought of Day Six as being particularly closely connected with Dante's poem and with his own Day One. For, while the ten-day structure of the *Decameron* is of course prior, there are also several indications that Boccaccio thought of Day Six as bringing a large aesthetic unit of his work to a formal, if temporary, conclusion:

1. The title *Decameron*, intrinsically at least, invites us to keep in mind the more usual medieval title, *Hexameron*, used for a treatise on the six days of creation.

2. Days One and Six both are Wednesdays and are thus associated with Mercury (*mercoledì*), the god of eloquent speech and thus, in general, of writers.

3. Days One and Six are linked by being the only two days devoted primarily to *motti*; for even if Day One is nominally a "free" day, starting with Filomena's third novella all the *novellatori* tell tales that demonstrate the force of a ready wit put into clever words.

Thus Day Six seems to have had for Boccaccio the function of rounding out, of completing, an important secondary unit of composition. To put this into a more speculative light for a moment, we might try to imagine how satisfying a composition the *Decameron* might have been had it contained only its first six days. I think we can sense that, had Boccaccio in fact written only his *Hexameron*, we would not find it an aesthetically disharmonious artifact.

Day Six is also more than usually reminiscent of Dante's *Commedia*. All of its first nine tales take place in Florence or its environs and probably reveal a greater feeling for the city during

Dante's time than the tales of any other day. (Surely the presence of Giotto and Cavalcanti as exemplary makers of *motti* is enough to make us think of Dante's treatments of these two figures in the *Commedia*.) And if we pause to think of Day Six as rounding out a Boccaccian week (Wednesday to Wednesday) of tale-telling, we will probably consider that the action of the *Commedia* also takes precisely a week (Thursday to Thursday).

With these brief and tentative remarks serving as introduction, let us turn our attention to Dioneo's account of Cipolla's successful deception of the populace of Certaldo. The fact that the friar is of the order of St. Anthony has drawn some commentary attention to Dante's invective against that order in *Paradiso* XXIX, 124–26. But the entire passage (67–126), with its attack on false preachers and their credulous auditors, is germane, although it will not be extensively revisited here. Like Beatrice's prevaricating preachers, frate Cipolla also uses *motti*; and Dante's words ("[With such practices] does Saint Anthony fatten his pig" [124]) probably yield a helpful gloss to Cipolla's assistant: Guccio Balena-Imbratta-Porco is surely a "pig" fattened by the corrupt order of Saint Anthony.

Boccaccio's closeness to Dante's text here is palpable, and if it is not the sort of obvious literary theft one can so easily perceive in Thomas Mann's later appropriation of Cipolla's name for his magician in *Mario und der Zauberer*, where it simply seems impossible to read Mann's story without recognizing the borrowing, it is perhaps still richer in its implications here. Frate Cipolla becomes, on the authority of Dante's text, the very emblem of fraternal fraudulence. Had Boccaccio's purpose been merely to continue Dante's values, however, he surely would have made his borrowing more evident. His imitation is a distanced one, visible enough once we have learned to see it, but not at once before our eyes. Clearly Boccaccio agrees with the moral force of Beatrice's denunciation. Yet he does so, it seems to me, with two disclaimers tugging at him. First, he must have desired to challenge Dante's firm sense of the gulf that separates false rhetorical extravagance from truthful rhetorical expression; second, he is more willing than Dante to explore the pleasures to be found in human behaviors that he admits are immoral. Thus Beatrice's outburst is used as a ground text for the situation of this novella, but does not completely control its final significance. Instead, and as we have seen in the first novella of the *Decameron*, Dante's *Commedia* becomes a text at issue, fervently admired, yet considered overly optimistic in its epistemological and moral assertions. Frate Cipolla, at our first perception of his Dantean provenance, is but a false Antonine, circumscribed by *Paradiso* XXIX. Yet, once we consider him more closely, does not this antithetic representative of Dante's most dearly held values as truth-teller and moralist become increasingly recognizable as the itinerant, lying rhetorician who is a latter-day version of the world's greatest itinerant poet, Dante Alighieri?

Cipolla's perversely lengthy *motto* is devoted to a description of his voyage, along the crusaders' route, to visit the patriarch of Jerusalem (VI, 10, 37–43). Branca has demonstrated that the place names pronounced during the first stage of his narrative of the voyage (37–39) respond to a series of *loci* in Florence itself, moving from east to west. Do we not think of Dante, who describes a visionary journey to still more distant worlds and who might have tested our credulity less had he been content to describe his (and Boccaccio's) city, a city so present in the preceding tales of Day Six? Cipolla continues on his way, through Truffia, Buffia, and finally to "terra di Menzogna," before leaping the sea. Do we not again think of Dante, who so frequently and emphatically swears to us that his journey was a true, and not an imaginary, experience? Is not the *Commedia* in Boccaccio's genially pugnacious view precisely a "terra di Menzogna"? Is not the relationship between Boccaccio and Dante in VI, 10, nearly identical to that between the "due giovani astuti molto" (one of whom, Giovanni del Bragoniera, bears a name at least partially similar to Giovanni Boccaccio's) and frate Cipolla? Boccaccio and the two Certaldesi are witty and playful audiences for marvelous rhetorical performances that they know are literally false but that they admire for their sheer magical audacity.

With this much as indication of Boccaccio's probable desire to put us in mind of Dante when we consider frate Cipolla, I would now like to turn to the two key words of this novella: *penna* and *carbone*. (These words occur a total of thirty-two times in Dioneo's tale, thus offering a qualitative judgment some quantitative support.) It is my contention that both are used with a lively awareness of their previous presences in the *Commedia*, where each does important service as a signifier of success or failure in aesthetic enterprise. Let us begin with *penna*.

Penna occurs in twenty-five *loci* in the *Commedia*; it appears twenty-eight times in the *Decameron*. In both works its most usual meaning is "feather," the *penne* found on wing of bird or angel. In the *Commedia*, on the other hand, the word five times signifies "pen," the tool of writer or painter; in Boccaccio it has such meaning six times. This meaning of the word is introduced to the *Commedia* in the beautiful extended simile that presents a peasant being at first discouraged by the hoarfrost (*brina*) that copies the snow: "but only a short while lasts the etching of its pen" (*Inferno* XXIV, 6). This remarkable image of nature imitating nature yields to a more usual sense for the word *penna* in *Inferno* XXV, 144. Dante, describing the super-Ovidian transformations of the thieves, begs our indulgence: "and here may the newness [of the phenomenon described] be my excuse if my pen seem to stray." The word returns in the celebrated passage in which Dante's poetic superiority is acceded to by Bonagiunta Orbicciani: "I well understand how your pens follow close upon the words of him who dictates—which was not true of ours" (*Purgatorio* XXIV, 58–60). Without pausing on the complex problems raised by this passage, we may simply note that the word has the same meaning here as in *Inferno* XXV, the authorial pen, made from a bird's feather, a natural object become the very sign of poetic making. Yet is it not Dante's claim that *his* pen is capable of faithful and truthful imitation? Justinian, retelling the history of Rome in terms of the flight of the imperial eagle, claims that its development under Julius Caesar was such "that neither tongue nor pen could follow it" (VI, 63). At *Paradiso* XXIV, 25, the word is employed with this signification a final time: "And thus does my pen pass over; I do not write it down." Dante's use of *penna*, then, in the sense of a recording instrument of reality, is obviously of some importance in the *Commedia*.

Boccaccio's deployment of the word is no less striking and is, as we shall see, cognizant of Dante's. It first appears in the description of frate Alberto, interestingly enough a self-disguiser who assumes the role of the angel Gabriel, punished as "uom salvatico," covered with honey and "empiuto di sopra di penna matta" (IV, 2, 52). Not only does the punishment fit the crime, the criminal looks forward to the similarly deceitful friar, Cipolla, who also seeks to identify himself with Gabriel. At V, 9, 37, the "penne, piedi, e becco" of Federigo's falcon become the sad and tangible sign of the poor man's love for Giovanna. The third use of the word in the *Decameron* occurs at VI, 5, 5, where we are introduced to Giotto, whom Boccaccio describes in the following enthusiastic terms:

> His genius was so surpassing that what he depicted, whether by means of stylus [*stile*] and pen or brush [*pennello*], so resembled what nature produces that it seemed less a likeness than the very thing itself, so much so that many times it happens that our sense of sight is deceived by his works, taking his depiction to be the thing itself.

The passage draws on Dante's exclamation of his wonder at God's art in the figurations on the pavement at *Purgatorio* XII, 64–66: "What sort of master of brush [*pennel*] or stylus [*stile*] was it that traced the figures and their features so as to make even rare genius marvel there?"

Perhaps no two passages in the *Decameron* and the *Commedia* more intensely present our authors' enthusiasm for the mimetic nature of art. Yet Dante insists on the inadequacy of even the greatest human sculptor or painter when his art is confronted with God's mimetic magnificence; Boccaccio, in evident polemic with his *maestro e autore*, insists on Giotto's supremacy as perfect mimic of nature. That is the sole mimetic task that Boccaccio would seem to be willing to admit to a human aesthetic capacity. Dante's passage itself reflects his judgments of painters pronounced some hundred lines earlier: Oderisi, having praised Franco Bolognese, goes on to report that Giotto has now surpassed Cimabue (XI, 94–96). Thus Dante's encomium of God's art in *Purgatorio* XII is implicitly a criticism of Giotto's merely human art. Boccaccio, imitating Dante's discussion of imitation and undoubtedly understanding the limited nature of Dante's praise of Giotto, now turns the argument back on its author.

Of Boccaccio's twenty-seven uses of *penna* in the *Decameron*, nineteen occur in VI, 10. There it always has the meaning "feather," referring to the parrot's feather (VI, 10, 46), which Cipolla claims is a feather from a wing of the angel Gabriel. We shall return to this *penna* shortly, after completing our inventory of *penne* in the *Decameron*. The next one we find is at VII, 8, 46, where the deceived husband Arriguccio is rebuked by his scathing mother-in-law. Her description of him includes the following details of his appearance: "with his stockings falling down around his ankles and with his pen stuck in his anus." Branca's note here refers us to the practice of a merchant or a notary who carries his *pennaiuolo* in his back pocket. Arriguccio's mercantile pen is a scabrously sorry object to imagine, the antithesis of Giotto's "stile . . . penna o . . . pennello," the petty bourgeois's pitiful (and probably falsifying) instrument for carrying out his *mercatura*. The word occurs four more times in the *Decameron*. Its next two uses are in the mouth of the vindictive scholar, boasting to the roasted widow of the power of his satiric *penna* (VIII, 7, 99) in ways that look forward to the *Corbaccio*. The *Conclusione dell'Autore* finally places the *penna* in the hand to which it most truly belongs: ". . . to give repose to pen and wearied hand" (1). His last use of the word asks that we grant his pen an authority equal to that which we allow the painter's brush: ". . . less authority is not due my pen than is due the painter's brush [*pennello*]" (6). We are reminded again of Giotto and of Boccaccio's sense of identity with him; and we have seen how much authority we should grant Giotto's mimetic capacity in the passage quoted above (VI, 5, 5).

Thus Boccaccio's varying uses of *penna* as the instrument of the artist would seem to establish a hierarchy. One's pen may resemble Giotto's brush (and Boccaccio's is obviously meant to be perceived as doing exactly that), or it may be the poor instrument of an inept merchant (VIII, 8), even the angry and wounding engine of a spurned scholar/lover (VIII, 7). In Boccaccio's hand it is the tool of the artist who has the power, like Giotto, to set before us the world as it is; this implicit claim has been honored by nearly all Boccaccio's enthusiasts.

Let us return to Cipolla. The parrot's feather that the friar would hold up as a relic is not referred to in terms that at first remind us of the six *loci* in the *Decameron* in which *penna* means "pen." Yet the fact that the actual object is the feather of a parrot is itself instructive, for that creature is the most talkative and mimetic of fowl. Cipolla is himself a sort of *pappagallo*, whose "tail feather" is redeployed by his fraudulent imagination on Gabriel's wings. This feather is metamorphosed by Cipolla's "pen," his artist's capacity for colossal untruth. As I have suggested earlier, Cipolla is presented as a sort of Dante run amok, a poetic wild man, although one, unlike Dante, who is willing to admit to his two Certaldese admirers that his "poetry" is *fabula* and not *historia*. It is the latter only for the groundlings at 3:00 p.m. on one 8 August in the early fourteenth century at Certaldo. The equations that we may derive from the *penne* found in the *Commedia* and the *Decameron* yield the following:

DANTE: True art = God's art = *Commedia*;
≠ Giotto's art.

BOCCACCIO: True art = Giotto's art = *Decameron*;
≠ Dante's art.

Giotto is a common element in each equation, with startlingly different results.

To conclude, we return to the second key word of *Decameron* VI, 10: *carbone*. It appears fifteen times in the work, fourteen of these here. Boccaccio's summary of VI, 10, runs as follows: "Frate Cipolla promises certain countryfolk that he will show them a feather of the angel Gabriel; finding coals in its place, he says they were among those that roasted Saint Lawrence." The struggle faced by Cipolla is to turn the *carboni*, left to him in place of the parrot's feather by his inimical friends, into spiritualized relics for the multitude. If a parrot's feather is, by comparison, fairly easy to pass off to the gullible as angelic, to make *carboni* seem sacral objects involves greater sleight of mind.

We have already seen how central to Dioneo's tale is Beatrice's assault on false preachers in *Paradiso* XXIX. Another of Dante's texts also beckons. *Purgatorio* II, 25–51, chronicles the advent of the Mercury-like angel who guides the triumphant crusading souls of the saved to the shore of Purgatory. Virgil orders Dante to kneel and pray in reverence before his "eternal feathers, which, unlike mortal plumage, are immutable" (35–36). This "uccel divino" (38) presides over a boatload of singing pilgrims. He leaves them after he has made the sign of the cross over them (49)—with his *penne*, we may reflect. Cipolla has described *his* crusade/pilgrimage to the Holy Land where he was given his angel's feather. After he sings "una laude di san Lorenzo" (VI, 10, 53), he too makes the sign of the cross on his auditors (a large one, requiring arduous laundering, we must reflect). Dante's arrival in Purgatory, a scene reflective of medieval pilgrimage to the Holy Land, probably stands behind Cipolla's false "pilgrimage" and his behavior as fraudulent angelic intercessor.

The *carboni* that he employs to sign these "crusaders" of Certaldo are also, it seems to me, of Dantean provenance. As he reveals them to the multitude, Cipolla refers to them as "carboni spenti" (51). The phrase, as far as I have been able to determine, has occurred only once before in Italian literature, *Inferno* XX, 100–102: "And I said: 'Master, your words are so sure to me and so gather my faith, that others would be for me burnt out coals [*carboni spenti*].'" Dante, seduced by Virgil's own denunciation of a passage in the *Aeneid* (X, 198–203) that would make Manto the mother of Mantuans, agrees to "desacralize" those verses of the *Aeneid*. *Carboni spenti*, in this formulation, become the very emblem of dead poetic activity. For a text to be a "carbone spento" is for it to contain no truth. Has not Cipolla (and Boccaccio!) given the final twist possible to Dante's phrase and its meaning? He has taken worthless objects, *carboni spenti*, and revivified them, made them, as it were, "penne." They even become, and specifically so, instruments for *writing*, indeed for writing the most sacrosanct of "words," the cross. Such is the nature of Boccaccio's supremely artful little joke at the expense of his beloved Dante.

If these reflections upon Boccaccio's reading of Dante have merit—and I confess that I myself am not so much convinced by evidence as intrigued by possibility—then there is a good deal more to be studied in the relationships between two of the greatest texts that mankind has ever received from its masters.

Nancy J. Vickers

The Body Re-membered
Petrarchan Lyric and the Strategies of Description

The speaker of Petrarch's *Rime sparse* characterizes his project as a specifically descriptive one, as an attempt to represent a woman loved and lost. In sonnet 309 he summarizes: "Love, who first set free my tongue, wishes me to depict and show her to whoever did not see her, and therefore a thousand times he has vainly put to work wit, time, pens, papers, inks."[1] Praise of Laura, an activity emblematized by the repeated play on *lauda-Laura*, springs then from epideictic roots, emerges from a rhetorical tradition of description as the center of celebration. The main moments of Petrarch's narrative—if indeed one can call it that—are consequently an instant of first appearance and a lifelong attempt at recreating, at making re-present, that instant. Laura's body is to be painted in verse, not only for the mind's eye of the age to come, but also for that of the speaker who loses her: "At the beginning," he reflects, "I thought to find through speech . . . some brief repose and some truce" (*RS* 73, 16–18). But truce is not lasting, and the effort to recapture Laura's lost *belle membra*, "beautiful parts," is an acknowledged failure—partial, fragmentary, empty.

Petrarch's speaker would depict a woman of indescribable beauty: it is, he tells us, the need to figure that beauty that makes him a poet, that loosens the knot that binds his tongue, that permits his speech; and it is the confrontation with indescribability that threatens that same speech. In this paradoxical context the act of describing necessarily questions the very possibility of description, questions the notion that perceived reality can constitute truth or that words can ever reproduce perceived reality. Sonnet 308 succinctly poses the question:

> Quella per cui con Sorga ò cangiato Arno,
> con franca povertà serve ricchezze,
> volse in amaro sue sante dolcezze
> ond'io già vissi, or me ne struggo et scarno.
>
> Da poi più volte ò riprovato indarno
> al secol che verrà l'alte bellezze
> pinger cantando, a ciò che l'ame et prezze,
> né col mio stile il suo bel viso incarno.
>
> Le lode, mai non d'altra et proprie sue,
> che'n lei fur come stelle in cielo sparte,
> pur ardisco ombreggiare, or una or due;
>
> ma poi ch'i' giungo a la divina parte,
> ch'un chiaro et breve sole al mondo fue,
> ivi manca l'ardir, l'ingegno et l'arte.

> She for whom I exchanged Arno for Sorgue and slavish riches for free poverty, turned her holy sweetness[es], on which I once lived, into bitterness, by which I am destroyed and disfleshed.

> Since then I have often tried in vain to depict in song for the age to come her high beauties, that it may love and prize them, nor with my style can I incarnate her lovely face.

> Still now and again I dare to adumbrate one or two of the praises that were always hers, never any other's, that were as many as the stars [scattered] across the sky;

> but when I come to her divine part, which was a bright brief sun to the world, there fails my daring, my wit, and my art.

This sonnet's first stanza specifies a turning point, a moment when sweetnesses (in which the speaker once lived) turned to bitterness (which presently kills): from that moment he has tried in vain to paint a portrait. The stanza structures itself upon a sequence of oppositions that are, at base, contrasts of fullness (presence) and emptiness (absence).[2] He has exchanged Arno

(Florence, mother country) for Sorgue (Vaucluse, exile); riches (although slavish) for poverty (albeit free); sweetness for bitterness; a body for dismemberment; union for separation. His rhymes point to a past place (the river Arno) and to two present, though fruitless (*indarno*), activities—he is at once stripped of flesh (*me ne . . . scarno*) and would give flesh to her (*incarno*). He acknowledges his inability to re-create Laura's absent face, and yet he maintains that he still tries, "now and again." Her praises—that is his poems—are but images he "dares to adumbrate," shadows "scattered," like their source, across the sky. Daring, wit, and art cannot fully re-present her to him: they fail before her divine part (presumably her soul), but they do sketch her other parts, "one by one," and thus generate an exquisite sequence of verse.[3] Indeed the rhymes of 308 might well be read as keys to both the objects (*parte/sparte*: part(s)/scattered) and the processes (*scarno/incarno*: I "disflesh"/I "inflesh") of Petrarchan description.

I will turn first to the related notions of particularization (*parte*) and scattering (*sparte*). A tension underlies Petrarch's entire sequence between the scattered and the gathered, the integrated and the disintegrated.[4] Moreover, in defining that tension—Petrarch's "poetics of fragmentation"—recent critics (Robert Durling, John Freccero, and Giuseppe Mazzotta) have consistently identified as one of its primary figures the particularizing descriptive strategy adopted to evoke Laura.[5] If the speaker's "self" (his text, his *corpus*) is to attempt a unity, it would seem to require the repetition of his lady's dispersed image.[6] We never see a totalizing description of Laura. This might not be exceptional if we were considering a single "song" or even a restricted lyric context: gothic top-to-toe enumeration seems, after all, more appropriate to narrative, more adapted to the "objective" observations of a third person narrator than to those of a speaker who ostensibly loves and perhaps even addresses the woman he describes.[7] But given an entire volume devoted to the "painting" of one woman, the absence of an attempt at a coherent or comprehensive portrait is significant. Laura is always presented as a part or parts of a body. When more than one part figures in a single text, sequential, inclusive ordering is never stressed. Her textures are those of metals and stones: her image is that of a collection of exquisitely beautiful, disassociated objects.[8] Singled out among them are hair, hand, foot, and eyes: golden hair trapped and bound the speaker; an ivory hand took his heart away; a marble foot imprinted the grass and flowers; starry eyes directed him in his wandering.[9] In terms of qualitative attributes (blondness, whiteness, sparkle), little in Petrarch is innovative. More specifically Petrarchan, however, is the obsessive insistence on the particular, an insistence that would in turn generate multiple texts on individual fragments of the body—whole sequences to the eyes, or entire sonnets on a foot. The goal, you recall from sonnet 308, was to "pinger cantando" ('to paint through singing'), not Laura's beauty, but her "beauties" (11. 6–7).

In the *Rime sparse* one verb places this particularization in the foreground: it is, moreover, a determinant verb for the entire sequence—*spargere*, "to scatter." *Spargere* appears in some form (most frequently that of the past-participial adjective *sparso* (*sparto*) forty-three times, and the pattern of its application is telling: nineteen (almost half) apply specifically to Laura's body and its emanations (the light from her eyes, the generative capacity of her footsteps); and thirteen (almost a third) to the speaker's mental state and its expression (tears, voice, rhymes, sighs, thoughts, praises, prayers, and hopes). The uses of *spargere* thus markedly gravitate toward not one but two poles; not just to Laura, but also to "I." His praises and her parts, as suggested in 308, are curiously coextensive: "Still now and again I dare to adumbrate one or two of the praises that were always hers, never any other's, that were as many as the stars scattered across the sky" (11. 9–11). The etymological roots of *spargere*, moreover, generate Laura's metaphoric codes. "I" figures the part-objects he would represent in terms of the connotations of "scattering": from the Latin *spargere* with cognates in the English "sprinkle" and "sparkle" and the Greek σπείρω, "I disseminate." Laura's eyes, for example, are generative sparks emanating from the stars; they sow the seeds of poetry in the "untilled soil" of the poet; and they sprinkle glistening drops like clear waters.[10] Her body parts metaphorically inseminate; his do not: "Song, I never was the cloud of gold that once descended in a precious rain so that it partly quenched the fire of Jove; but I have certainly been a flame lit by a lovely glance and I have been the bird that rises highest in the air raising her whom in my words I honor" (RS 23, 161–66).

Within the context of Petrarch's extended sequence, then, the lady is corporeally scattered; the lover emotionally scattered; and the relation between the two is, by extension, one of mirroring. "I" tells us that he stood fixed to see, but also mirror Laura; he offers to eliminate the only source of sadness for the lovely eyes—their inability to see themselves—by mirroring them; and he transforms the coloration of the lady's flesh into roses scattered in snow in which he mirrors himself.[11] The specular nature of this exchange explains, in large part, the often disconcerting interchangeability of its participants. Even the key rhyme *rimembra/membra* ("remember/members") reflects a doubling: twice the *membra* are his (RS 15 and 23); once those of the lost heroes of a disintegrating body politic (RS 53); and twice hers (RS 126 and 127). In reading madrigal 52, a text in which the speaker equates his voyeuristic pleasure in witnessing the laundering of Laura's veil with Actaeon's voyeuristic pleasure in seeing Diana's naked body, Giuseppe Mazzotta demonstrates this textual commingling; he points out that Diana's body, in the first tercet, is completely naked (*tutta ignuda*) in a pool of icy waters (*gelide acque*), but, by the last line, her observer's body is all atremble (*tutto tremar*) with a chill of love (*un amoroso gielo*).[12] Mazzotta goes on to note that male/female roles often alternate in Petrarch's figurations of the speaker/Laura relationship: he is Echo to her Narcissus, Narcissus to her Echo; she is Apollo to his Daphne, Daphne to his Apollo, and so on.[13] The space of that alternation is, of course, a median one—a space of looks, mirrors and texts.

In a recent study, Michel Beaujour suggestively comments, "The contradictions of language in description, of space in time, lead to an imitation of process and passage which yet is not narrative: we might call it a metamorphosis."[14] Drawing examples from the *Roman de la Rose*, he elaborates: "The fountain of Narcissus, then, is something like an allegory of the descriptive mode in general, . . . the fountain is a textual emblem of ekphrasis," a surface that dually orients desire "toward an object and toward the self as it is reflected in the mirror."[15] Returning to Petrarch's sonnet we do indeed read process: we read verbs that describe and characterize the act of description: "I" would "inflesh" (*incarno*) a lost body but cannot; and inversely a speaking body is being "disfleshed" (*scarno*). A metamorphosis takes place before our eyes; but within which mythical construct, within which frame of reference?

In his twenty-third *canzone*, the *canzone* of the metamorphoses, Petrarch's "I" narrates his history of changes: he was Daphne (a laurel), Cygnus (a swan), Battus (a stone), Byblis (a fountain), Echo (a voice), he will never be Jove (a golden raincloud), and he is Actaeon (a stag). He has passed through a series of painful frustrations, now experiences a highly specific one, and never was granted the sexual fulfillment of a god capable of transforming himself into a golden shower and inseminating the object of his desire. His use of the present in the last full stanza— the Actaeon stanza—is telling, for it centers his text and his sequence on the juxtaposition of what the speaker was and what he now is: "Alas, what am I? What was I? / The end crowns the life, the evening the day." The end also crowns the song, and this song paradoxically abandons its speaker in the form of a man so transmuted that he cannot speak.

Petrarch's account of Actaeon's story closely follows the subtext that obviously subtends the entire *canzone*—Ovid's *Metamorphoses*. Actaeon is, like Narcissus, a hunter. Like Narcissus he seeks rest and shade in a grove and sees, by chance, a beautiful body in a pool. For Narcissus that body is his own; for Actaeon it is that of Diana, chaste goddess of the hunt. In Ovid, Diana is surrounded by protective nymphs, but Petrarch makes no mention of either her company or of Actaeon's. He thus focuses the exchange on its principal players. Actaeon is transfixed (a stance Petrarch exaggerates), and Diana, both in shame and anger, sprinkles (*spargens*) his face (*vultum*) and hair (*comas*) with water. Although in Petrarch Diana is silenced, in Ovid she utters these words: "Now you can tell (*narres . . . licet*) that you have seen me unveiled (*posito velamine*)—that is if you can tell (*si poteris narrare*) (*Metamorphoses* III. 192–93). Diana's admonition simultaneously posits telling (narration and/or description) as the probable outcome of Actaeon's glance and negates the possibility of that telling. Her vengeful baptism operates a metamorphosis: it sequentially transforms Actaeon from horn to hoof into a voiceless, fearful stag (*Metamorphoses* III. 193–98). It is at this moment that Petrarch, with a characteristic iterative present, situates his speaker: "No other sight appeases me"; "I am transformed"; "I flee" (*RS* 23, 152, 159–60). The speaker *is* Actaeon, but, more important, he is a self-conscious Actaeon: he knows his own story; he has read his own text; he is defined by it and even echoes it in enunciating his suffering. What awaits is annihilation through dismemberment, attack unto death by his own hounds goaded on by his own devoted friends.

It is perhaps logical to examine Petrarch's use of a myth about seeing a woman—a goddess, but still a woman—in order to reexamine the strategies he adopts to describe a woman seen. The Diana/Actaeon story is, after all, not only one of confrontation with forbidden naked deity, but also with forbidden naked femininity. Here the "metaphor of appearance," to use Mazzotta's phrase,[16] that is so central to Petrarch's volume, is paired with a myth of appearance: the fateful first perception of Laura—an image obsessively remembered, reworked, and repeated—assumes a mythical analogue and mythical proportion. What the reader must then ask is why that remembered image, like the rhyme (*rimembra*, "remember"/*membra*, "members") that invokes it, is one of parts. An answer, I think, may be found in the pattern of relating imbedded in the myth itself.

The Diana/Actaeon story is a story of identification and reversal: Actaeon hunts; Diana hunts; and their encounter reduces him to the status of the hunted.[17] Petrarch further underscores this equation by having his Actaeon describe the first perception of Diana in terms more animal than human or divine: "I followed so far my desire that one day, hunting as I was wont, I went forth, and that lovely cruel wild creature (*fera*) was in a spring naked when the sun burned most strongly" (*RS*, 147–51). This fated meeting, this instant of midday recognition, is one of fascination and repulsion, for it is ultimately a confrontation with difference where sameness might have been expected and desired. It is a glance into a mirror that produces an unlike, a different, a deeply threatening image. In order that the reader not miss this implication, Ovid's Actaeon, once transformed, literally repeats the specular gesture. Prefiguring Narcissus, he looks into another pool and sees the stag he acknowledges to be himself. The sight before him provokes horror, not love. Whereas Narcissus fails to recognize and adores an image, Actaeon knows and despises an image: "But when he sees his features and his horns in a clear pool, 'Oh woe is me!' he tries to say; but no words come. He groans—the only speech he has—and tears run down cheeks that are not his own" (*Metamorphoses* III, 201–03). His transmuted body signifies his sin and suggests his punishment; he recognizes himself as the prey of his own hunt, as a body identical to those he has so often mutilated.

Actaeon sees Diana; Diana sees Actaeon; and seeing is traumatic for both. She is ashamed, tries to hide her body, and thus communicates her sense of violation. Her observer consequently knows that pleasure in the sight before him constitutes transgression: he deduces that transgression, although thrilling, is threatening. Their initial communication is a silent look. Subsequently signifying media fill the gap between them: in Ovid, "She stood, turning aside a little, and cast back her gaze; and though she would fain have had her arrows ready, what she had she took up, the water, and scattered it (*spargens*) on the young man's face and hair" (*Metamorphoses* III, 187–90); and in Petrarch, "I stood to gaze on her, whence she felt shame and, to take revenge or to hide herself, sprinkled water (*mi sparse*) in my face with her hands. I shall speak the truth" (*RS* 23, 52–56). She shatters the mirror of likeness and defends herself with scattered water; he, with scattered words: "You who hear in scattered rhymes (*rime sparse*)the sound of those sighs with which I nourished my heart, during my first youthful error, when I was in part (*in parte*) another man from what I am now" (*RS* 1, 1–4).

But Ovid's telling of the Diana-Actaeon encounter differs in important ways from Petrarch's. In Ovid, Diana is the only person to speak once Actaeon has caught his first glimpse of her: *narrare* is her word; she pronounces it; she even repeats it. "Now you are free to tell (*narres . . . licet*) that you have seen me unveiled—if you can tell (*narrare*)" (*Metamorphoses* III. 192–193). She cannot (or would not?) prevent him from seeing, but rather from telling. Consequently, that Petrarch erases both her speech and the verbal object of her interdiction (*narrare*) from his own narration is significant. A review of the evolution of the Diana-Actaeon sequence of *Rime sparse* 23, a text at many points explicit in its verbal echoing of Ovid, shows that "I shall speak the truth (*dirò*)" initiates the primary and final versions of line 156. Two intermediate variants read: "I narrate the truth (*narro*)."[18] What that rejected present, *narro*, affirms in a mode perhaps too obvious to be acceptable even to Petrarch, is that his speaker, as Actaeon, does precisely what Diana forbids. Laura, too, forbids: "Make no word of this," she insists earlier in the same *canzone* (*RS* 23, 74). Not only does Petrarch's Actaeon thus nullify Diana's act, he repeats her admonition in so doing. To the measure that he continues his praises, he persists in inverting the traditional economy of the mythical exchange; he persists in offending: "Not that I do not see how much my praise injures you," he says to the eyes, "but I cannot resist the great desire that is in me since I saw what no thought can equal, let alone speech, mine or others" (*RS* 71, 16–21).

Petrarch's "modern" Actaeon is in a median time: he is fearful of the price of seeing yet to be paid—dismemberment—but still pleased by what he saw. The remembered image is the source of all joy and pain, peace and anxiety, love and hate: "Living is such heavy and long pain, that I cry out for the end in my great desire to see her again whom it would have been better not to have seen at all" (*RS* 312, 12–14). He perpetuates her image in speech that is on the brink of silence: he repeatedly tells us that he "cries out in silence," that is to say, "cries out with paper and ink."

A body is displayed to Actaeon, and his body, as a consequence, is literally torn apart. Petrarch's Actaeon, having read his Ovid, realizes what will follow: his response to the threat of dismemberment (*me ne scarno*) is a neutralization, through descriptive dismemberment (*incarno*), of that threat. The description of what was seen, consequently, is informed less by the status of an external body than by the status of the speaker who would speak it; who depicts and shows it to "whoever did not see" it; who—if successful—transforms his listener or reader into yet another Actaeon. He would accomplish a complex incarnation—her flesh made words (made flesh). His description would not only "re-member," restore substance to a lost body, it would safely guarantee remembering:

> Chiare, fresche et dolci acque
> ove le belle membra
> pose colei che sola a me par donna,
> gentil ramo ove piacque
> (con sospir mi rimembra) . . .
>
> Clear, fresh, sweet waters, where she who alone seems lady to me rested her lovely parts, gentle branch where it pleased her (with sighing I remember) . . . (RS, 126,1–5).

Even this image, imprinted in the book of memory, is not that of a lovely face mirrored, Narcissus-like, in the limpid stillness of a pool but rather that of exquisite parts poised in the "clear, fresh, sweet waters" of the river Sorgue, a medium that moves but does not change, that is constant but in flux. Petrarch's descriptive project—"to paint in song Laura's high beauties"—similarly sets her *belle membra* in a medium of process and of passage. Like the speaker we are left to wonder at the futility of any attempt to construct unity through re-membering, but we must acknowledge that by insistently painting in the waves the poet generates a portrait destined to resist not only coherence but also completion, a portrait that must forever be begun.

Murray Krieger

Presentation and Representation in the Renaissance Lyric
The Net of Words and the Escape of the Gods

I begin by trying to convey some idea of the exhilaration I feel as I respond to the dynamics within the linguistic forces set and maintained in motion by the English Renaissance lyric at its best. Let me suggest two rather different, if not opposed, modes of verbal behavior.

Here is the first movement I seek to follow: A word seems about to turn into another word. It is very exciting to watch it happen. But how can the transformation occur? Here is the word in the process of overrunning its bounds, destroying its own sense of territorial integrity along with its neighbor's. It is undoing the very notion of "property," whether we relate the term "property" to that which defines an entity or to that which defines a possession, so that it is defying the operational procedures of logic and law—and those as well of language itself. For property is the elementary basis for the differential principle underlying the operation of language, which in turn underlies the operations of both logic and law.

Still, in the face of such impressive resistance, the word seems to pursue its errant career, if we know how to watch it perform. At which moment does a word stop being its own sealed self and begin to merge with its neighbor? Can a system of conventionally accepted meanings continue to function if any of them turns unstable and thus slides into fluidity? All these difficulties are exacerbated if the differences between the terms being transformed into identity are—more than merely different—wholly contradictory: if they are nothing less than binary oppositions that are forced into a fusion. Often, it is through the exploited coincidence of the arbitrary phonetic properties of words that such fusion is apparently achieved. (It would take another paper to deal with the complicated process by which the act of silent hearing is incorporated into the reading habits of the educated reader when confronted by a poem.) Because words, however different in meaning, sound alike—or almost alike—they are forced, as we hear by watching, to become alike. Often it occurs in the coupling act of rhyming or—more extremely—of punning. But often the poet slips from word to word and from sound to sound in a continuing parade of subtle echoes.

We find this extraordinary poetic tactic in many English Renaissance poems. We can begin with an obvious example. In Ralegh's "Poesy to Prove Affection is Not Love" ("Conceit, begotten by the eyes, / Is quickly born and quickly dies"), the poet deals with the death-in-life of affection, the "conceit" that "within the Mother's *womb* / hath his beginning and his *tomb*." This collapsing of the womb-tomb opposition into a womb that is also and at the same moment a tomb becomes an enabling act for the poem's complex claim.

Or a more subtle example. In Ralegh's "Nymph's Reply" to Marlowe's "Passionate Shepherd," in the line "Time drives the flock from *field* to *fold*," we find a simplicity that should not hide its density. The single alteration of the vowel from "field" to "fold" carries with it the equation within the course of nature's seasons as well as within man's life: from open freedom to coffinlike enclosure, under the driving hand of time, the second ("fold") already implicit (inscribed) in the first ("field")—in its very letters. And, a bit later, the line, "Is fancy's spring, but sorrow's fall"—following "A honey-tongue, a heart of gall"—uses its chiastic pattern of alliteration ("fancy's" and "fall" on the outside, "spring" and "sorrows" on the inside) to hold its oppositions and yet convert them into the sameness of echo.

Let me cite one last quotation from Ralegh, this one at a desperately and conclusively late moment in the magnificent "Nature, that washed her hands in milk." Having created an elegantly balanced ideal mistress at the behest of love, nature must suffer her delicately wrought creature to be undone by time, which "Turns snow and silk and milk to dust." The sequence of alliteration and internal rhyme leads to the crumbling of language into a negative, universal equation. Nature earlier turned away from earth, using snow and silk instead, as she propagated the moist by excluding the dry, but the moistness of snow and silk and milk ends with the alliterative equivalent of the *drying* that is a *dying*: ends, like earth, in *dust* with the collapse of all distinctions. (Pages could be written on the destructive power that Ralegh—in more poems than this one—imposes on the alliterative extension of words beginning with the letter *d*.)

Shakespeare everywhere reminds us of the transformational power of words, their appearing to defy their own distinctness by overlapping and changing places with one another. As he suggests in Sonnet 105, his verse, "One thing expressing, leaves out difference." The sonnets are full of examples. I'll cite just a few, choosing almost at random. I have dealt with some of these, often at length, in other places, so that it should be enough for me to do barely more than mention them here.[1]

There is the obvious collapse of the line between truth and falsity, as well as the multiplication of the meanings of those terms *true* and *false*, in the lines from Sonnet 72, "O, lest your *true love* may seem *false* in this, / That you for *love* speak well of me *untrue*." Or there is the collapse of the line between opposition and advocacy in Sonnet 35: "For to thy *sensual* fault I bring in *sense*— / Thy *adverse* party is thy *advocate*." In Sonnets 6 and 9 we find a verbal play that muddies distinctions among use, interest, waste, and abuse: "That *use* is not forbidden *usury*" (Sonnet 6, line 5) and, later, "But beauty's waste hath in the world an end, / And kept *unused*, the *user* so destroys it" (Sonnet 9, lines 11–12). In Sonnet 71, the calculating world of material self-interest, in its concern to feed the body, is quickly identified with the feeding *off* the body by those most materialistic inheritors of the grave: ". . . that I am fled / From this *vile world*, with *vilest worms* to dwell." The vileness of the world is totally realized only in the superlatively consistent activity of the vilest worms, which correct the spelling (*world* to *worms*) and extend vileness to the ultimate degree.

Opposites are turned into one another even more extremely in the fully realized pun, in which two words—violently at odds with one another—share a single phonetic entity. Thus, in Sonnet 87, "Farewell! thou art too dear for my possessing," "dear" must embrace and identify that which is dear in the marketplace with that which is dear in our unworldly affections. The mixed argument that follows springs from both sides of this doubleness of "dear." We find in a good number of sonnets a similar use of puns to bring together into a phonetic identity meanings that are normally differentiated or even opposed—for example, in "state" in Sonnet 124 ("If my dear love were but the child of state") and in "refigured" in Sonnet 6 ("Then let not winter's ragged hand deface"): "Ten times thyself were happier than thou art, / If ten of thine ten times refigured thee." The device of having one word turn into another, under the pressure of the poem's dynamics, is only exaggerated in the pun that forces at least two words to be one another at the same time. Words seem to undermine themselves and the way they are supposed to function, as if they insist on reminding us that their meanings, with oppositions flowing into one another, must be as inconstant as the experience they would record. Most of my examples, from the inconstant "conceit" of Ralegh onward, have related the inconstancy of these words (despite their pretense to be fixed entities) to the inconstancy of time, so that words as fixed entities would be an inaccurate representation of experience under the fickleness of time. The purely poetic device cannot escape having thematic consequences—indeed must be seen as the consequence itself of a thematic cause. The thematic and the poetic are circularly related, like the chicken and the egg. The words, as a conceit, may seem to be a fixed or static formula of meaning, but Sonnet 15, furnishing me my final example of the movement from one word into another, indicates how unfixed the verbal formula becomes after all: the sonnet refers to "the *conceit* of this *inconstant* stay" (line 9), forcing the conceit itself to collapse into inconstancy.

But I mentioned at the start that I would point out two rather different, if not opposed, modes of verbal behavior, and so far I have spoken of one only. Now for the second. Instead of our watching as meanings come together in violation of the law of differentiation or even binary opposition, we may find what seems to be the reverse operation occurring. As we watch, a word finds itself at odds with itself, falls out with itself, indeed negates itself, in effect canceling itself out; it undoes the integrity of words upon which the operation of language depends. A stunning example occurs in Shakespeare's Sonnet 116 ("Let me not to the marriage of true minds"): ". . . love is not love / Which alters when it alteration finds / Or bends with the remover to remove." The negative repetition ("love" to "not love") is indeed a self-denial of language, a self-cancellation. Language in effect wipes itself out as everything is made relative, contingent, arbitrary. The poet must protest a language that operates this way, though this seems to be the inevitable consequence of the function of language.

A similar expunging of the word occurs in Thomas Campion's song, "Thou art not fair," when the poet threatens the beloved to take away her nature (that is, change his mind about her) if she is less than constant: ". . . thou shalt prove / That *beauty* is *no beauty* without love." Or Ben Jonson's "Slow, slow, fresh fount," in which time forces the acknowledgment, "*Our* beauties are *not ours*." If, in the first poetic manipulation of language that I have described, differences collapse into apparent identity in a way that violates the notion of verbal boundaries and property, in this second operation we find the most immediate linguistic entity losing identity, falling itself into difference—now at a distance from itself, so that there is no single, undifferentiated verbal self.

Perhaps the most striking example of this second device is found in *The Phoenix and Turtle* in the climactic cry of reason, which, in its admiring acknowledgment of the impossible union it has witnessed, in effect denies its own name: "Love hath reason, reason none, / If what parts can so remain." The miraculous destruction of number in love is a violation of the operation of reason, and love's very existence changes what reason must be as it changes the way in which language can work—in effect, by insisting that, in the way we usually understand it, language cannot work at all.

But this final example should indicate to us that our two seemingly opposed modes of poetic devices are themselves in the end identical and mutually reenforcing. The line "Love hath reason, reason none," emphasizes both the falling apart of a verbal entity ("reason none") and the growing together of opposed entities ("love hath reason"). Despite my separating these two devices, it should have been clear throughout that there is a similar, if reverse, duplicity operating in both, a duplicity that forces our observation to see every movement of words toward identity as accompanied by an equally urgent movement in them toward differentiation, each from itself as well as from every other. It is precisely this need to hold both awarenesses at once—the identifying and the differentiating—that makes these movements we have been observing so exciting in their stretching of the resources of linguistic operation.

Probably no example can serve more forcefully to reflect this duplicity than those lines I have already quoted from Ralegh's "Nymph's Reply": "A honey tongue, a heart of gall, / Is fancy's spring, but sorrow's fall." The mingling of the move to identity with the move to differentiation among fancy and fall, spring and sorrow, or rather spring and fall, fancy and sorrow (echoing the cross-relations within the parallels of the preceding line) is only the more forceful when we remind ourselves that these lines are preceded by the lines, "The flowers do fade, and *wanton* fields / To *wayward* winter reckoning yields." The unpredictability and indiscriminacy of unlimited fertility turn into the unpredictability and indiscriminacy of unlimited death, the "wanton" into the "wayward," words that overlap as much as they are distinguished, as they are applied to "fields" and the alliterated "winter." Hence, in "honey," "heart," "tongue," "gall," or "fancy," "fall," "sorrow," "spring," the interlacings of parallelism and chiasmus, of meaning and sound, join opposition to dissolution.

These duplicitous manipulations of words, as they are made either to move outward to interanimate one another or to move inward to cut off from themselves—or to manage somehow to do both at once—such manipulations arise from the poet's struggle to win from language a representational power that he does not trust words normally to provide. By exploiting the sensory side of words—their sound, which is their only material aspect—the poet tries to invoke the illusion of their presence. This is for him to use the sensible to transform the intelligible. It is his way to overcome our impression of verbal absence—inspired by an exclusive interest in the merely intelligible aspect of words—our impression of words whose object is elsewhere as they mean, often vainly, to point to it. Thus their auditory character, normally most arbitrary in that it has no relation to their meaning, seems—by means of devices such as those I have suggested—to turn words substantive, in effect allowing them to take on the illusion of body. So, apparently acknowledging normal language to be a verbal parade of arbitrary meanings, of empty, bodiless counters, the poet seeks to turn the arbitrary into the necessary and the functional—into the materially present. It is as if he uses the sound of words as the most extreme symbol of their arbitrary character, forcing those apparently insignificant phonetic elements to prove the poem's power to break through arbitrariness to substantive inevitability, to transform our awareness of words' absent, though intelligible, objects to their own material, fully sensible presence.

I can point—as I have elsewhere[2]—to Sir Philip Sidney's Sonnet 35 ("What may words say, or what may words not say"), which I might refer to as his semiotic sonnet in that it deals explicitly with the problem of representation and the futile contribution made by our usual words to solving it. The poet is worried that even our noblest words—names of our most glorious abstractions—can have no meaning because the living reality of Stella forces them to contradict and hence negate themselves. In the sonnet we find example after example of the second of the two devices I described earlier, the self-denial by words of their own entityhood ("Love is not love . . ." or "Love hath reason, reason none"):

> What may words say, or what may words not say,
> Where truth itself must speak like flattery?
> Within what bounds can one his liking stay,
> Where Nature doth with infinite agree?
>   What Nestor's counsel can my flames ally,
> Since Reason's self doth blow the coal in me?
> And ah what hope, that hope should once see day,
> Where Cupid is sworn page to Chastity?

How can words have meaning if Stella's very being forces truth to speak like flattery, forces nature to be one with infinity, forces reason to be the sponsor of desire, forces Cupid to be "sworn page" to chastity? And then the climactic inversion: instead of a person growing through achieving fame, ". . . Fame / Doth even grow rich, naming my Stella's name." The invocation of the one true name, the one word in the language that encloses its own essential value, is the only act that authenticates language, gives it a reality. Fame can grow rich in the act of naming Stella's name; and the poem itself guarantees the claim by at that moment naming Stella's actual name, Rich, following it with her mythical name, Stella. (Is the double name the reason for the poet's repeating the word "name"?) So fame has aggrandized itself; it becomes "rich," in effect becomes Stella. The one way for other verbal names (truth, nature, reason, chastity, fame) to have substance is for them to share the substantive magic of the one true name, the name that *is* its meaning (thanks to a fortuitous pun). Otherwise words are without substance, empty. And the sonnet's conclusion follows: it is she who teaches wit what perfection is, and it is she who raises praise to the level of being itself praised in the moment of being praised herself: "Not thou by praise, but praise in thee is raised: / It is a praise to praise, when thou art praised." Once Stella herself has entered the poem by way of her name to en-rich fame, she is able, similarly, to convert the incapacities of words ("wit," "praise") to a new power, although she licenses them only for the single act of serving her own reality, her being finally bestowing meaning upon them.

The poet has in this sonnet indulged—and in this sonnet sequence freely indulges—the magical act of invoking Stella's name to convert all other names, those unmagical nouns that fill both our language and our empty poetic conventions, from nonsense to meaning, a living meaning attached to her living being. In sonnet after sonnet we find the magic word *Stella* incanted and then watch the transformations that follow from that incantation. From the first sonnet in the sequence (and the first sonnet itself is a splendid example), the poet is struggling with a halting, recalcitrant, and inoperative language that will not do the job of representation, and resolves his struggle by breaking through to the substantive image of Stella, a reality carried in the image and usually invoked by the name, the latter being the one signifier that suffers no separation from its signified. Stella, her being as well as her name, must be made by the poet to invade the unreal net of words—and to invest it with substance. In this one case, the nominal reality becomes the fleshly reality, a language that enables this poetry to speak as man otherwise cannot. Thus, in Sonnet 74 ("I never drank of Aganippe well"), the poet, a "layman" forsaken by the antique, figurative muses and unfit "for sacred rites," has his mouth inspired by the mouth of Stella, a fleshly muse who gives speech through oral embrace: "My lips are sweet, inspired with Stella's kiss." The introduction of Stella's kiss, in the final couplet, is an invocation of a present and literal muse indeed. The poet's invocation is an act that puts the sonnet in the present tense, and, since her name alone is substantive, she is to enter the poem with her name.

It is as if the poet has discovered the built-in futility of our usual attempt at verbal representation. That futility is carried in the prefix, the *re* of *re*present. Words are empty and belated counters because it is their nature to seek to refer to what is elsewhere and has occurred earlier. Any pretension by them to present reality is frustrated by the *re*, which requires that what they would represent—what has already presented itself in person—

has had its presence, its presentness, elsewhere and earlier. But the poet would dabble in verbal magic, calling upon a sacred name that would overcome belatedness and introduce a living, bodily hereness that would make language more than properly representational, that would make it nothing less than presentational.

What, in Sidney's enraptured fiction, makes Stella's name so special in its powers, at once exempted from the empty inconstancies of words and able to reendow language with a vital function? The name is to remind us that the language around it has long been deactivated, even as it creates for us a new dispensation under which words can be reactivated, given substance, *her* substance, once again. But what permits the name to function in this remarkable way? Clearly, as in much Renaissance lyric poetry that reaches ambitiously toward presence, what is paramount is the analogy to Christian paradox, with its insistence on the participatory magic by which spirit partakes of, and becomes one with, body. Unlike the now-absent gods that once inhabited verbal abstractions often represented by the gods in Classical mythology (truth, reason, love, and so on), Stella *is* her name and constantly remains so, just as that name actively intrudes upon, and participates in, these poems, both as name, with its heavenly trappings, and as the physically present lady herself.

In Sonnet 28 ("You that with allegory's curious frame"), the poet rejects the use of allegorical structures and references in favor of the plain and literal statement, in favor of "pure simplicity." Though he speaks extravagance enough in the poem, it is—because he speaks of Stella, because he speaks the name *Stella* and speaks under its aegis—to be taken as literal simplicity. Thus, "When I say Stella, I do mean the same / Princess of Beauty. . . ." And the conclusion: "But know that I in pure simplicity, / Breathe out the flames which burn within my heart, / Love only reading unto me this art." That direct speech should be so apparently metaphorical and simplicity so apparently extravagant is attributable—as in other sonnets—to Stella and the poet's invocation of her rather than to any empty appeal to "allegory's curious frame." But, guided by her powers, the speech remains direct and simple, whatever it may seem; for it is literal speech. After all, the invoked name, Stella, like the lady herself, is at once her name and an *apparently* allegorical reference to the star (thus qualifying her poet-lover as an Astrophil, or star-lover). But, the sonnet is insisting, this too is no allegory; it is simply what she is (and what, consequently, she makes him). Again he would have her participate in, and become consubstantial with, these meanings (as he did with the abstractions in Sonnet 35), claiming a new dispensation for language, not unlike the typological identities being claimed for a semiotic controlled by the Christian paradox.

But, with Stella enacting the role of his goddess, why not this claim? It *is* an outrageous joke for the poet to deny using allegory at the very moment he is speaking her apparently allegorical name ("When I say, Stella, I do mean . . ." and mean nothing more; but what he says he means is more than enough—"princess of beauty" and the rest). Still, his very point is that all that he says is what, simply and literally, she *is*. Whatever he has given away is won back through her; whatever he has given away in language is won back through her name. It all pours into her and out of her—*as* her name. And, as this new dispensation for language, that name is the only language he speaks—and really the only word, since all other words are to be read—or rather reread—in light of it. No wonder, then, that, as he tells us in Sonnet 19, no matter what he tries to write, "My very ink turns straight to Stella's name." And Stella, with all that name means and is, is captured in the poem and, once in it, reconstructs its meaning and its action.

On the other side, in the cynical poem by Fulke Greville, one of Sidney's close contemporaries (Ralegh was another), "Away with these self-loving lads," there are the following lines:

> My songs they be of Cynthia's praise,
> I wear her rings on holy-days,
> On every tree I write her name,
> And every day I read the same.
>   Where Honor, Cupid's rival, is
>   There miracles are seen of his.

> If Cynthia crave her ring of me,
> I blot her name out of the tree.

Where there is inconstancy, a failure to overcome the ways of the world under the sway of time, there no name is sacred; a name cannot replenish the emptiness and arbitrariness of language but only shares in it. Names, like all words, come and go, are written and subsequently erased, are interchangeable. Honor is the rival of Cupid and, so long as Honor holds out, justifies the miracle of the lady's name written and each day ritualistically adored. But the eventual victory of Cupid and inconstancy leads to erasure and substitution.

One can look upon such apparently light, if bitter, love poems as serious attempts to treat man's desire as the extreme emblem of the earthly, of the absolutely arbitrary, with the interchange of names representative of the interchangeability of words within a failed and impotent language. Sidney himself is, in some sonnets expressing failure, aware of the failure of his magic, of his attempt to invoke the sacred name and, with it, Stella's presence. Nowhere is the invocation of the name more explicit, or the failure—and Stella's continued absence—more starkly acknowledged than in Sonnet 106:

> O absent presence Stella is not here;
> False flattering hope, that with so fair a face,
> Bare me in hand, that in this orphan place,
> Stella, I say my Stella, should appear.

The lack of response leaves the poet, his world, and his language, untransformed as, in the balance of the sonnet, he comes close to (but resists) the temptations of Greville's fickle world of change.

It is the poet's double awareness that concerns me here: he knows, as a result of his impatience with language's representational—to say nothing of its presentational—failures, that he must indulge the pious attempt to use the poem to invoke and contain its object, its goddess; but he knows also the illusory nature of his attempt, the recalcitrance of language, together with its refusal, after all, really to give way. So he knows also the transcendence of the gods, their abandonment of the world and of the world of language. But he continues to try and to cultivate his (sometimes ironic) poetic illusions.

The sonneteer's invocation of the poem's object, bringing her into the poem as an active presence through the use of verbal devices such as those I have examined, returns me to a theme that has been central to all my writings on Renaissance poetry and especially on the English Petrarchan sonnet: the phonetic struggle for an illusion of presence that we find in it reflects the poet's effort to force into the network of language the elusive object that words—his words of love—have not been able to capture. Here is what I have referred to as the poet's quest for a representational power or—more extremely—a directly presentational power that he finds words normally lack. The referent—as the beloved, the poet's goddess, his Platonic heaven—insists on remaining transcendental to the poet's words that would enclose her in order to transform her state from one of absence to one of presence. After all, the fictional given of the Petrarchan sonnet is precisely that which demands such an effort on the part of the poet-lover. He writes his poem out of his lack, his want, of his beloved, who is—and threatens to remain—at a distance from him, like the absent god from the supplicant. But, as we have seen with Sidney, in his poem the poet can do more than complain of this absence, though complain he surely does; he can seek to use the poem to close the breach between his sacred object and himself, to make her responsive and hence present by having her enter the poem by way of her invoked name. So the poem can be as much an entreaty as a lamentation, as much an act—and a call to action in return—as a sorrowful recitation.

What the poet is trying to bring about—whatever his skepticism about the chances for his literal success—is a miracle of linguistic presence as much as a miracle of quasi-religious presence. His task, and the breakthrough he hopes to accomplish, partake of the realm of semiology as well as that of love's theology. The beloved goddess, who is absent from him and who is beseeched by his poem, must be brought bodily into it by having her name break through the emptiness of words to fill them with itself and—through name magic—with herself. As Sidney's Sonnet 35 ("What may words say, or what may words not say") has shown us, it is the language process itself, with all its unmagical incapacities, which must be reconstituted in the act of naming the beloved. To the extent that the poem would succeed, it must transform the naming process of language in order to retain the present goddess trapped within it. Thus, as I earlier pointed out, in Sonnet 74 ("I never drank of Aganippe well"), we see the actual kiss of Stella's lips by the poet's lips replace the empty allusions to the muses with the actual consequences of physical presence.

So the absent goddess sought by the Petrarchan poet is one among the absent signifieds to which the normally dualistic process of language testifies. It is for this reason that I have claimed the poet's trial to be at once semiological and theological, if—indeed—love's theology is not being reduced to a problem in semiology. The world of references stands outside the network of words that seeks in vain to capture it. As the Petrarchan poet conceives the problem, chief within that world, the all-dominating transcendental signified among a host of transcendental signifieds, is the beloved-as-goddess. If the poet can work the magical breakthrough into presence for her, the others will follow within a remade language process.

I see the poet, then, as setting himself the objective of capturing the absent god (or goddess) within a verbal network that he knows cannot hold him (or her). The poet works his magic, changes lamentation to invocation, sometimes claims success; but we see him start the next poem anew as if the task has to be performed all over again. This is a Sisyphus-like concession to the failure of his word-magic to produce more than a momentary illusion of a breakthrough to presence. The absent goddess and the world of being that she dominates are out there still, still resisting capture by his words, whatever he may momentarily have appeared to bring about with his phonetic word play and the invocations that it permits.

The path I have been traveling has led us back to my title,

which is my theme: "Presentation and Representation: The Net of Words and the Escape of the Gods." My reference there was to the language of Ben Jonson's "Why I Write Not of Love," which I have discussed at greater length on another occasion.[3]

> Some act of Love's bound to rehearse,
> I thought to bind him in my verse;
> Which when he felt, Away, quoth he,
> Can poets hope to fetter me?
> It is enough they once did get
> Mars and my mother in their net;
> I wear not these my wings in vain.
> With which he fled me, and again
> Into my rhymes could ne'er be got
> By any art. Then wonder not
> That since, my numbers are so cold,
> When Love is fled, and I grow old.

The poet has set himself the task of binding Cupid in his verse, and Cupid is equally determined to evade capture. And, of course, momentarily the poet does have him—indeed has him as a speaking character. The god reminds the poet of Homer's earlier capture, in *his* net of words, of Venus and Mars in their lovemaking. It is significant that Cupid is attributing the act of binding to the poet rather than to the irate Hephaestus, who in the narrative forges the net (of metal and not of words) to display the lovers. The responsibility, so far as Cupid is concerned, is Homer's: Cupid is looking beyond the narrative cause in the jealous god to the ultimate metapoetic cause in the poet. He is looking, then, to the net of words that, for Cupid's purposes on the present occasion, is more substantive and threatening than the net forged within the frame of the story. Cupid's escape from the present poet follows, and the poet's verse must do without the erotic god.

But the god is referred to in the poem, not as Cupid, but as Love. And what makes the poem work so brilliantly is the gradual movement—anticipated in the poem's title ("Why I Write Not of Love")—that allows Love also to take on all the roles of love as it functions in the poet's life. When the god Love is fled, so is love, leaving an old, cold poet, with his verses emptied of the god—and of desire. If he does not have Love (the god) in his verse, he cannot have love, consequently cannot write of love. Presentation must accompany representation. The language of myth is given life by being made participatory, as literary allusion and living immediacy are made one. Isn't this very much the unified doubleness we saw in Stella as she functioned in her several ways in Sidney's Sonnet 28, with its denial of allegory? Stella's function as star, goddess, and beloved is similar to Cupid's function as erotic god and the poet's desire. The god is both the mythological creature and the existential force that the mythic name represents, so that she or he forces herself or himself into presence and beyond allegory, beyond *re*presentation.

Still, despite the entry into experience by myth, as the poet describes it the mythic god himself struggles against the poet to maintain his absence, to remain transcendental to the words, to keep them from filling themselves with divine presence. So once again, as with Sidney's Sonnet 35, Jonson's poem is concerned with its subject and theme by virtue of its being concerned with semiotics, with what its words—or what words in general as signs—can mean and can enclose, as well as with what escapes words to remain unreachably outside discourse, to remain the gods and transcendent.

In his well-known song, "Drink to me only with thine eyes," Jonson explicitly raises the question of the divinity of the object of desire, prefers her fleshly humanity, and then—if only ironically—suggests the divine consequences of her earthy powers. Early in the poem, the rhyming words "wine," "divine," and "thine" carry the contrast and permit the inversion.

> Or leave a kiss but in the cup,
> And I'll not look for wine.
> The thirst that from the soul doth rise
> Doth ask a drink divine;
> But might I of Jove's nectar sup,
> I would not change for thine.

The lady's kiss is preferred as a substitute for the sacrament of wine, the "drink divine," as the speaker seems—in an anti-

Petrarchan vein—to insist upon her as an antithesis to divinity. It is this un-divine nature that is for him precisely the source of her power. But, in the second half of the song, the speaker attributes the transubstantiating power to the lady's effect on the flowers, which, if we are to believe him (he says, "I swear"), can be nothing less than miraculously divine, even though that effect is restricted to the world of sense (how the flowers smell).

> I sent thee late a rosy wreath,
> Not so much honoring thee,
> As giving it a hope that there
> It could not withered be.
> But thou thereon didst only breathe,
> And sent'st it back to me,
> Since when it grows and smells, I swear,
> Not of itself, but thee.

The poem is utterly good-humored about its insistence upon the ungodly, sensual appeal of the lady: it halfheartedly seeks to make her his goddess by virtue of that appeal, and, having found the words that—through a rhyming exchange—could effect her transformation, it relaxes its pressure in order to keep itself within the realm of the sublimity of human limitations. In the contrast and exchange between the wine and the kiss, I am reminded of Sidney's "I never drank of Aganippe well" (Sonnet 74), in which the kiss functions as the earthly substitute for the muse—literal inspiration (mouth to mouth) for empty figurative inspiration. The bodily world of sense is accepted through the exalted metaphors of myth, although those metaphors now appear in their literal nakedness, as deconstructed equivalents of transcendental signifieds brought inside human language for the purpose of functioning in a thoroughly human experience. The poet's lofty language, for all its reductions, does not fail, because his application of it, accompanied by a wink, is restricted to a world from which transcendence has been excluded. The creatures and the actions he has constructed are verbal only, since he implicitly acknowledges the incapacity of his words to do more, though we may—for the occasion—rest in the satisfactions and momentary persuasions of the fusions and transformations his language seems to have worked upon us.

I return to Ralegh's "Nature, that washed her hands in milk" for a final observation about the attempt of a poem to construct an artful object of idolatry within its verbal bounds, and its confessed failure to do so. But, I must insist, if it is thematically about failure, it is a failure that only supports the poem's confidence in its own artifice, which is to say, in its own illusionary success.

> Nature, that washed her hands in milk,
> And had forgot to dry them,
> Instead of earth took snow and silk,
> At love's request to try them,
> If she a mistress could compose
> To please love's fancy out of those.
>
> Her eyes he would should be of light,
> A violet breath, and lips of jelly;
> Her hair not black, nor overbright,
> And of the softest down her belly;
> As for her inside he 'ld have it
> Only of wantonness and wit.
>
> At love's entreaty such a one
> Nature made, but with her beauty
> She hath framed a heart of stone;
> So as love, by ill destiny,
> Must die for her whom nature gave him,
> Because her darling would not save him.
>
> But time (which nature doth despise
> And rudely gives her love the lie,
> Makes hope a fool, and sorrow wise)
> His hands do neither wash nor dry;
> But being made of steel and rust,
> Turns snow and silk and milk to dust.
>
> The light, the belly, lips, and breath,
> He dims, discolors, and destroys;
> With those he feeds but fills not death,

> Which sometimes were the food of joys.
> Yea, time doth dull each lively wit,
> And dries all wantonness with it.
>
> Oh, cruel time! which takes in trust
> Our youth, our joys, and all we have,
> And pays us but with age and dust;
> Who in the dark and silent grave
> When we have wandered all our ways
> Shuts up the story of our days.

This poem may serve as an allegory of what I have tried to describe in this essay—and, pace Sidney's sonneteer, critics may resort to allegory and its transparencies even if poets should not. Speaking about this poem, I commented earlier on the rejection of earth for the moist-smooth-whiteness of milk and snow and silk as materials to be used in nature's attempt—in response to "love's request"—to "compose" an ideal mistress for the pleasure of "love's fancy." But this mistress, which nature—with whatever self-contradiction—has composed artificially, is a perfect Petrarchan creation since with her beauty nature has given her an unnatural "heart of stone" (unnatural though conventional—that is, thoroughly in accord with Petrarchan convention). The consequences for love and his ideal mistress are controlled within a "real" world that runs in accordance with enmity and its spite. Nature's cold creature kills love, for whom she was created, and time—nature's enemy—in turn destroys nature's prized creation: "His hands do neither wash nor dry; / But being made of steel and rust, / Turns snow and silk and milk to dust." Even worse, time's destructive action is not even a special damnation, specially enjoyed, contrived for a most precious creation slated for extinction. It is no uniquely prized victory. Instead, the action is, like time itself, automatic in its application: he feeds her specially created parts to death indiscriminately, like any of nature's less endowed creatures, so that death is fed but hardly filled by her.

> The light, the belly, lips, and breath,
> He dims, discolors, and destroys;

> With those he feeds but fills not *d*eath,
> Which sometimes were the foo*d* of joys.
> Yea, time *d*oth *d*ull each lively wit,
> And *d*ries all wantonness with it.

The poem preciously and delicately composes nature's creature, an absolute poetic creation supposedly responsive to love's poetically conventional desires. That her "heart of stone" is unresponsive to love's actual needs is in accord with the convention that dictates her creation and is a result of nature's foregoing of earth for more delicate, if cool, materials. As a creature of artifice, there is no earth in her, and so no earthiness in her response to love. But the creature, this superb work of art, is reduced—with all of earth—to dust (and I recall my observation about Ralegh's deadly use of the alliterated "d," each instance of which I have italicized in the above quotation). The extravagant metaphor invented by nature to constitute the creature, with all its substitutions of milk and snow and silk for earth, collapses; it dissipates, with the rest of us, into a negative residue. With the metaphoric attempt thus shown to be only a fragile illusion, no more than an aesthetic construct, time takes the stage to give us the sense of an ending that converts the deconstruction it has traced into a narrative that finds formal closure. The metaphor may have failed to sustain itself, since the creature is no more than earth after all, but the illusion it permitted before its deflation is one of the most glorious of the stories that, at the end, time closes off. Which is why the poet has chronicled it.

By the final stanza the characters have been eliminated, one by one: love, the mistress, and—by implication—nature itself. Only time is left at the end to tell the story by ending all stories, supplying the closure for all our stories:

> Oh, cruel time! which takes in trust
> Our youth, our joys, and all we have,
> And pays us but with age and dust;
> Who in the dark and silent grave
> When we have wandered all our ways
> Shuts up the story of our days.

"Shuts up the story of our days"—an echo of "Time drives the flock from field to fold" in "The Nymph's Reply": it sees the flock of all of us shut up by time in the "fold," the universal coffin.[4] In effect, then, time brings even itself to a close in that, although still standing onstage, beyond the last line even it must cease to exist. For the closure, the shutting up the story of our days, is absolute. Ultimately—which is to say beyond the last line—it is only the final negating character, death, time's agent, that remains. Only death remains—together, of course, with the words of the poem ("the story") that seems to have eliminated everyone but itself, now emptied of all it has created narratively and metaphorically, though insistent upon its own verbal presence as testament of what is lost.

I have tried here to center our concern upon English Renaissance poets wrestling with the problem of verbal representation. They see that it is the nature of signifieds—gods and beloveds among less glorious ones—to continue to be transcendental, as it is the struggle of poets to use their specially wrought net of words to capture them and to keep them trapped within discourse. All things that come before the poet's present, belated discourse—whether in language or outside it—stand like elusive gods outside it and its attempt to name them. In Sidney's Stella, Jonson's Love, and Ralegh's creature, we have seen various methods by which the poet both closes and reopens the gap between transcendence and participation, between stand-off and breakthrough—in other words, between failed representation and satisfying presentation.

Renaissance poets seemed capable of giving themselves a secular mission that was to demystify language as language operates outside the theological realm. When they were most self-conscious, which was not infrequently, they were aware of the deceptive tendency of all language to deify its would-be objects. Their own obligation was to expose this deception and confess the abandonment of language by the gods. But at the same time they had, themselves, to undertake to create a language that could truly tame the gods and bring them inside. So the poet had to acknowledge what language normally cannot do, what words may not say. He had to manipulate them, in hopes of turning them into *his* words, magic words, so that, in spite of their usual incapacities, he could enrich them, endow them with the power to speak after all, the power that attested to a present signified, a captured god within.

But the transcendent god is never caught, after all, however well the verbal net seems to be forged. The poet has sought to open up that net in order to seize and return with its would-be signifieds; to open it up and then, as with "the story of our days," to shut it down. He tries to display them and succeeds in giving us an awareness of the semiotic exhilaration that would accompany such an entrapment. He may even give us a momentary sense that he has them and that we have caught a glimpse of them. But a higher linguistic reality is there too, one that the poet uses to remind us of his sleight of hand, as he shuts up his own story, packs up his verbal magic, and walks off, leaving our gods intact and far away, as we return to our babbling. Fortunately, however, we may still be rescued from time to time; for the poems remain, a permanent presence, ready to perform.

Thomas M. Greene

Erasmus's "Festina lente"
Vulnerabilities of the Humanist Text

The term "vulnerabilities" in my title may well appear perverse in connection with one of Erasmus's *Adagia*, that most notorious of all Renaissance *florilegia*, a vast, baggy, shapeless hulk of a book, its 4000-odd entries apparently innocent of organization and proof against all its indexes, unread today for the most part and perhaps in its entirety unreadable. To deliver a wound, even to strike a blow, one wants to know where one is aiming, but this interminable leviathan—literally interminable—presents us no fore or aft. One might lop off a decade of entries here, a century there; no sequence would be interrupted. To assault this amorphous monster, even to talk about it, seems nothing if not quixotic; "Fluvius cum mari certas"—being no more than a river, you contend with the sea. Yet for all its formidable, swollen, and treacherous mass, one can discern a kind of structure organizing individual entries; one can also appropriately describe certain features of the *Adagia* as vulnerable, features that are endemic to the Humanist enterprise and inseparable from the peculiar type of Humanist mimesis.

The rough history of the *Adagia* is well known: its modest beginning with a paltry 800-plus entries in 1500, near the opening of Erasmus's literary career; its first large edition in 1508 with over 3200 entries, nourished by its author's improving Greek as well as his access to Italian libraries and to the press of Aldus Manutius; then its frequent re-editions throughout the remainder of its author's life, each new edition containing more entries and interpolations inserted in the older ones, more autobiography and more polemic as the author discovered his book's potentialities. Each entry includes a proverb, a figure of speech, an enigmatic cliché familiar in antiquity, followed by a commentary that is primarily, ostensibly philological, citing the passages or authors where the phrase can be found and indicating its ancient meaning and evolving range of meanings. In some cases this purely philological commentary fades into a discussion of potential applications within Erasmus's contemporaneous world. In roughly twenty cases, this in turn leads to a longish essay capable of introducing almost anything Erasmus cared about. Thus any entry consists of two unequal parts—the original adage proper, inherited from antiquity, and its unfolding, its explication, at greater or lesser length, with greater or lesser inventive freedom, always subject to expansion.

Seemingly one of the freest of all the adage-commentaries is that produced by the little oxymoronic injunction "Speūde bradéos, Festina lente," "make haste slowly," which first appeared in the big Aldine edition of 1508. Erasmus privileges this adage not only by the length and range of his commentary but also by his enthusiasm. He writes that no other proverb is as worthy as this one, so absolutely concise, so fertile, so gemlike, so applicable to every situation in life. In fact, he writes, it deserves to be called "royal," *regius*, partly because its wisdom is needed by kings, but also, one gathers, because this is the king of all the adages. We observe, however, that the genealogy of this royalty is more obscure than befits most kings. Erasmus cites an expression from Aristophanes, "make haste hastily," and conjectures that somebody later wittily reversed the adverb. At any rate, Octavius Caesar is known to have used the phrase repeatedly, and the emperor Titus had a coin stamped bearing a dolphin and an anchor to express the same thought. The mention of this medal opens up alternative, older, and mistier genealogical reaches, back into the hermetic lore, the *prisca theologia* of the ancient Egyptians, who according to Plutarch and "Suidas" produced a so-called hieroglyphic wherein a circle enclosed a dolphin entwined around an anchor. Since a circle symbolized eternity (this symbolization permits a digression on the metaphysics of finite and infinite lines), since a dolphin symbolized speed and an anchor delay, the hieroglyphic is to be read: "Always hasten slowly." After elaborating on each of these mystic meanings in turn, Erasmus modernizes hieroglyph and adage by referring to his printer, Aldus Manutius, who has made the anchor and dolphin his trademark. Nor, writes Erasmus, is there any falling off from the imperial coin to the printer's page, since this particular printer seems born to restore true ancient learning. Aldus typifies the Humanist hero-archaeologist-necromancer who restores the ruinous and the dead to life. No nobler work can be imagined.

> It is indeed a Herculean task, and worthy of a kingly spirit, to restore to the world so divine a thing, out of such complete ruin; to investigate what lay hidden, to bring to light what was concealed, to call to life what had perished, to fill up gaps and emend a text corrupted in so many ways.[1]

In conclusion Erasmus offers three overlapping interpretations of this royal adage: first, "it would be better to wait a little before tackling a matter; when a decision has been reached, then swift action can be taken"; second, "the passions of the mind should be reined in by reason"; third, "precipitate action should be avoided in everything." Erasmus ends his commentary by expatiating on each of these sententious truisms.

This sketchy summary of mine recompresses a text that presents itself as a decompression and that underscores its own leisurely, digressive, serpentine progress, pulling in allusions, quotations, erudite bric-a-brac, souvenirs, and anecdotes to enlarge its substance and lengthen its course. How are we to understand the relationship of this garrulous paraphrase to the tiny ur-phrase which instigated it? What is the logic of this fusion of *copia* and brevity, and what structural principle, if any, orders it? The impulse, whatever it was, that produced this text and its thousands of companions has to be regarded with some curiosity, since the *Adagia* stands, whether or not we read it, as one of the fountainheads of Humanism. In fact, each paraphrastic, dilative unfolding can be considered as a microcosm of the Humanist enterprise.

The search for an organizational center should properly begin with Erasmus's love of verbal jewelry. At the opening of the "Festina lente" essay, he says that proverbs in their concision and brilliance should be as clear-cut as gems (*gemmae*). This particular adage he finds especially gemlike. The analogy recurs frequently. We meet it again in the adage-essay "Herculei labores": "Proverbs are like little gems, so small that they often escape the searcher's eye unless you look very carefully. They are not ready to hand but lie hidden, and it is a matter of digging them out rather than collecting them" (p. 196). To search out these tiny stones of meaning is for Erasmus precisely a Herculean labor, and we can guess which one when he compares the ignorance and laziness of commentators to dung concealing gold. In the prefatory epistle to the *Parabolae*, which itself amounts to a book-length catalogue of similes, the same metaphor returns.

I have not chosen what was ready to hand, nor picked up pebbles on the beach; I have brought forth precious stones from the inner treasure-house of the Muses. The barber's shop, the tawdry conversation of the marketplace are no source for what is to be worth the attention of the ears and eyes of educated men. Such things must be unearthed in the innermost secrets of nature, in the inner shrine of the arts and sciences.

This unearthing is worth the labor, writes Erasmus somewhat surprisingly, since "almost all the dignity of language stems from its metaphors."[2] In his fascination with the hard, secret, precious, time-resistant capsule of signification, Erasmus seems to attribute to it something theurgic, mysteriously and uncannily powerful. The amulet of meaning carries an aura of potency all the stronger if the meaning is enigmatic or figurative or paradoxical. Thus in "Festina lente," what Erasmus calls the force and fecundity of the words lies in their oxymoronic conflict: "verbis inter se pugnantibus." The absolute brevity of the paradox produces its "precii miraculum," and we should not, I think, try to diminish the wonder of the writer before the *miraculum*, this talismanic marvel.

The same fascination with the apparently irreducible kernel can be found in Erasmus's devotional writing. The Christian, like the Humanist, betrays this wonder, although he adjusts his metaphors. In the adage-essay "Sileni Alcibiadis," he writes:

The parables of the Gospel, if you take them at face value—who would not think that they came from a simple ignorant man? And yet if you crack the nut, you find inside that profound wisdom, truly divine, a touch of something which is clearly like Christ himself. . . . The real truth always lies deeply hidden, not to be understood easily or by many people. (P. 276)

This principle of verbal expression is also the principle of biology, even of what we might call human ontology.

In trees, it is the flowers and leaves which are beautiful to the eye: their spreading bulk is visible far and wide. But the seed, in which lies the power of it all, how tiny a thing it is! how secret, how far from flattering the sight or showing itself off! Gold and gems are hidden by nature in the deepest recesses of the earth. Among what they call the elements, the most important are those furthest removed from the senses, like air and fire. In living things, what is best and most vital is secreted in the inward parts. In man, what is most divine and immortal is what cannot be seen. (Pp. 274–75)

This secret ontology of man is also the ontology of the kingdom of heaven, which "has as its symbol a grain of mustard seed, small and contemptible in appearance, mighty in power" (p. 273). That principle must be kept in mind by the interpreter of scripture. The *Enchiridion* compares God's secret law to manna. "The fact that it was only a small thing signifies the paltriness of language, the vast mysteries contained in words which are, so to speak, crude and inadequate." Later Erasmus invites the reader to "break through the husk and find the kernel."[3] It is hard to resist pairing this sacred kernel of the *Enchiridion* with the potent gem of the *Adagia*: both are verbal Silenus boxes whose resistance to understanding has to be pierced for the initiate to participate in their latent semiotic infinitude.

Yet the "Festina lente" essay reminds us that this absolute brevity, "absoluta brevitas," is *not* absolute; the irreducible gem is further reducible, since the essay alludes to that pseudo-code that the Renaissance called "hieroglyphics" and that, following Plutarch's example, it credulously attributed to ancient Egypt.

[Hieroglyphics] is the word for the enigmatic carvings which were so much used in early times, especially among the Egyptian seers and theologians, who thought it wrong to exhibit the mysteries to the vulgar in open writing, as we do; but they expressed what they thought worthy to be known by various symbols, things or animals, so that not everyone could readily interpret them. But if anyone deeply studied the qualities of each object, and the special nature and power of each creature, he would at length . . . understand the meaning of the riddle. (P. 175)

From this passage it is clear that the hieroglyphic is superior to the adage on three counts: first, it is even more compressed; second, it does not signify idiosyncratically—its meaning is not dependent on historical accident but remains perennial; third, it points directly to the essence of its referent. In this account of the hieroglyphic, we can discern a kind of nostalgia or envy of a semiotic gem still more durable, economical, powerful, and hermetic than the adage. The hieroglyphic, as we meet it here, *is* the absolute signifier; the adage is a creature of history, subject to debate, to interpretation, to a variety of uses—the coin of the emperor Titus, the trademark of Aldus, the essay of Erasmus. The Aldine edition contains for the first time a preface that define the adage or "paroemia" as a proverb adapted to certain times and circumstances ("accomodatum rebus, temporibusque proverbium");[4] thus the time-bound character of the adage is for Erasmus a part of its definition. Its meaning is not available, without special help, to all ages. Hieroglyphics represent semiotic perfection; they present the ultimate code, and thus they dramatize the imperfection, the vulnerability of language. It is clear that for Erasmus their perfection is related to the restriction of their use; their purity remained pristine because the Egyptian seers thought it a crime or sacrilege, *nefas*, to expose their age-old wisdom to the crowd. Erasmus indeed adds a revealing parenthetical clause: ". . . to expose the mysteries to the crowd in ordinary writing, *as we do*" ("quemadmodum nos facimus"). The *we* of this clause, the *nos*, can refer to the members of the Christian church; or it can refer to those contemporaries we would call Humanists, who taught and interpreted the wisdom of antiquity, whose profession was divulgation; or this *nos* could be read as an authorial "we," referring precisely to the writer compiling the *Adagia*, exposing all these precious stones to public view. Judged by the conduct of the Egyptian seers, Erasmus writes his book, as the adage has it, "illotis manibus," with unclean hands. Erasmus's divulgation, like all Humanist divulgation, would be a kind of pollution.

Because, for better or worse, he is not a guardian of hieroglyphics, because with clean or dirty hands he is involved in a massive, historic dissemination, because he depends on that everyday writing, *literis communibus*, which is vulnerable to historical contingency, Erasmus cannot leave his amulets pristine and hidden. He must, on the contrary, dilate his metaphors and oxymorons with commentary and interpretation. In this respect he plays the role of the antipriest, and he makes no attempt to conceal this role; the imagery of dilation, expansion, diffusion is very common in the *Adagia* and especially prominent in the "Festina lente" essay. Expansion, of course, is the foremost activity in the *Adagia*. Not only is each entry the expanded explication of a single phrase, but this entry is likely to be lengthened in later editions as the number of entries is also tirelessly, heroically, pitilessly increased. The "Festina lente" essay itself is expanded by a long digression added in 1526 that I have yet to discuss. In a less concrete sense the announced aim of the work is a widening of knowledge, a literal dissemination that was a part of the Humanist mission. The opening page of "Festina lente" concretizes this disseminative impulse. These words, writes Erasmus,

should be cut on every pillar and written over every temple porch, inscribed in gold on the double doors of princely halls, chased on episcopal rings, engraved on royal sceptres; . . . they should recur on every monument everywhere and be spread abroad and celebrated, so that such an important thing should be so much under the public eye that no single mortal could avoid acting on it. (Pp. 171–72)

Erasmus's enthusiasm leads him to vast fantasies of planetary dissemination: "Happiness like this far outflows the boundaries of empire, and is spread abroad throughout the most far-flung peoples of the world" (p. 172). Expansion like this can of course only be accomplished by the printing press, the instrument of the essay's hero, Aldus Manutius. Aldus, we learn, "is building up a sacred and immortal thing, and serving not one province alone but all peoples and all generations. . . . [He] is building up a library which has no other limits than the world itself" (pp. 180–81). Aldus's library, extended immeasurably, becomes analogous to the verbal core of the essay, the two words paraphrased and dilated by Erasmus's spiraling commentary. The centripetal nostalgia for the absolute, hermetic, closed point is thwarted, but a centrifugal alternative emerges that is at once textual, semantic, sociological, and geographic. Never is Erasmus more quintessentially Humanist than in this paraphrase, dilation, dissemination perceived to be faithful to an origin, which is to say not, in our terms, Derridian.

It would be tempting to find in this movement outward the structural principle we were looking for. Expansion in all its various meanings is celebrated in the 1508 essay as a healthy exercise of power. Even the somewhat sententious close is quickened by an image of dynamic growth from Pindar. But in the late edition of 1526 a long addition makes its appearance in the "Festina lente" essay, roughly half as long as the original version. This addition is devoted to the risks of divulgation, which according to the aging Erasmus has been overtaken by disaster. This is due in part to the avarice of collectors but chiefly to the greed of the disseminators. The heroism of an Aldus has been debased and travestied by a swarm of lesser printers, thriving particularly in Germany, who care nothing for textual accuracy, who are lazy, unscrupulous, even illiterate, who print and circulate anything. Now the wave of centrifugal world-wide diffusion becomes an abominable danger. "To what corner of the world do they not fly, these swarms of new books?" These cursed printers "fill the world with books, not just trifling things (such as I write, perhaps), but stupid, ignorant, slanderous, scandalous, raving, irreligious and seditious books" (p. 182; p. 184). Only in a passage such as this can one fully gauge how much power Erasmus and his world attributed to the written and printed word. The vision in fact becomes apocalyptic. The meretricious printer becomes the agent and synecdoche for universal chaos.

If things go on as they have begun, the result will be that supreme power will be concentrated in the hands of a few, and we shall have as barbaric a tyranny among us as there is among the Turks. Everything will give way to the appetites of one man or of a few, and there will not remain the slightest vestige of civilized society, but all will be under the rule of military force. All noble disciplines will wither away, one law alone will operate. (P. 183)

The church is threatened with impotence, the family with dispersal. And much of the mischief comes from the printers' "unbridled license." The press, once an instrument of enlightenment, threatens the globe with Armageddon.

Thus the process of sociologic and geographic expansion lies open at once to the sacred and the sacrilegious. It is both Herculean and vulnerable. But in a different sphere one can say the same for the textual, semantic expansion enacted by the text before us. As the adage-commentary grows into the adage-essay, its relation to the tiny, verbal gem presented as its center becomes more problematic. Here too the process of indefinite widening involves the threat of chaos, and not least in this meandering divagation away from the most royal and most privileged of all the adages. The commentary presents itself throughout the volume as a faithful unpacking of compressed but determinate meaning, as the translation of a trope, a paradox, ostensible nonsense, into the nonfigurative, discursive, lucid sense of the nonfigurative. The commentary supposedly supplies the solution to the miniature problem posed by the verbal kernel; it proposes to fill in the signification, smooth over the paradox, by means of dilation, thus transforming mystery into wisdom. But as the dilation proceeds further and further, as it reveals all the abundance, the *copia*, of the adage proper, the kernel becomes progressively indeterminate; it fails to center the essay. The act of spinning out meaning begins to look arbitrary and subjective. We come to realize that each writer might provide his own particular enlargement, just as each historical age would provide its own counterparts to ancient experience. The original trope begins to look utterly protean, to the point where the plenum of meaning may be indistinguishable from a void of meaning. Perhaps the adage proper is only an inkblot test, a starting place for random association. Failing to be a hieroglyphic, failing to possess that absolute, essential, perennial meaning that history cannot erode, perhaps the adage reveals only a pretense of meaning. According to this view, its dissemination *would* be Derridian. In the Erasmian terms employed by Terence Cave, this cornucopian text would betray its poverty of nourishing substance in its very cancerous growth, its failure to be *uber* as it becomes more visibly a *tuber*.

This risk is undoubtedly present in the adage, and it is all the more threatening in the shifts of perspective and moral emphasis that divide it. On one page a hymn to the dolphin, with its "almost incredible energy of movement," becomes a hymn to what the dolphin is said to symbolize, the ardent and dauntless vigor of the [human] mind ("acrem illum et indomitum animi impetum"). But on another page, the last, the dolphin is taken to symbolize the folly and ungovernable impulse of the mind ("socordia . . . vel immoderato impetu"). The adage-essay shifts its terms and values like an essay by Montaigne, but it lacks the putative center of those later wandering texts, a changeable yet knowable self. Thus we are left to ask if there is any way at all to recuperate some structural firmness for the adage, for this particular, exemplary adage or for all the others in this endless, Borgesian library of a book. The answer, if it exists, will concern not only this work but the intellectual and cultural movement for which it speaks.

One response to this structural question, one fashionable response, would point to the way many of the adages can be read as self-referential. We have already met explicit self-referentiality in the adages "Herculei labores" and "Sileni Alcibiadis." If "Festina lente" combines awe for the mind and fear of the mind, a celebration of the press with horror of the press, it is, arguably, merely acting out its originating oxymoron. Any number of other adages might be read, with only a minimal amount of nudging, as metaphors for their own compilation. To compose the *Adagia* may require the writer "cum larvis luctari," "to struggle with ghosts," or "a mortuo tribuum exigere," "to demand tribute from the dead." To compose the work may be a privilege, since "non cuivis homini contingit adire Corinthum," "not everybody is lucky enough to visit Corinth." But the work is also burdensome, since it deals with "difficilia quae pulchra," "things beautiful because difficult." Perhaps the writing of the book is essentially futile, as futile as transplanting an old tree: "Annosam arborem transplantare." With this thought, in fact, a host of monitory adages present themselves: "Thesaurus carbones erant"—"charcoal instead of treasure"; "catulae dominas imitantes"—"whelps aping their elders"; "ne sutor ultra crepidam"—"the cobbler shouldn't aspire beyond his last"; "felix qui nihil debet"—"happy is he who owes nothing." It would be an instructive game to work through a century of adages, interpreting each as auto-descriptive or more frequently auto-refuting. Perhaps a scorpion sleeps under every stone ("sub omni lapide scorpius dormit"), even if the stone is precious. But ultimately this game would pall, and some of the four thousand entries doubtless would resist even the ardent and dauntless vigor of the most ingenious interpreter.

This leaves us still without a structural center. But I want to argue that each adage does contain a center of sorts, and in coming to recognize it we will be in a position to recognize Humanist mimesis. This center will prove to be wobbly; as an organizing principle it will be vulnerable, but it will serve, in a rough way, to protect most Humanist texts from cancer. Margaret Mann Phillips, the best-informed student and translator of the *Adagia*, writes of it: "The aim . . . is to give [the proverb's] whole pedigree, to show it living a continuous life from one author to another, changing in scope and meaning" (p. 77). What Phillips calls a pedigree lies at the beginning of every adage-commentary; it offers a crude basis for structure that is philological. Each commentary, each essay, is arranged around a history of its concrete usages and applications, a history in which the modern instance takes its place, or rather a history from which this new usage, with all its congeries of associations, is in the process of emerging. The real center is not the static gem but rather the dynamic, wavering, but persistent continuity through history. The adage turns, like most Humanist texts, upon an uncertain, unsteady axis stretched backward through time, an axis that is anything but straight, that excludes long periods of history, that combines divination with science, but that allows the modern text to situate itself with all the limitations and the actuality of its own historical moment. Thus the "Festina lente" essay draws its own axis from the ancient theology of Egypt, from Aristophanes, from the emperor Augustus and the emperor Titus, down to Aldus and finally to its own successive, agglutinative incarnations. Following Phillips, one can call this succession a pedigree or genealogy; I prefer to call it an *etiology*, by which I mean a retrospective explanation of a textual coming-into-being, a process of accumulated significations through time (which does not of course exclude a concurrent loss of signification).

To see this wobbly axis as an organizing element is not to deny Erasmus's historical separation from his imputed origins, or to deny his own, individual eccentricity in the unfolding chronology. His essay is his own; no other contemporary would have written it as he did; doubtless no other contemporary would have made out precisely the same etiology. Later ages, including ours, would bend the axis in new directions. But one can recognize this separation and this eccentricity without accepting a purely random dissemination. The line from the supposed ancient seers to the Erasmus of 1526 is not a straight line, but its curves and shifts of direction are more or less contained by cultural history. Culture always presses the mind to moderate its haste, always wants to guide and limit intellectual change, which is semiotic change. The given trope, like all Humanist topoi, carries a past with it that it violates only within given parameters. The adage-essay is really about an emergence from a fragile, constructed line of continuity informed with retrospective awareness. Although Erasmus's metaphysics of the line includes only two kinds, the finite straight line and the infinite circle, his essay really adumbrates a third kind—incomplete, meandering, perpetually becoming.

Thus the adage-essay acts out a version of history; it supplies an imitation, a mimesis of history. This version is of course grotesquely foreshortened; it may also be inaccurate, as we know the myth of hermetic theology to be inaccurate. The text offers us at best a stylization of history. But it does cast back into time its etiological umbilical cord, whose curves lie within the boundaries of cultural change. Other Renaissance texts are less explicitly informative; one has to subread their etiologies; they allude rather than name, imitate rather than cite, but they also ask to be understood in terms of an emergence out from a long line of development. Each line is a special representation, epitomizing and interpreting history, and therein lies the mimesis. That is the peculiar technique of Humanist reference. It bears roughly the resemblance to the actual course of history that the stylized world of a novel bears to an actual society. "Festina lente" posits an original era of hermetic wisdom, a practical wisdom in imperial Rome, a void of wisdom during the Gothic darkness, a new heroic necromancy in the age of Aldus threatened finally by imminent apocalyptic chaos. Within that construction it dramatizes its own appearance, which contributes at least one fact to the story. The story becomes a metaphor or synecdoche for the vast, confusing movement of crude history. The one story maintains a rough parallelism with the other, and in that wavering parallel lies whatever mimesis Humanism could produce. The *Adagia* as a whole consists of several thousand mimetic histories.

The retrospective sketch of a past such Renaissance texts contain remains, in a sense, a fiction. It is constructed on insufficient knowledge, and therein lies part of its vulnerability. Its version of history stems from a union of philology and invention. It suffers from all the confusions and errors of history, both the kind that is written and the kind that is enacted. It is also exposing its own enterprise to potential criticism, including the criticism of its named predecessors. By continuing the life of the adage down to his own moment, his own scope, his own moral style and expansive interpretations, Erasmus was taking a risk. He was wagering that his own moment and his own prolongation would not diminish the tradition, that they would not pollute it with unwitting parody or bathetic anachronism. The Humanist text that imitates or paraphrases an ancient model or topos assumes deliberately its own concrete historicity, the perspectives, the prejudices, the semiotic vocabulary of its age, "accommodated to times and circumstances." This again involves a vulnerability. The text accepts the particularity, which is to say the limitations, of its historical situation. Erasmus accepts the printing press, which enlightens and vulgarizes, instructs and corrupts. More important, he reflects ways of understanding, interpreting, and symbolizing that are not those of his masters; if they were, there would be no history. This assumption of a difference is the admission of a risk, the risk of being smaller, of appearing blind, of betraying a degeneration, of falling into travesty or pollution. We don't have to look far to find Renaissance texts that lost their wager and that did betray helplessly their own inequality to their models or subtexts. But in those Renaissance works that bring the wager off, the vulnerability proves to be a source of strength. The concrete historicity reveals its fertility. "Virescit vulnere virtus."[5] Strength is renewed by a wound.

The constructed etiology of the Humanist text provides at best a simulacrum of order, a flexible, shaky order that remains in the realm of becoming. (This is especially true of the writing of Erasmus, who was skeptical of historical patterns and who tended to ignore theories of circular *chronos* for spontaneous occurrences of specific *kairoi*.) But the etiology serves in any case to contain any drift toward purely haphazard dissemination. And by presenting the emergence of modern meaning as a progressive exfoliation, it responds to the charge of perpetual deferral. This is the charge that Professor Cave has brought, with great learning and skill, against Erasmus's writing along with other writing of the Renaissance.

The perpetual deferment of sense encourages—even constitutes—*copia*, defined as the ability of language to generate detours and deflections. Textual abundance (the extension of the surface) opens up in its turn an indefinite plurality of possible senses. The intention (will, *sententia*) which was supposed to inform the origin of a text and to guarantee the ultimate resolution of its *sensus* remains for ever suspended, or submerged, in the flow of words.[6]

The perspective changes if one shifts the origin of the text to a wavering line of succession in which the authorial will takes its place. The text can then be read as a progressive realization of modern meaning defining itself as it becomes present. This coming into being is never properly completed, which is to say the final word is never written; no ultimate closure is ever imposed. But the requirement of some ultimate closure, some switching off of textual generation, reflects a rigidity of the twentieth-century mind. It isn't clear why we should want that utopian "ultimate resolution" that contemporary readers miss; it isn't clear how we would recognize it if we found it; it isn't clear why its absence should be a symptom of cancer. To embrace history is to embrace contingency, incompleteness, the vulnerability of the contingent. But it is not to succumb to an incurable disease.

The *Adagia*, of course, present a double orientation—toward the modern variation and toward the beginning of the etiological line. The "Festina lente" essay begins with its conjectural speculation about a phrase from Aristophanes and later reaches further back into pre-Roman Egypt. Most of the adages supply firmer beginnings. But the quest for one is a constituent element. Phillips writes: "The important thing is the correlation of the proverb with the event or point of view which gave it birth, finding 'fabulam proverbii parentem' (III, x, 98)" (pp. 13–14). We are free to consider this quest misguided; we are free to quote the adage "Facilius sit Nili caput invenire"—it would be easier to find the source of the Nile. The source or the parent-fable of the adage may be another construct, another fiction. But it reflects an enduring impulse of Humanism that deserves our attention. We might indeed learn from the Humanists the crucial role of "the point of view which gave [the text] birth," if by "point of view" we understand the entire, specific, semiotic world, the specific habits of attributing meaning peculiar to a given historical moment. Every literary work bears the imprint of that given formative moment, and it asks to be read according to those habits; it asks to be read *appropriately*. Thus the reader is obliged to seek to recapture the presuppositions, the signifying habits, of the text's origin; these are not always as imprecise as are a proverb's.

Thus the "Festina lente" essay records its era's love of compression and its will to diffusion; these and other features help us to *date* the essay and they oblige us to recognize its diachronic specificity. The text asks to be read with a sensitivity to its origin, which is to say with the historical imagination. The reader who abandons that task is guilty of hermeneutic narcissism, even though admittedly the task will never fully be accomplished. The exemplary heroes of this effort of historical understanding are Erasmus and his fellow Humanists.

Thus, in opposition to Derridian dissemination, with its deteriorating dispersal, diaspora, metempsychosis, oriented toward a destructuring future, might be set the orientation of an Otto Rank toward the trauma of birth, a textual birth whose marks, scars, circumstances help to determine textual destiny. Rank argues that all psychic experience and all culture constitute a series of responses, displacements, sublimations, symbolizations of the trauma of individual, biological birth. One can appropriate that psychoanalytic theory, right or wrong, as a metaphor for the determinacy each text receives, not from conscious authorial intention, but from the conditions of its origin. The text bears the inscriptions of a particular historicity and a particular semiotic world, and these inscriptions, however obscured by the text's passage through history, remain constitutive. Erasmus assumed a dissemination that is not Derridian because he assumed with his fellow Humanists the determinate power of its beginning. It is this determinacy that shields it from uninformed, irresponsible, whimsical readings, Cave's "indefinite plurality of possible senses." The meaning of the text is available for new reflection, fresh updating, enlarged significance, but this is only possible because the text possesses an inherent quality, knowable or unknowable, because it has had a certain origin, knowable or unknowable. Its history is a function of that determination. Even if, in the case of an adage, the will to reach the beginning leads to mythology, this failure need not be absolute and universal. Without a theoretical essence, the essence of origin, there can be no displacement or dispersal; even a destructuring dissemination must assume some seminality.

For Rank's human being, the concealed burden is the birth trauma. For the inherited text, the concealed burden is the remoteness of birth, the mystery of a birth that remains nonetheless decisive. We can never know fully the product of another semiotic world. Every text aspires to be a utopia of perennial meaning; to some degree it always fails. Humanism, like modern scholarship, was dedicated to mitigating the textual burden, to protect us from the difficulty of understanding, without narcissism, texts whose origins are remote. We need that philological protection, even if it is never altogether successful. Some texts and some critical schools presuppose utopias of pure synchronism; they are misguided. It is the strength of so much Renaissance writing that it settles for less than the utopian. As we gauge the endeavor of the Renaissance to cope with its own separation from its imputed sources and masters, we can recognize its need and its courage in stringing up precarious lifelines, imitations of cultural sequence, defining each work, each essay, as a vulnerable extension out of the remote into a self-creating, self-vindicating present. "Vitiat lapidem longum tempus"—"even stone is worn away by time"; that is the basis of Humanist pathos. The basis for hope is more tenuous but it remains available: "Viam qui nescit ad mare, eum oportet amnen quaerere"—"whoever can't find a [straight] road to the sea should follow the [circuitous] river."

Terence Cave

The Mimesis of Reading in the Renaissance

The hypothesis that I would like to present in this paper is that the sixteenth century, in northern Europe at least, witnesses a major shift in the status of the reader: reading becomes, in various senses, a much more prominent activity.[1]

In order to set any such hypothesis in motion, it is necessary to suggest, as a preliminary generalization, that relatively low priority is given to the reader in the theories and paradigms of discourse that have become established, in both scholastic and humanist quarters, by the beginning of the century. This would certainly be true, for example, of nominalist grammar and logic, with their emphasis on the formal processes of signifying and on the truth-value of propositions. Yet there are a number of apparent exceptions to (or limitations of) the general claim.

In the first place, from the patristic era onward (as many of the contributions to the present volume point out), the problem of reading correctly gives rise to theories of authorial intention, and to complex rules for reading designed to recover the authentic meaning of a text (scriptural or classical). In particular, the techniques of allegory define the reader's activity in considerable detail. However, the very fact that this activity is prescribed in advance means that reading is assigned a subordinate status. The mimetic task of allegorizing a text (the allegorical rewriting of Ovid's *Metamorphoses*, for example) is at least in principle closed and static, producing a copy of what is presumed to have been hidden inside the original text. We may of course regard such readings as transformations, but the theory implied by allegorical method gives little scope to the transformational potential of texts and small license to their readers. One might remark also that the product of allegorization is always a series of moral and theological commonplaces. This feature persists in later periods (it is no doubt still with us), but will in certain important stances, as I will try to show, assume a different function.

In the second place, the humanist methods of philological and contextual commentary that are already becoming established by the end of the fifteenth century are also, one might argue, deeply concerned with the activity of reading. Erasmus and other northern humanists interest themselves above all in the education of a skilled reader, prescribing in some cases a lifetime's work as preparation for the supreme exercise of reading Scripture. But here again the text itself would seem to have absolute priority, transcending in its venerable antiquity the local, time-bound, and marginal figure of the reader. Indeed, the humanist stress on the priority of the text is the greater in that it is designed to counter what the humanists claimed to be the arbitrary glosses of the scholastics. As an example of this emphasis in the Scriptural sphere, one might cite Erasmus's Christocentric theory of reading, in which the reader would ideally be transformed into the text and thus identify himself with the divine Logos: Erasmus here owes a great deal to Augustine, whose notion of scriptural reading has as its logical conclusion the disappearance of the reader as a "willful," independent subject and the epiphany of grace (*caritas* equals *claritas*).

The theory and practice of secular rhetoric more evidently emphasize the act of communication. The notion, for example, that the audience will not be moved and persuaded unless the speaker is himself genuinely moved by his topic dramatizes the production and consumption of discourse in quasi-theoretical terms: the reader is here explicitly present. Or again, the Neoplatonist theory of inspiration, another major *topos* of humanist reflection on discourse, provides a metaphysical version of the same scenario: the poet, like a rhapsode, transmits his supernatural "enthusiasm" to the listener, who is activated by the energy of the text.

Yet the study of rhetoric is designed primarily for writers and speakers, not for readers, and the theory of inspiration is an attempt to explain the production of discourse rather than its consumption.

Finally, it is certainly the case that all three accounts of communication—allegory, rhetoric, Neoplatonist theory—may be considered to be heuristic in the sense that they aim ideally at the moral improvement of the reader, not by direct instruction, but by changing his state of mind or affections, or giving him a mental discipline that he in the end must put into effect for himself; this would be true also of the systematic spiritual exercises devised in the sixteenth century, and of their medieval antecedents. But the power and privilege of a master text, and of its author or speaker, remain unshaken: reading is a mimetic act that seeks to restore the totality and integrity of the original discursive performance. Nowhere is this clearer than in the so-called Ciceronian imitation of the Renaissance, where a closed discipline of reading is prescribed in order to guarantee a perfect representation of Ciceronian discourse, and presumably of the Ciceronian *sententia* enclosed within it.

In the course of the sixteenth century, however, other accounts of reading begin to impose themselves, accounts that make the task of the reader more central and correspondingly change the status and function of the text. In a sense, this is perhaps already a generally accepted hypothesis: for example, it is well known that Protestant theories of Scriptural reading, as well as humanist stress on the return *ad fontes*, release the reader from the constraints of what one might call institutionalized allegory and glossing. Or again, in a more literary context, studies like those of Walter Kaiser, Barbara Bowen, and Rosemary Colie have demonstrated how such procedures as irony and paradox become dominant in certain sixteenth-century texts, radically changing the nature of the relationship between writer, text, and reader. I don't propose to rehearse these conclusions, although they should be borne in mind as a corroboration of some of the points I shall be making. I want to focus more precisely on the ways in which sixteenth century writing defines or imagines the reader, the ways in which the *figure* of the reader emerges in textual practice. That the figure does emerge, becoming a predominant topic of writing on his own account, is of course one of the main points.

My point of departure, then, will be the thematization in Renaissance texts of the act of reading. At the most straightforward level, one notices that characters in such texts spend a great deal of their time engaged in reading, or in similar activities such as quoting and citing. One might take as an initial paradigm the *Heptaméron* of Marguerite de Navarre, where Boccaccio's device of the framework story is expanded to a point at which the game of storytelling is no longer the end but the means: the stories are there to be read and discussed by the *devisants* (narrators who have become readers). A detailed analysis of this example might draw attention to the leitmotif of Biblical readings which run parallel to the secular storytelling, thus multiplying the intertextual possibilities; to the quotation by the storytellers / readers of other texts (the *Roman de la rose*, Plato, Scripture); to the way in which readings of one story generate the narration of the next story; and to the *mise en abyme* of the whole process in the Prologue, which refers to a "real," but unrealized, storytelling project proposed by Marguerite de Navarre at the French court, in which all the stories—unlike Boccaccio's—were to be true. In general terms, what is most visible, however, is that while the content of the storytellers' readings may easily be reduced to a set of moral, religious, and courtly commonplaces, this content is presented in such a way as to highlight the heuristic activity of reading. A dialogue of readers has invaded the terrain of narrative.

Among other examples one might cite Erasmus's *Convivium religiosum*. This is a dialogue that I analyzed in *The Cornucopian Text* in terms of its transformation of interpretation into a pursuit of sense, a mobile scenario in which no reading is ever foreclosed and some readings are ostentatiously unresolved. It is, in fact, another dialogue of readers, although what they are reading is not narrative fiction but a set of emblems and quotations. The mimetic function of the dialogue in this case is not the production of glosses said to represent the true sense of an authoritative text; it is rather the representation of reading itself as an activity that can be dramatized, assigned a life of its own beyond the confines of the text or texts being read. These examples seem to me to embody a totally different conception of "represented reading" from what one finds, for example, in the *Ovide moralisé*, where the allegorizer, having narrated a segment of the narrative, appears on the scene adding his glosses as an external accretion. They are also quite different from the procedure used in the *Roman de la rose*. There, the lover is certainly a personification of reading as he moves through, and attempts to interpret, his allegorical scenario. But, sealed as he is within the narrative, he is the perfect counterpart of the reader himself, who likewise is obliged to move in linear progression through the arcade of emblems and personifications in search of the single *telos* reserved for him by the text (the fact that Guillaume de Lorris's version is, as it happens, unfinished is immaterial in this respect). If the *Roman de la rose* is regarded as having a heuristic structure, what it encourages the reader to discover is the art of repetition, the virtue of hermeneutic transparency or symmetry. The unfinished and generative readings of the Renaissance examples, by contrast, while still rehearsing *topoi*, begin to assert the otherness, the irreducible asymmetry or discontinuity of reading, and the ultimate priority of the reader.

The enactment of reading in Rabelais may be said to work in the same way. Here my primary example will be the first meeting between Pantagruel and Panurge in *Pantagruel*, IX.[2] This episode is narrated in dialogue form as an instance of noncommunication: Pantagruel asks questions to which Panurge replies in a series of foreign languages that his interlocutors cannot understand. It thus highlights the role of the reader: unsuccessful reading necessarily makes the content of the text subordinate to the attempt at comprehension. Panurge's foreign-language speeches are of course not a narrative or a poem or scriptural text in need of elucidation, so that the word "reading" might seem misplaced here. However, the relation of the whole episode to reading emerges when one observes, first of all, that what Panurge enunciates in disguised form is a number of quotations, *sententiae*, and adages: in other words, excerpted readings. In the second place, it can be shown that the encounter is a parodic inversion of a recurrent episode in the *Odyssey*, namely, the reception of a stranger by a host who invariably offers hospitality before asking the stranger who he is and where he comes from (Pantagruel does the reverse). Thus the shadow of a displaced narrative, itself a consecrated text, falls across the dialogue: its absence allows an activity to take the stage that would be germane to glossing, were its product also not partially occulted. The product is of course Panurge's set of *topoi* on the themes of charity and the priority of moral action over language. The whole episode might thus be reconstituted by the reader as an evangelical, humanist gloss on the *Odyssey*, except that what is represented here is not the inner meaning of a venerable text: the charade performed by the characters peremptorily changes the terms of reference of reading. The visibly imperfect reading within the text obliges us as readers to play an active role: not simply the solving of a riddle, although that paradigm has some relevance, but the rehearsal of the characters' performance at one or more removes. A similar function can, I think, be ascribed to the "misreadings" of Panurge in the *Tiers Livre*, although there the heuristic procedure is still more apparent because its repetition structures the greater part of the book.

In Montaigne's *Essais*, too, the reader is personified, not only through Montaigne's often ironic, second-person asides, but through the writer's self-personification as a reader of other texts and of his own. I shall be returning to this question shortly, but I prefer to approach it by a slightly different route, that of imitation theory, which is undoubtedly central, whether as cause or as symptom, to the shift I am attempting to characterize.

The debate over the imitation of consecrated authors—the classics, Scripture, a few moderns such as Petrarch—necessarily implies contrasted views of what reading is and does. The so-called Ciceronian position, represented in the sixteenth century by writers such as Dolet and Scaliger, stresses the universality of nature as located in, and perceived by, the human mind; this universal may be more or less perfectly represented in discourse, so that the reader's task is to seek out and dwell on its most perfect representation. It is illuminating in this respect to find that in Scaliger's grammatical theory (*De causis linguae latinae*, 1540), the authenticity of concepts ("universals") as reflecting the nature of reality is reasserted, despite the powerful legacy of nominalist grammar in this period. Thus—as I indicated earlier—reading, for the Ciceronian, is the repetition of a perfect or near-perfect discourse; the reader should, as it were, disappear or efface himself in favor of the paradigm text. By contrast, the anti-Ciceronian position, which one might as well call in this period the Erasmian position, since it is developed in its most detailed and penetrating form by Erasmus,[3] extends virtually *ad infinitum* the range of texts to be read and stresses, not universal nature, but the individual nature of the reader as the agent by which this assemblage of materials is gathered, selected, and given meaning. This is probably the most pervasive single aspect of the reorganization of discourse in terms of the subject that is generally attributed to Renaissance humanism. In Erasmian theory nature is plural and protean; it shifts to the side of the imitator or of the "copy," generating new meanings and new texts.

It is important to notice, however, that Erasmus does not quite say that each reading of a text displaces that text in a direction determined by the context and nature of the reader: the displacement occurs for him at the moment of rewriting. The reverence for ancient texts and for their original, authentic meaning, which is an equally potent part of the humanist approach, here provides a constraint, as it will also for Montaigne's much more open approach to reading. What I think it possible to argue is that imitation as a theory of writing contributes to a change in habits of reading. If venerable texts are to be fragmented and eventually transformed by the process of rewriting, it becomes visibly less necessary to regard them as closed and authoritative wholes.

Evidence for the decline of the authoritative status of such texts is provided by two recent studies. Antoine Compagnon discerns in the sixteenth century a shift from the citing (*allégation*) of *auctoritates*, a procedure akin to glossing, to free quotation. In one case, the reader of the ancient text sees his own reading and his own discourse as wholly subservient: it is a humble activity carried on very precisely in the margins. In the other case, of which Montaigne is the prime example, the reader as an independent subject is beginning to impose himself and his own discourse as primary: the quotation is integrated into a new context authorized by the rewriter. According to Compagnon, this is a transitional stage: by the later seventeenth century, the signs of "borrowing" will have virtually disappeared, and the new text will thus be wholly the responsibility of its author. Marc Fumaroli corroborates this hypothesis from another point of view by his discussion of "quotation rhetoric," which he regards as the predominant mode of writing among the *magistrature* of the sixteenth century, but which becomes outmoded in the course of the seventeenth.[4]

The production of the new texts in the late Renaissance according to the principles of Erasmian imitation or quotation rhetoric might, then, be said to give the reader an entirely new role. Precisely because such new texts contain (and, as it were, enclose) fragments of *auctoritates*, reading can no longer consist of systematic glossing or of mimetic repetition. The gloss has swollen to the point where it has visibly engulfed the master text. What works such as Montaigne's *Essais* represent is not an inert original meaning but a process, a displacement or transformation. This is already true of certain of Erasmus's works (the *Adages*, for example), and of Rabelais's fiction, where innumerable fragments of canonical writings are cited and quoted by both narrator and characters in constantly shifting contexts, often provocatively unexpected ones. I don't, by the way, share the view of those who would argue that Rabelais's use of such devices wholly subverts the authorities quoted; the text implies rather that whatever may be of value in these quotations is only realized by a positive act of appropriation on the part of the reader. The displacement mimed by the text *is* so mimed in order that the reader will operate a further displacement beyond its margins.

Reading thus becomes a kind of rewriting, because what is

read is itself perceptibly a reading in something like the modern sense—that is to say, a provisional exercise. This possibility is most explicitly envisaged by the *Essais* of Montaigne. Montaigne does, as I suggested earlier, retain the notion of an original, intended meaning, and attacks glossing as a deviation. But what he objects to is perhaps that the gloss, instead of recognizing that it is a deviation, claims perfectly to represent the master text. In virtually all of Montaigne's accounts of reading, deviation is in fact accepted and recognized as potentially productive. The appropriation of alien texts adumbrated in the imitation theory of Erasmus and Du Bellay is systematically put into practice in the *Essais*. Montaigne misquotes, disguises his quotations, quotes without identifying the text, provides a radically new context for his quotations, and in addition makes all these operations explicit.

This subject has been fruitfully explored by Compagnon, Lino Pertile, and most recently Mary McKinley, so I will not cite specific examples here.[5] I would like instead to indicate two aspects of the way in which the *Essais* imagine their own reader. The first is the oscillation between strategies of obstruction and exclusion on the one hand and the theme of desire for an ideally sympathetic and alert reader on the other. Montaigne speaks of his text as being only suitable for his family and friends, as being not worthy of the reader's attention, as being difficult to read, and as requiring a reader who falls into no pre-existing category. At the same time, he persistently addresses the reader, courts him, and plays the game of irony with him; he says that he is "affamé de [se] faire connaître," and hopes that the book might eventually find for him a sympathetic friend to replace the one he lost in Etienne de La Boëtie. It isn't my purpose to dwell on the psychological or even the rhetorical content of this twin perspective, or to propose that any contradiction or paradox is involved. What is interesting is rather the fact that these two types of presentation together undermine the conventions of reading that contemporary readers were likely to adopt, and begin to open up a space—still hypothetical and on the horizon of Montaigne's perception—for a different kind of reading. Such a reading would at once be uniquely attuned and sympathetic to the displacement enacted by the *Essais*, and for that very reason be capable of a new and as yet unpredictable displacement. An example that embodies these characteristics, although it is not one in which Montaigne is speaking explicitly about the reception of the *Essais*, is a passage from I.xxxv ("D'un defaut de nos polices").[6] Montaigne here reports his father's suggestion that every town should have a register in which people could announce their reciprocal needs and thus contact one another, as for example "I want to sell some pearls, I want to buy some pearls . . . so-and-so seeks a servant of such-and-such a type; someone else seeks a master." He even uses the word "advertir," thus anticipating verbally as well as by the general conception the system of advertisement. Like an entry in the personal columns of a modern newspaper, the *Essais* is a text in search of exactly the right reader.

The second point is one that I owe in part to a reference in Pertile's article on Montaigne, but principally to an as yet unpublished thesis by Professor Frederick Hodgson.[7] When Montaigne says "I only speak others in order better to speak myself" (I.xxvi, p. 146), and later in the same text "It's no longer Plato's idea but my own, since he and I understand and see it the same way" (p. 150), he is rephrasing Seneca's remark in the *Letters to Lucilius* (16.7) about his own habit of abundant quotation: "I make generous use of other people's writings. But why do I say 'other people's'? Whatever has been well said by anyone, is my own." It is of course relevant that Montaigne is here himself quoting without acknowledging his source (he even puts in Plato as a red herring), and that the rephrasing shifts the sense, replacing Seneca's reference to an appropriated commodity with an intersubjective use of personal pronouns ("he and I"). But what matters above all is that a passing remark in Seneca's writing reappears as a focal point in an entirely new context, as an extreme consequence of imitation theory. The constantly reiterated enactment by the subject of the *Essais* of reading as appropriation or displacement obliges the reader to imitate the writer's gesture and displace his text according to the vector of his own will or desire.

At the beginning of a passage that virtually rules out the possibility of an adequate reading, Montaigne asks the rhetorical question "And anyway, who are you writing for?" (II.17, p. 640). The use of the second person momentarily casts the reader in the figure of a writer, a personification that is echoed in many other passages on the potentially indefinite extension of the *Essais*, whether by Montaigne himself or by his readers. The subject once again abrogates the text, and here the subject is seen to shift deictically with the substitution of pronouns ("you" for "I"). In this sense, the subject is a blank space, always ready to be filled with displaced *topoi*;[8] at the same time it is the only guarantee for Montaigne of the authentic production of meaning. In order to be properly read, the *Essais* must be misread, contested, dismantled, deformed and reformed in the name of a new subject. And this, Professor Hodgson argues, is precisely what Pascal does to them. Pascal picks up Montaigne's rephrasing of Seneca ("It's no longer Plato's idea but my own . . .") and recasts it as follows: "It isn't in Montaigne but in myself that I find everything I see there" (*Pensées*, Lafuma no. 689). The deictic shift is now still more marked, since Montaigne's implication of a sympathy between Plato's view and his own ("he and I") has given way to an abolition of the writing subject: the reading (or rewriting) subject has invaded the whole of the text. The violence of this usurpation is in fact appropriate to Pascal's reading of Montaigne in its entirety: it penetrates, challenges, and reorientates the *Essais* under the aegis of a radically different project. If this is hardly the response Montaigne would have liked his advertisement to solicit, it constitutes a perfectly plausible transformation of Montaigne's own reflections on reading.

Considered as a mimetic text, the *Essais* gives priority to— even perhaps fabricates—the writer as subject; at the same time, it proposes heuristically the transformation of that subject, inviting the reader to constitute himself as subject through the act of reading. The never-ending sequence of *topoi* in which the *Essais* take their place by discussing moral virtue, old age, Socrates, the functioning of the imagination, education, and so on, is now no longer presented as an encyclopedia of learning; the book is not a substitute memory. It is the means, as Montaigne would put it, by which an individual judgment may be formed and through which an individual *forme maistresse* may be perceived. Pascal's approach is more uncompromising. Many of the *topoi* are still there, and the appropriating subject appears to be there, too; but Pascal's metaphysics—precisely in a fragment that precedes in the manuscript the one I quoted earlier—designates the self as a place filled only with appearances. The disquieting blank space foreseen at certain moments in the *Essais* is now a vertiginous void in which the *topoi* of human *divertissement* are engulfed. What else are *topoi*, after all, but *divertissement*? This disappearing trick that Pascal performs on the reader himself (and of course his own text), leaving nothing but the chance of an unspeakable transcendence, is again part of a heuristic exercise. Even if one doesn't accept its metaphysical assumptions, it is impossible not to admire the rigor with which Pascal exposes reading, at this most extreme point,[9] as an all but empty scenario.

In case it should seem that I believe the affiliation that I have traced so far—the one running from humanist imitation theory via Montaigne to Pascal—to be the dominant development in the late Renaissance, I should like now to give a brief account of two other paradigms of reading that present the reader in a quite different light but have equally far-reaching implications.

The first is not directly connected with the question of representation, but it is crucial to the formation of an appropriating reader, of the reader as consumer. It becomes possible at a stage in the development of humanism at which virtually the whole canon of classical writings is available in good editions, and translation (Greek into Latin, Greek and Latin into the vernaculars) has enormously extended the circle of potential readers. It foreshadows what the twentieth century will, in the most general sense, call literary criticism: that is to say, an aesthetic and moral appraisal of privileged texts, based on a presumption of shared good taste and fine discrimination. Informal judgment either of whole works or of their distinctive features replaces the application of rhetorical or allegorical categories serially to fragments of the work; in addition, the preferred language of the critic is emotive and figurative.

Significant instances of this type of reading, which has classical antecedents,[10] occur in humanist prefaces and orations on individual writers and their works, while in the later part of Scaliger's *Poetices libri septem* (1561), literary judgment is treated on a systematic basis in relation to a Virgilian paradigm. Montaigne's demonstration of the art of reading in "Des livres" (II.x) and other essays is, by contrast, deliberately extempore and discontinuous, but all these approaches bring the same principles into play. In passages such as the comparison of Latin poets in "Du jeune Caton" and the analysis of a mythological scene from Lucretius in "Sur des vers de Virgile," Montaigne is already using the techniques that nowadays characterize practical criticism: he pays close attention to the detail of word or phrase that governs a certain effect, and he uses carefully graded comparisons to persuade other readers to accept his order of literary merit. Another procedure germane to these, and also widely used by Montaigne, is the collocation of life and works, either as a hermeneutic device or as a source of ethical considerations. All of these approaches present reading as a pleasant exercise of the intelligence, a leisure activity for cultivated *magistrats* who can thereby display their easy command of *bonae literae*. Reading is a pastime, analogous—though no doubt superior—to hunting: "History," says Montaigne, "is more my quarry, or poetry, of which I am particularly fond" (I.xxvi, p. 144). The expression of personal taste is a discreet display of one's social and intellectual credentials.

My final paradigm of reading begins with the rhetorical figure that casts the reader in the role of spectator or eyewitness to a dramatic scene, that is to say, *enargeia* or ecphrasis (this figure may of course include other devices such as prosopopeia or *sermocinatio*, together with a wide range of tropes—metaphor, apostrophe, use of present tense for past—which contribute to the double effect of brilliance and actuality). It is important to remember that in humanist rhetoric, enargeia is a powerful but local device: the momentary illusion that it creates is harnessed, in theory at least, to a persuasive or epideictic function. In other words, a clear distinction needs to be made between the rhetorical figures of eyewitness representation and the general conception of a poem, play, or other text as an imitation of reality. That general conception is debated, at least until the mid-sixteenth century, in terms of *topoi* such as Plato's view of poetry as inauthentic mimesis, or the poetry/painting analogy: the example of the painter Zeuxis, used by Cicero and elaborated in the commentary of Marius Victorinus, is a particularly favored commonplace, recurring prominently, for example, in Erasmus's *Ciceronianus*. At this level, the question turns on the representation not so much of particulars, or of an illusion of presence, but of universals, and the mind of the speaker as a repository of such universals. Rhetoric is or should be a *speculum animi* or *effigies animi*. The mimetic function of *enargeia* would have a strictly subordinate role in these more privileged and global modes of representation. Likewise, enargeia is quite distinct from Aristotelian mimesis, which begins to be discussed at length only in the later sixteenth century with the dissemination of the *Poetics*.

If one preserves these distinctions, it becomes clear, for example, that the ecphrases of sixteenth-century drama are not part of a general effect of *vraisemblance*. Usually, they are moments of bravura in a rhetorical movement designed to create pathos, as in the concluding act of *Les Juifves*, where the slaying of the children and the blinding of Sédécie are narrated. It is possible also to cite other, more exclusively scenic, instances: in *Henry V*, the Chorus's speeches take the place of stage illusion, explicitly inviting the audience to accept ecphrasis as a substitute: precisely for this reason, they are again visible as a local device; they do not disguise themselves in order to become part of a total illusion.

On the other hand, it seems that, in Neoclassical tragedy, eyewitness illusion is no longer simply a momentary effect or rhetorical category: it has become the organizing principle of the play as a whole. Ecphrasis, it is true, remains as a verbal device in the exposition and (especially) in the tragic *récit*. But, as Timothy Reiss argues so cogently in his book *Toward Dramatic Illusion*,[11] the audience is progressively constituted as a spectator or eyewitness, a purely passive recipient, it would seem, of the illusion. In any further investigation of this development (which clearly lies beyond the scope of this paper), one of the most central issues would be the kind of interaction between visual and discursive representation discussed by John Lyons in his contribution to the present volume; and one would need to look also at the theater as a visual system imposed on a discursive system, or vice versa. My purpose here is only to point to a configuration that assigns to the reader the status of a spectator who watches silently, from outside, the enactment of a dazzling illusion.

The sixteenth and earlier seventeenth centuries, then, saw the emergence of some radically new conceptions of reading, although it would be wrong to assume that they entirely supplanted established principles such as systematic allegorization or the reverence for *auctoritates*. In the first place, the notion of what one might call a "generative reading" coincides with the progressive fragmentation of the medieval encyclopedia and its humanist counterparts as a *speculum mundi*. Instead of acting as a universal and permanent memory, the text performs a heuristic exercise, proffering *topoi* that the reader may appropriate and reorganize in relation to an unforeseen mental horizon. With hindsight, we can now clearly see that this horizon was to be that of the subject, hypostatized by the writer in such a way as to force the reader to constitute himself in his turn as subject. This accident in the history of discursive practice first becomes fully legible in Montaigne's *Essais*: its future will lie primarily in the realm of first person narrative (autobiographical and other), even if such narrative as we now know it does not formally invite the reader to displace and rewrite the text. But there are other variants of the "generative" paradigm: indeed, the terrain we are concerned with here is to a considerable degree coextensive with what is commonly called "moralist" writing, and is perhaps more vigorously explored in French than in any other vernacular. In addition to examples such as Pascal's *Pensées* and Diderot's dialogues, one might cite also the rise of narratives with ingenuous protagonists: in the *Lettres persanes*, *Candide*, and *L'Ingénu* the central figure is a naïve reader set loose on the text of the world. The moral and philosophical *topoi* have changed since the sixteenth century, but Usbek and Candide, as readers, have more in common with Pantagruel and Panurge or with Montaigne than with the lover of the *Roman de la rose* or Christian in *Pilgrim's Progress*.[12] Allegorical readers move toward the *telos* of a synthesis of knowledge, generative readers undo syntheses and perceive *topoi* as fragments. This development, it would appear, is played out by the end of the eighteenth century, although it may be said perhaps to reemerge, shorn of its practical and moral orientation, in later twentieth-century notions of the dialogic, non-mimetic text and of reading as rewriting.

The other two views of reading I have touched on both conceive of the text as a closed and integral unit: in one instance, it is an object to be appraised and judged, ethically and aesthetically; in the other, it is a flawless illusion sustained by an interlocking set of mimetic conventions. Each in its own way makes it possible to speak of a category called "literature," as distinct from the very much broader category of *bonae literae* or *literatura* that is adopted by humanist writers and readers. And this brings me to my final point. Different—even radically opposed—as the "generative" and the "mimetic" modes may seem, they complement one another as marking the failure of discourse to organize itself coherently as a mirror of reality. Late medieval nominalism (which is by no means forgotten in the sixteenth and seventeenth centuries) already heralds this failure in that it brackets external reality and concentrates on imposing coherence on an avowedly arbitrary set of discursive relations. Renaissance skepticism, carefully delimited as its terrain may be, operates in the same way. Discourse is seen to be fluid, erratic, always potentially mendacious, despite the Ciceronian argument, and despite the attempts of dialecticians like Valla, Agricola, and Ramus to overcome its defects. One solution to this predicament is to allow discourse to exhibit to the reader its own characteristics, which is what Rabelais's fictions and Montaigne's *Essais* preeminently do. They mime their *own* reality, putting on the scene the activities of both writer and reader; but, unlike their modern equivalents, they propose a moral or practical function for the performance: "the true mirror of our discourse," says Montaigne, "is the course of our lives" (I.xxvi, p.168). Something is presumed to go on "outside"; it may be generated by the text, but by definition it can never be fully represented in discursive terms. The other solution is to define a text as illusory representation while expecting of it a virtuoso repression of every element that might make its illusory character visible: this is the neoclassical paradigm.

The two solutions—the one that displays and the one that conceals—are thus complementary, even perhaps necessary to one another. Their dialogue does not itself constitute literature as a category in the modern sense: it is only with the rise of scientific discourse that literature is assigned its privilege and its limits as a product for leisure consumption and for university study. Nevertheless, I would propose that a great deal of what we now understand as the activity of reading is made possible by the shifting representations of the reader in the Renaissance.

John D. Lyons

Speaking in Pictures, Speaking of Pictures
Problems of Representation in the Seventeenth Century

> I used to tell my friends that the inventor of painting, according to the poets, was Narcissus, who was turned into a flower; for, as painting is the flower of all the arts, so the tale of Narcissus fits our purpose perfectly. What is painting but the act of embracing by means of art the surface of the pool?
>
> —L. B. ALBERTI, *De Pictura*[1]

Alberti is generally credited with the discovery of linear perspective, and thus of the system that still governs most of our visual representation. Perspective permits the projection onto flat surfaces of seemingly accurate depictions of objects in a way that is "scientific"—that is, in a way that does not permit the whimsy of the artist nor judgments of spiritual or affective value to alter what is seen by the eye. Perspective is thus objective. But at the same time perspective depends on the cooperation of the subject, the painter/viewer, who adopts a certain position to make and view the picture and whose individual point of view becomes the single permissible one. Perspective is thus subjective, or, rather, it converts the relationship between persons and things into the relationship between subject and object, defining both in a mute and immutable contract.[2] It is highly appropriate that Alberti, the inventor of perspective, should designate Narcissus the inventor of painting, for it draws our attention to an image in which the subject is its own object and discovers in the act of representation its own destruction.

The tale of Narcissus remains pertinent to painting, and particularly to perspective images, two centuries after Alberti's discovery, for in the seventeenth century the subjective and self-destructive aspects of this invention come to the fore, again with some help from the poets. The seventeenth century experienced a particularly intense preoccupation with visual perception. Galileo's telescope, Descartes's works on optics, the theoretical work of Gérard Desargues and Blaise Pascal, who discovered between them, it has been said, the "two basic theorems of the modern geometry of perspective"[3]—all this testifies to the seriousness of the scientific interest in visual phenomena, and particularly to the determination to find "truth" in visual apprehension of the world. But this very passion for truth, for a mathematically sound and impersonal vision, led to the creation of images that seem to be completely opposed to the common conception of truthful representation of the seen, the anamorphic art that swept Europe in the sixteenth and seventeenth centuries.[4] Anamorphic painting, by extending the Albertian conception of the subjective element of perspective in an implacably mechanical way, finishes by creating images that are not merely less satisfying but indeed completely without sense unless they are viewed from the most narrowly defined viewpoint. Anamorphic art develops the spatially prescriptive element of Alberti's system in such a way that the viewer is not only invited to contemplate the work from a particular point, but punished, if he does not do so, by being confronted with meaningless form. By locating the unique viewpoint in nontraditional ways—for example, far to one side and not on a line crossing the painted surface—the anamorphic artist reminds the viewer of the active role that the viewer must take in deciphering the image. The viewer will walk first to one side and then another, trying to find the viewpoint, while initiates watch and giggle with delight, or he will squint through peepholes or tilt the printed plate at unhabitual angles, holding it mere inches from his nose. In this way anamorphoses—and, it might be added, much baroque architecture—force on the viewer an attitude of obedience, although anamorphic art, unlike baroque art generally, instills in the viewer the consciousness of the viewer's individual activity.

Contemporaneous with this activity in optics and perspective studies, there was a general wave of verbal use of the concept of visual representation. Poets, and to a lesser extent, novelists, incorporated into their texts references to paintings and to mirrors. Critics have found a rich vein in the precept *ut pictura poesis* and have described at length "pictorialist" literature of this period.[5] Emblem books continued to appear in great numbers. A rhetoric of "paintings" flourished, as Fumaroli has recently noted, in the sermons and writings of the Jesuits.[6] The study of hieroglyphics was both an esoteric and a popular pursuit.[7] And the telescope invaded the world of letters in the guise of an Aristotelian telescope.[8]

It would seem that in confronting seventeenth-century literature in France as elsewhere we are overwhelmed with vivid pictorialism, with *enargeia*, with a "talking picture" (*peinture parlante*, an extremely common metaphor for language). But there is a reaction against this exuberant adoption of the image as paradigm for verbal representation or indeed for conception in general. The first chapter of the Jansenist *Logic, or the Art of Thinking* (1662) of Arnauld and Nicole addresses the widespread habit of treating thought as mental picturing.[9] The word *idea*, the authors note, is so clear that one cannot explain it by other words. But one can at least try to keep oneself from restricting its meaning "to that single manner of conceiving things which occurs when we turn our mind to the images which are painted in our brain, and which is called imagination" (p. 40). Painting pictures in our mind is a trope that reappears obsessively in the first chapter of the *Logic*, each time with an insistence on the impossibility of understanding thought as painting. For example, if one should wish to create a mental picture of a thousand-sided geometrical figure, one would fail, "because the image that I would try to paint in my imagination would just as much represent any other figure with a large number of angles as it would a thousand-sided figure" (p. 40). Another example of thinking that cannot be adequately represented by the concept of painting is the act of affirming or denying: "someone who believes that the earth is round and someone who believes that it is not round both [have] the same things painted in their brains" (p. 41). Citing the authority of Augustine, Arnauld and Nicole underline the impossibility of drawing all our ideas from the world of the senses. They compare the doctrine of the sensual origin of all ideas to the absurdity of saying that a picture draws its origin from money simply because "a painter may be motivated to make a picture by the money promised him, yet one cannot for that reason say that the picture has its origin in the money" (p. 45).

The denunciation of the dangerous metaphor of painting and of the faculty—the imagination—to which it is linked pervades the work of Pascal. Imagination, taken in its strongest sense, as the faculty of producing images, and thus in opposition to the intellective faculty, is not only disparaged as "that dominant part of man, that mistress of error and of falsity" (p. 44), but denounced specifically in the metaphor and concept of painting: "What vanity is painting, which draws admiration by the likeness of things that one doesn't admire in themselves!" (p. 40).[10] Pascal uses painting, however, and specifically perspective, as a cure for the very delusion that imagination can cause. He reminds the reader of the subjective element involved in the interpretive act by which an image is understood: "Thus pictures seen from too far or from too near. And there is only a single indivisible point which is the true place. The others are too near, too far, too high or too low. Perspective assigns it in the art of painting, but in truth and in morality who will assign it?" (p. 21). There are many other comments on painting in Pascal that question its representational properties and the conditions we must accept in order to view a painting.

However, in the literary domain, there is a more extensive reflection on visual representation, a reflection that, like Pascal's, is based on the demonstration of the subjectivity of such representation. The portrait and the picture—that is, the painted story or *historia*, to use Alberti's term—have an important place in the novels of Madame de Lafayette. Lafayette's work is by far the most widely read today of French seventeenth-century narrative, particularly her *La Princesse de Clèves* (1678). Her two novels deal in interesting ways with the relationship between the characters' attempts to grasp general or abstract truths and their perception and communication of fragmentary individual experience. The failure of experience and belief or of action and desire to join in these novels lays bare the ontology on which representation, and particularly visual representation, is based.

The earlier of Lafayette's novels is *Zayde, histoire espagnole* (1670–1671).[11] Consalve, one of the heroes, has found survivors of a shipwreck on the lonely Spanish coast where he has taken up his retreat. He does not speak the language of these two survivors, nor do they speak his. However, he falls in love with one of them, Zayde, and she not only smiles reassuringly at him, but seems to recognize him. Consalve forms the hypothesis that her sadness is due, not simply to her being shipwrecked on a foreign coast, but to the resemblance between himself and a lover of Zayde, perhaps one lost in the shipwreck. In his attempt to draw Zayde's attention to himself and to communicate his fear that she loves another, Consalve makes use of a picture, a seascape with tempest and shipwreck. He asks the painter to modify the first state of the image by adding three figures: a young and beautiful woman bending over a male corpse stretched out on the sand, and "another man" kneeling next to her, trying to bring her away from the corpse. When he shows the painting to Zayde, she looks angrily at him and then brushes out the figure of the dead man. Consalve's first interpretation of her action is that she does not love another man, that she has no dead *lover*. His second interpretation brings him less satisfaction: that she does love another, but that he is not dead. She has no *dead* lover. The limitation of the pictorial statement is that it does not permit negation, or more precisely, that it cannot indicate being or nonbeing.

Before looking at the way Lafayette pursues this problem, let us consider in more detail the way the painting is produced and used. Lafayette has gone to considerable length to include within the initial description of the painting an evocation of the relationship between persons and the image. The mere execution of the seascape calls into play the relationship of Consalve, his host Alphonse, and a painter. This last is reduced to the role of executant, for the content of the image is entirely determined by a series of commands. Alphonse's initial command was for a view of the sea as seen from his windows. His order inscribes within the image an entirely proprietary or subjective view of the world, the world as *he* sees it from a position that only he (or those to whom he grants the privilege) can occupy. This command controls the action of the painter, limiting his freedom of selection and imposing on him the subjectivity of another. Moreover, Alphonse's command imposes a certain stance towards the represented world on all who see the painting, for they must accept Alphonse's proprietary vision. In this way another term is introduced in the relationship of persons—which now appears as a relationship of roles—namely the viewer, whose future presence is made explicit by Alphonse's next command, to render the painting more *agréable*.[12] This *agréable* is of a very special sort, suggested by a convention of the period, the *topos* of the shipwreck familiar to readers of romances, of libertine poetry, and of the poetry of solitude. Within this *topos* it is important to note the sharp distinction between the subjective and "objective" poles, for the viewer/patron, the one from whose point of view the vision is seen, is himself absent from the representation, leaving a trace only as the *point* of view. Here the true authority of Alphonse over the depicted object becomes apparent, for he plays a godlike role in what he orders. But "to paint a storm" means in this context depicting an arrangement of human figures and their property at the moment of their destruction—"one saw men trying to swim to safety and one saw those who had already perished and whose bodies the sea had tossed on the beach" (p. 94). The superiority over such fellow beings makes the scene agreeable (as in the poetry of Saint-Amant).[13] Beginning with an apparently realistic impulse, to paint the sea in a specific location and to include the statement of the patron's position in that reality, the design of this painting moves towards a fictive definition of the patron/viewer as superior to other human beings—reduced to the status of human figures—who are about to pass, or who have just passed, from the status of living to that of dead figures, their creation or property destroyed in order to permit the patron/viewer to enjoy his property, his creation, his power—in short, his *absence* from the scene of destruction.

Consalve's modification of Alphonse's project changes completely the arrangement by which the subject, the viewer/patron, is absent from an image that is fully objectified. Alphonse's image is relatively flat and simple. The figures within the image have no particular assigned relationship to one another except in degree: they are more or less dead, but are otherwise distributed randomly in respect to one another. Their functional relationship is to the viewer (here giving an aesthetic value, the "agreeable," though within the conventions of such painting the image could produce different effects, such as the sense of futurity in the *memento mori*). Consalve's image has a depth that comes from the relationship among the figures as well as from a relationship to the viewer. In Consalve's image the viewer, instead of being agreeably absent, is figured within the image in the form of the young woman looking at the corpse, while the young man facing her is the figure of the patron. Thus the viewer/patron roles, fused implicitly in Alphonse's image, are split in Consalve's. Where Alphonse's image would impose upon the viewer the point of view of Alphonse himself (as he sees from his windows), Consalve's image imposes on the viewer a point of view toward the patron of the image, who appears as *another man*, and forces the intended viewer to see herself. The human figures in Alphonse's image were fully objective; they had no subjective role; there is no indication that they directed their gaze towards the viewer/patron nor toward one another. In Consalve's image the two subjects looking at the painting are engaged within the painting in a struggle between themselves as potential viewers and viewed. The viewer within the image, the figure of the young woman, refuses to direct her gaze toward the figure of the patron who wishes to become the object of her vision. The figure of the young woman also is the point of contact between the two versions of the image, Alphonse's and Consalve's. Like the viewer of Alphonse's image, she directs her gaze at an object that cannot respond and from whose glance she will always be absent, a corpse belonging to the *topos* of the shipwreck. However, she also belongs to Consalve's interactive vision, for, like the "other man," she is both subject and object, both seeing and seen.

Zayde's gesture of effacing the corpse at first reassures Consalve that she does not have a lover, but his subsequent interpretation leads him to believe that she does have a lover who is alive (p. 98). The effacement of the corpse removes the figure from the power of Consalve; only painting the figure into the frame confers power, establishes the authority of the patron and viewer over what is contained in the image. The representation of the corpse is furthermore a means for Consalve to exercise *self-control*, which he loses when the removal of the image allows the imagination a limitless productivity and deprives him of any means to act on the imagination of Zayde. With the reinterpretation of Zayde's gesture, Consalve must return to his earlier problem, which is precisely a problem of self-representation, and, at the same time, a problem of the self *as* representation—that is, the feeling that he has no meaning for Zayde in himself but only as the image of another. Because Consalve is jealous of a supposed lover who resembles himself, the very glances that should reassure him of Zayde's love incite him to further jealousy. Only the inclusion of the corpse can rid him of the jealousy he feels for his own likeness, because this dual image permits him to kill off his likeness. Paradoxically, therefore, painting as the art of representation, the art of making resemblances, serves here as the means of destroying resemblance, or of destroying that which resembles and allowing that which remains to be sole and unique. It is thus Consalve's hope that the transference of likeness to the image will free him from being himself merely a likeness, merely the image of another. Consalve thus becomes a kind of ironic anti-Narcissus, compelled to seek the person who resembles him, compelled to project his likeness onto canvas, but at the same time repelled by that "other self," whom he would not embrace but destroy. Representation would then itself be abolished in favor of *presentation*.

Consalve's problem, the fissure in his conception of his appearance, is due to the inadequacy of another kind of painting, the portrait. When Zayde eventually learns Spanish and Consalve learns Greek so that they are able to talk to one another, Consalve remains jealous of the person who resembles him. Zayde believes that she is destined to marry the Prince of Fez and that Consalve resembles the Prince of Fez, whose portrait she had seen. Just as the painting posed an insurmountable problem of interpretation for Consalve, so the portrait was misinterpreted by Zayde. The interpretive problem raised by the seascape was based on the inaptitude of the visual representation to *negate*; the problem raised by the portrait is the failure of the image to *specify*. As the portrait is understood or misunderstood by Zayde, it is a representation of a specific individual. A portrait in this sense is quite different from other types of images that contain a human figure—for example, the icon of a saint. An icon in the religious sense does not resemble a historic person; it merely refers to that person. The religious icon thus stands on the boundary of representation and reference. On the other hand, the portrait both refers to and resembles its object. One might even say of a portrait of the Prince of Fez that it *is* the Prince of Fez: "And thus one will say about a portrait of Caesar without forethought and carelessly that it *is* Caesar" (*Logic*, p. 156). The portrait that Zayde had seen before meeting Consalve seemed to her to specify an individual. A seer connected the image with the title "Prince of Fez," when in fact the portrait was of Consalve. The portrait's reattribution to the hero occurs at the very end of the text and restores to him his own unalienated appearance or self-resemblance. No longer need he fear those admiring glances directed toward him by Zayde, while Zayde need no longer fear the person portrayed and to whom she believed herself bound by destiny. These twin fears were both effects of a misconstruction of the portrait as sign, an assumption that resemblance, the basis of the image as sign, is adequate grounds for representation. Only the repossession of the portrait by language permits correct interpretation and adequate representation.

The inadequacy of the portrait to bridge the gap between resemblance and representation, its failure to specify, is also suggested by Consalve's gesture of writing Zayde's name and his (assumed) name on the surface of the painting: "he took the painter's crayon and wrote the name 'Zayde' above that beautiful person and the name 'Theodoric' above the young man who was kneeling. Zayde, who read what Consalve was writing, blushed when he had finished" (p. 95).[14] It is only after Consalve adds these names that Zayde brushes out the figures, suggesting that for Lafayette the representational function does not come into play until words are added to the image. The portrait resembles Consalve but does not "represent" him until language intervenes. Similarly, in the painting the figures resemble the two protagonists but do not "represent" them until the words are inserted into the image.

Both in the painting and in the portrait an attempt to substitute visual for verbal language fails. Only the word can properly specify the relationship of resemblance to being, can exorcise the alienation of self-resemblance imposed by the image. The power of the image depends on the circumstances of its reception, on the way in which the viewer uses it. In *Zayde* the *use* of painting is to mediate between persons. And this mediation fails because of the poverty of painting before the complexities of being. It is worth adding that there is little that is decorative about the visual arts in *Zayde*. They are subordinated to the desperate attempt to bridge the distance separating persons in a world in which knowledge, which is within, and experience, which is without, cannot be joined with any certainty and where painting is the paradigm of the failed attempt to deal externally or objectively with operations that are only possible in the intellect, within a subject.

Lafayette's other novel, the *Princesse de Clèves*, also concerns a portrait and another painting, and here too the images serve an important mediating role between hero and heroine. In the *Princesse de Clèves*, moreover, the pictorial or visual qualities of the image are even more markedly displaced or effaced in favor of the production and conveyance of images in an attempt to reach across the chasm of the world that separates one mind from another, or even separates mind from itself. In *Zayde* a figure is effaced and a portrait misnamed; in the *Princesse de Clèves* a portrait is stolen and a painting is misappropriated.

The portrait is that of the princess herself. It is stolen in full view of the court. The dauphiness had decided to have miniatures made of all the beautiful people of the court, including the princess. On this occasion the princess asks the painter to correct a detail of an earlier portrait of herself that belongs to her husband. Her suitor, publicly undeclared, the Duke of Nemours, takes the opportunity to steal the portrait, specifically the portrait that belongs to the husband. This is how he does it:

The Dauphiness was sitting on the bed and speaking in a low voice to Mme de Clèves, who was standing in front of her. Mme de Clèves noticed, through the curtains, which were only half drawn, M. de Nemours, his back against the table at the foot of the bed. She saw that, without turning his head, he was adroitly taking something from the table. She had no trouble guessing that it was her portrait, and she was so agitated by this that the Dauphiness detected that she was not listening and asked out loud what she was looking at. M. de Nemours turned at these words; his eyes met those of Mme de Clèves, who was still looking at him. He thought that it was not impossible that she had seen what he had done. (P. 302)

This episode is stated with extreme precision. The location of each character—again a triangle—is carefully established in a space that recalls that of the theoretical stage and that of painterly perspective. There are two moments to this episode. In the first there are four audiences and four spectacles. The dauphiness faces the princess whose reactions she can scrutinize. The princess thus offers a spectacle to the dauphiness, while she constitutes an audience to the dauphiness who is speaking to her. At the same time the duke, framed by curtains, involuntarily presents a spectacle to the princess while he is attempting, in a fully theatrical way, to perform for the unnamed multitude elsewhere in the room. To the latter group he offers the spectacle of a man leaning against a table. But he presents an entirely different sight to the princess, who, in her turn, having seen his act, will cease to perform the proper role of respectful attentiveness before the dauphiness. This evident lack of attention sets off the second moment of the episode in which the duke turns towards the princess, ending one performance by becoming in turn the spectator of what was happening "behind" him. But in this web of spectacle, there are in fact two privileged spectacles that are successive. Initially the duke, who is both consciously performing and framed by curtains, is the object of the princess's gaze. It is his action that bears the new information, or assures the progress of the narrative. Furthermore, the princess is the subject, the one who sees, while the duke is object—he does not see her. In the second moment the duke turns to see the princess, and the relationship is reversed. It is the princess who is the object of the duke's observation. It is the sight of the princess that brings new information to him, despite the overlapping glance by which her "having seen" is constituted as the theme of his seeing.

Theater and painting have in common, among other things, that they were linked to the Renaissance technology of perspective (for example, the Palladian Teatro Olimpico, Vicenza). For these arts space is no longer an aggregate but a system, as Panofsky reminds us.[15] They both impose upon spectator and spectacle a specific relationship within which, and only within which, meaning can be found. They proceed by reduction or exclusion, for in both cases what is not seen (the off-stage) is as important as what is seen. It is sometimes said that northern European painters favored a perspective of emphatic subjectivity, in which the peculiarly partial, oblique, and proximate view would give the viewer a sense of participation within the space of the picture. The fact that the viewer could not see everything was guarantee of the realism of the depiction, for the imperfection and "subjectivity" of a human viewpoint were fully conveyed to the viewer instead of being corrected by a painter bent on transcending individual human limitation to give a distant and more complete representation of the object (Panofsky, p. 170). Lafayette has similarly disposed this episode to indicate exclusion. It is important that the duke's act be visible *only* from the princess's point of view. It is important that her reaction to what she sees be incomprehensible to the third party, who does not occupy the privileged position. It is essential that the meaning of the vision be based, not only on the viewer's vision of the object, but on the viewer's consciousness of the privileged relation established between subject and object, for the subject is constituted *as* subject only by that relationship.

This whole episode is organized around a disappearance. The visual representation of the subject (the princess) is part of the object of her gaze (that is, the "scene" of the duke taking and concealing her portrait). She sees "herself," or that representation of herself that belongs to the Prince de Clèves, being taken, or rather she sees something being taken and has no trouble guessing what it is, what she perhaps both fears and desires that it be. The disappearance of her portrait, as the subsequent paragraphs make clear, permits the "appearance" of the duke's love for her. The silence with which she covers the event permits the duke to understand her love for him. Thus a symmetry occurs in two occlusions: disappearance of the image and suppression of the words that reason (*raison*) requires of the princess. The invisible and the unheard bring forth in this way a higher message.

In the most important recent article on the *Princesse de Clèves*, Kurt Weinberg has commented subtly and convincingly on the second of the three principal episodes of voyeurism in the novel, the incident in which the duke witnesses the nocturnal contemplation of his image in the painting of the *Siege of Metz*. In the pavilion the duke sees the princess weaving yellow ribbons around his *canne des Indes* and then going to stare closely at the painting in which he figures. Here the apparent invisibility of the object, the princess, permits the viewer to discover what is normally concealed, as does the celebrated confession episode in which the duke overhears the evidence of passion. But the evidence thus obtained is of no use to the beholder because it is not communicable to another; it remains strictly limited to the viewer. The very attempt to intrude upon the scene, to approach the object of one's gaze, destroys the scene. At his movement toward her, Mme de Clèves flees from the pavilion. In the case of the portrait, the vision remains only because the viewer, the princess, refrains from attempting to interfere with the theft.

The princess's evening in the pavilion is very much a replica of the duke's theft of the portrait, for she has obtained his image and his *canne des Indes* through third parties. In seeing her with them the duke discovers himself possessed as an object of representation, just as the princess had been the solitary viewer of the spectacle of her own possession as object of representation. Thus the viewer of both scenes finds himself/herself as portrayed *en abîme* within a spectacle.[16] The external spectator of these scenes is therefore both within and without, both included as painted object and excluded from the spectacle of the object's possession. The viewer of this spectacle is furtive, intruding unbidden upon a scene, stealing a glance, and the spectacle itself is one of furtive possession. In both cases they are sights that literally immobilize the viewer and deprive the viewer of speech (the duke "was so beside himself that he remained immobile looking at Mme de Clèves. . . . When he had recovered a bit, he thought that he ought to wait to speak to her" [p. 367]). Later neither the princess nor the duke can say to anyone what they have seen.

The role of the portrait and of other paintings in Lafayette's novels bears an interesting resemblance to aspects of Port-Royal's critique of representation. The Jansenist emphasis on the role of the subject and the preoccupation with the problems caused by the sign or external mark by which thoughts are transmitted between two subjects can help form suggestions for the further understanding of the case of the vanished portrait.

We have already noted the strong denunciation of the imagination and of images as paradigms for ideas at the beginning of the *Logic*. This criticism is motivated by a desire to separate the operations of the mind from the outside world. Port-Royal not only denies the old maxim that "nihil est in intellectu quod non prius fuerit in sensu" (p. 49), but goes further to argue that the truth is contained within our ideas themselves if only we attend to the separation of the clear from the confused. This evidently Cartesian concept is a secular presentation of grace, and of a grace that is not only sufficient but efficacious. We do not need signs to recognize truth; it reveals itself by itself:

> Just as there is no need of marks to distinguish light from darkness, except for light itself which makes itself felt, so also there is no need of other marks to recognize truth except for the clarity itself which surrounds truth and which subdues the mind and persuades the mind in spite of itself (malgré qu'il en ait). (P. 20)

The *Logic* begins with the conception of ideas, the first action of the mind, before moving on to judgment, which is the mental operation "by which, joining together different ideas, [the mind] affirms of one thing that it is the other or denies of one thing that it is the other, as when, having the idea of the earth and the idea of 'round,' I affirm of the earth that it is round or I deny that it is round" (p. 37). If judgment is seen as the joining together of ideas, then it is not surprising that Port-Royal should conceive of the verb as being "a word which signifies affirmation (vox significans affirmationem)" (p. 112). The *Logic* breaks down all propositions into a form of the verb *to be* (or not *to be*). *Pierre vit* becomes, in an analysis that has become familiar to us through Chomsky, *Pierre est vivant*. The principle that permits this rewriting is fundamental to judgment and therefore to the whole process of representation. Arnauld and Nicole cite as Aristotle's definition of the verb, "vox significans cum tempore," a word that signifies with time (p. 110). The difference between this definition and the *Logic*'s is that it does not make explicit, as Arnauld and Nicole do, that an act of judgment, the act of a mind, is taking place in any verbal construction. Sentences seem to make statements about the world, but what they really tell us is what goes on in a mind. They are made out of two ideas, "one for the subject and one for the attribute and of another word that marks the *link that our mind conceives*" (p. 168). The problem of thinking is to understand the operation of our mind, and then the problem of communication is to bring this conception from one mind into another, taking into account the various kinds of interference that will occur within and between these minds. Signs exist for this purpose, and especially words, defined in the

Logic as "distinct and articulated sounds, of which men have made signs to mark what is happening *in their minds*" (pp. 103–4). In understanding what is said we again encounter the problem of an inward confusion, on account of the capacity of words to have numerous secondary effects beyond their strict meaning, "that distinction necessary between the ideas awakened (excitées) and the ideas precisely signified" (p. 101).

Thus the *Logic* repeatedly reminds us of the subjective aspect of knowledge, the distinction between what is in the mind and what is outside the mind. This is so fundamental that all verbs are defined as statements of a link that is made in the mind by the application of the verb *to be*. This insistence on the separation of what is in the mind from what is outside the mind is particularly notable in all our efforts to bridge the gap between two minds. In this desert of signs, both natural signs and conventional signs, there is nothing but uncertainty. All certainty depends on the mind, and the *Logic* attaches itself in a particular way to some of the most irritating cases of the indefinite—for example, to the problem of the pronoun. In the chapter entitled "About ideas which the mind adds to those which are precisely signified by words" (I, xv[a]), Arnauld and Nicole deal with the problem of *hoc*. How can one say what *this* is? Here is a clear case of the intervention of the mind to supplement the deficiencies of the world of signs. Another problem is posed by the "equivocal by error (l'équivoque d'erreur)," when a term designates a single and unique thing but people do not agree to which thing it refers, despite their acceptance of its unicity (*Logic*, I, viii). Furthermore, a thing can both represent and be represented; it can even be a representation of itself:

> Every sign requires a distinction between the representing thing and the thing represented, yet it is very possible that a thing in a certain state may represent itself in another state, as it is very possible that a man, in his room, may represent himself preaching; and thus the mere distinction of states suffices between the representing thing and the thing represented: that is, that a thing may be in a certain state the representing (figuring) thing and in another the represented (figured) thing. (Pp. 53–54)

One can begin to see that the problems raised in *Zayde* are not without echo in the *Logic*. Consalve's problem is how to traverse the space separating his mind from Zayde's, and the fiction of two lovers who do not share the same language is only slightly more unusual than some of the examples used in the *Logic*. The failure of the painting is owing to the indefiniteness of signs generally but also to a particular inadequacy that makes the visual sign inferior to the already perilous verbal sign. The painting cannot perform the fundamental operation of judgment; it cannot affirm or negate. One cannot paint a verb, or at least one cannot paint the *substantive* verb, as Arnauld and Nicole call *to be*. Without this foundation of all verbs the image must remain without a clear mark of its relationship to being, as that relationship is made by the affirmation of a mind. The dead lover can be in the painting or can be absent from the painting, but, as Consalve finally realizes, not being in the painting—that is, the effacement of the figure—can convey no information about the outside world and cannot reveal what is happening in the mind of Zayde. While both Consalve and Zayde have modified the image in an attempt to affirm and negate respectively, they have not communicated a statement. They have, at the very most, been able, each separately, to conceive an idea, the first mental operation, but they have not been able to state a judgment.

Significantly, the seascape with figures, like all of the paintings in the two novels, contains the image of the protagonist. The particular need of creating an external representation of oneself is recognized by Port-Royal as part of our fallen and concupiscent state. Is this need not perhaps the source of all subsequent representations? Is not the separation of the inner light from the outward sign the abyss that creates the distinction between the *chose représentante* and the *chose représentée*, such that man becomes a sign for himself and of himself? The man in his room represents himself preaching in a division that recalls the internal scission in Consalve between his representation of himself and of his rival. Lafayette, however, has gone considerably further than the *Logic* in stating the manner in which our need for self-representation can lead to a repetitive and imprisoning concern with the externalization of our own subjective emptiness. The desire to escape from this state in which one perceives oneself as sign leads to a proliferation of images that only exacerbates the division. In commenting on the "confused and obscure" ideas conceived in our minds, Arnauld and Nicole attribute the proliferation of representations to our fallen state:

> [Man] has also lost by sin true greatness and true excellence and hence to love himself he is forced to represent himself to himself other than he really is; to hide his miseries and his poverty and to include within his idea of himself a large number of things which are entirely separate in order to swell this idea and to make it more grand. (P. 78)

The result of the projection outward of the unsatisfied desire within us, the void that remains when our first parents lost grace, is a number of "idols" or "fantoms." Our need for others depends not so much on our need for them in themselves as for our need of their image of us. Solitude—let us recall that Consalve had sought solitude when he took refuge on the coast—is intolerable to most people because it deprives us of the *judgments* of others. Others are necessary to reflect the sinner's image and "to heighten the idea they have of themselves" (p. 82). As Nicole writes in another work, "Man looks at himself no less according to a certain being that he has in the imagination of others . . . based on the view of images of himself (*portraits*) that he discovers in the mind of others."[17]

Consalve's problem is doubly a problem of estrangement through a sign of himself. His portrait has been misattributed to another. He himself is then seen as the image of this portrait. His attempt to capture and contain the image of which he has become the image takes the form of creating still another image, and he attempts to reduce the other to a sign in order to release himself from the status of sign. The visual image is, we have seen, Port-Royal's antimodel for the proper conception of ideas. In Lafayette's further questioning of the image as sign, the apparent objectivity of the image becomes, despite all the characters' attempts at establishing the point of view, the reference; and the origin of the image, an insurmountable barrier to the individual subject's judgment. The consistency of the portrait of the supposed "Prince of Fez" is such that Consalve is seen, up until the very last pages of the novel, as the one who resembles the portrait instead of as the one whom the portrait resembles. The hero has fallen into a state similar to that described by Nicole when he sets forth the extreme example of absence of self-knowledge: "What would one say of a man who, seeing his image in a mirror every day and looking at himself constantly, never recognized himself and never said, 'There I am'? Wouldn't we accuse him of a stupidity little different from madness?"[18] Louis Marin's comment on the representation of the self in Port-Royal is here highly applicable to *Zayde*: "The loss of self, from the moment of birth, in exteriority is accompanied by an interiorization which is not contrary; what is interiorized is the self alienated in exteriority."[19]

The portrait and painting episodes that recur in the *Princesse de Clèves* demonstrate the way in which we are possessed only as signs and in signs. The princess sees the duke take the portrait of herself, but he never possesses her—is it theoretically possible to do so? The duke sees the princess plunged into contemplation of his image in the painting of the *Siege of Metz*, but cannot introduce himself into this scene. Even though the appearance of these signs should in itself be a source of satisfaction, the gap will always remain. Even the two confessions, the one the duke overhears the princess make to her husband and the one she makes directly to the duke when she a is widow, after the duke has posed as a painter in order to be able to see her from the window of a Parisian house—these confessions satisfy neither the duke nor the princess. Part of this is due, as I have suggested elsewhere, to the criticism of induction that characterizes both Lafayette and Port-Royal. This questioning of induction is itself a symptom of the suspicion of outward appearances, which are not the things themselves but only signs.

There are, then, certain resemblances between the Port-Royalist consideration of knowledge and signs, on one hand, and what happens, on the other, in Lafayette's novels. But how does this relate to the lively interest in emblems, hieroglyphics, optics, and anamorphoses in the seventeenth century? Anamorphic art is in one sense a purely rational construction with scientific aims. It is the logical outcome of linear perspective, and it is not surprising that advances in mathematics should lead to refinements in perspective representation. On the other hand, anamorphoses are linked to religious, ascetic tendencies in both the objects represented—frequently skulls—and the reminder that the world of appearances is deceptive.[20] Holbein's *The Ambassadors*, with its curious blur in the foreground, ultimately reveals a reality beyond the surface image of a vain prosperity, but only if the viewer knows the way to look beyond that surface by adopting the proper viewpoint. The blur becomes a skull. A portrait of Charles I, now in Sweden, is a catoptric anamorphosis, one that must be viewed through a mirror in order to reveal the likeness of the king. Viewed directly it reveals only a blur surrounding a skull. Francois Du Breuil published in 1649 a plan for a catoptric anamorphosis of a skull, one which would reveal the skull clearly only in a mirror. Beyond the representation of a skull, a well-known *topos* of religious meditation in the late Renaissance, anamorphic art is of religious significance because of its reminder of the distinction between appearance and reality. Such a reminder in turn leads the viewer to an awareness of his own role in penetrating the appearance. The viewer's role is therefore an extremely active one, as is the religious meditator's, in that the external world is only a storehouse from which specific, internal, thematic constructions can be made if one is guided by a certain method. Therefore, the most objective and rational system of representation meets the most subjective tendencies by placing the emphasis on the active role of the individual mind (one should note that "subjective" is not used here in the sense of random, capricious, or unmethodical).[21] Because confusion can only be dispelled by occupying a single point in space, one person only can generally view an anamorphosis correctly at one time. There is something distinctly individual and even lonely about anamorphic art. It is monadic in its way of forcing the viewer to take cognizance of a vision that is not available to all or not to all at the same time. Small wonder that Leibniz should have been interested in anamorphoses.[22] Furthermore, anamorphosis depends on the reduction of both viewer and object viewed to their purely spatial relationship; point of view and line clearly dominate color. Anamorphosis is therefore a highly rationalized, methodized, and solitary art that unites one of the supreme achievements of visual representation with the reminder that perspective representation depends for its meaning on the viewer. At the same time, it makes of the viewer, not a freely inventive individual, but a subject in two senses—not only the one who sees within a subject/object dichotomy, but subject also in the sense of the one subjected, controlled by the image in the discipline that it requires. It suggests the limitations of our perception, or at least of our unaided, spontaneous perception. We must be educated to our position in relation to the world of appearances.

Neither Lafayette nor the authors of the *Logic* would be likely to dispute Alberti's claim that Narcissus was the inventor of painting. They would, however, have extended the metaphor of the pool. Everything, including other beings, becomes a surface for the portrait that Nicole claims we seek in other people's judgments, or, as Pascal says, "We want to live in the ideas of others an imaginary life and we thus force ourselves to appear" (806). This *vie imaginaire* is for the seventeenth century, strictly speaking, a life of images, the images we project outward at the expense of the true life. ("We work incessantly to embellish and to preserve our imaginary being and we neglect the true one" [*Pensées*, 806]). The denunciation of color in painting is closely linked to the urging that we not be fascinated by the image in itself but that we look *through* it to the mind that created it and to the thought that the painting embodies.[23]

The frequent appearance of the skull—figure of vanity and of the illusion of material things—in anamorphic painting, the rationalism of such painting, and the general criticism of the illusionistic painted image seem to me therefore to be congenial to the Jansenist critique of the visual sign. We are asked to look actively through the first appearance and to take account of our own role in the distortions—and in the corrected view—of the world of material experience.[24] In the work of Lafayette it is clear that what had been blinding us was our own attempt at self-representation. In *Zayde*, for example—if we step back for a better view—we recall that even in words the male protagonists of *Zayde* had attempted, in numerous internal narratives, to represent their lives as they perceived them and then attempted to draw from this representation a general description, a maxim, of human conduct. But not realizing that their representations of the world were flawed by an inability to take into account their role in the representation, they failed to pass from representation to understanding. This understanding can only come from within, from an interiority that is made inaccessible by its dim reflection in the outside world.

In the conclusion of the *Princesse de Clèves* the heroine, like her portrait, vanishes, retreating from human society because the only cure for Narcissus is to remove his image. Thus, paradoxically, the cure for narcissism is solitude.

Michel Beaujour

Speculum, Method, and Self-Portrayal
Some Epistemological Problems

Dialectica est ars artium scientia
scientiarum ad omnium methodorum
principia viam habens.
                PETRUS HISPANUS (quoted by P. Tataretus)

I have recently come across one more book I should have read earlier, namely, Wilbur Samuel Howell's *Poetics, Rhetoric and Logic* (Ithaca, 1975), which deals elegantly, if a bit sketchily, with the Aristotelian distinction between two species of literature: the mimetic-poetic, on the one hand, and the rhetorical-logical on the other. Literary self-portraits, such as Montaigne's *Essays* or Cardano's *De vita propria* (not to mention Descartes's *Discourse* and *Meditations*, which raise difficult questions), clearly belong to the rhetorical-logical branch of literature, although their status in this category may appear somewhat problematic. But let us assume, for the sake of this argument, that the books of Montaigne and Cardano (and perhaps Descartes) are in some ascertainable fashion related to Aristotle's *Rhetoric, Topics*, and *Analytics*. According to Howell, beside history "the types of non-mimetic discourse as Aristotle enumerates them by implication, comprise all forms of expository, scientific, philosophical and argumentative prose" (p. 51). If such is indeed the case, we can more readily understand why self-portrayal, as a rhetorical-logical kind, is a subject-oriented variant of such other rhetorical-logical kinds as the encyclopedic *speculum* and the impersonal discourses on method, which are evidently related to specific parts of the Aristotelian corpus.

Within the loose time frame of what we call the Renaissance, we should therefore not be surprised to find literary self-portraits standing in some sort of close relationship to the many works that purported to do over, or to supplant, the Aristotelian *organon*, from Agricola to Ramus, Bacon, and Descartes. In other words, self-portrayal is inherently involved in epistemological speculation because it questions the validity of the procedures that program its own dialectical invention, as it attempts to map out a new field of inquiry: the individual thinking object, and the very process of thinking. Conversely, the epistemological evolution of Renaissance science can be read—at least on one level—as an elaboration of new methods conferring upon the individual scientist as philosopher a personal responsibility for his inferences, and for testing—logically or experimentally—their validity.

If we follow Jean Piaget, three cardinal notions are involved in the analysis of knowledge: the objects, the subject, and valid structures. The question of validity, implicit in all discussions of method, can be approached in one of two ways: either the valid structures are examined from the point of view of the results they yield, or they may be studied from the perspective of their formation, which involves a study of the subject's cognitive activities. This, of course, is the purpose of Piaget's own discipline, genetic epistemology. It was also, in an earlier period such as the Renaissance, the task undertaken by the self-portraitist, whether by means of introspection (Montaigne) or retrospection (Cardano, Descartes), a process conducted according to procedures derived from dialectical or rhetorical invention. For Piaget,

an analysis of the knowing subject can yield only *two* kinds of findings: either the discovery of *norms*, the validity of which is affirmed by the subject, or the discovery of facts, in the form of cognitive behavior or mental processes. If it is a question of validity, only logical analysis is competent to deal with it, and philosophical speculation is left behind.

If, on the other hand, it is a question of pure facts—including the fundamental fact that the subject always comes to give himself, or to recognize (valid or invalid) norms—it is clear that objectivity and honesty impose external controls and warn against the illusions inherent in self-observation.[1]

According to such stringent criteria, it may well be that Montaigne's or Cardano's (and even Descartes's) self-studying is of slight scientific value. But the Renaissance does not, to my knowledge, yield any more reliable observations of the actual process of cognition.

Montaigne's *Essays* can therefore be seen as a description of cognitive behavior and a documented challenge to accepted logical norms. In this respect, the *Essays* record a negative moment in the dialectics of passage from Aristotelian scholastic science to modern scientific procedures as they are variously adumbrated in the works of Bacon, Descartes, and the Royal Academy. This negative moment witnessed the turning around of heuristic procedures from a storage-retrieval orientation to discovery in the modern sense. And Cardano's sketchy description of his own research procedures draws our attention to the epistemological confusion of the times, when observation yielded results for which neither Aristotelian logic nor Neoplatonic metaphysics could satisfactorily account.

It should be mentioned in passing that the *objects* of Renaissance science were not the same as ours. This is of course well known in principle, but modern prejudice sometimes makes us reluctant to remember that physics, metaphysics, theology, and ethics could be studied with the selfsame methods: these disciplines formed a unified, if polymorphous, philosophical field. The accepted methods, whether logical or dialectical, were better adapted to systematic lecturing and academic *disputatio* than to research in our sense. Hence the difficulty of accounting for unprecedented, divergent, empirical findings. Cardano's description of his quasi-Aristotelian method within his own self-portrait (*De Vita Propria Liber*, chap. 44)[2] distinctly suggests that his acknowledged scientific discoveries (in physics or medicine, for instance) were not actually the result of scholastic, methodical procedures, which he reserved for lecturing and debating. To Cardano, dialectics was a methodological alibi, since, as he states so disarmingly, he had "received all things whatsoever [he had] known through the channel of the spirit" (chap. 47).[3] The slow, methodical—and perhaps sterile—progress of the Aristotelian scientist is short-circuited, in Cardano's case, by an illumination from above whose suddenness and unintelligibility led Cardano to believe that he had been, like Socrates, attended by a benevolent spirit. Under the circumstance, any systematic procedure involving the senses, the imagination, reason, and the will became incidental to a dazzling gift for which the subject was neither responsible nor accountable. Like the mystic achieving a vision, the scientist is the undeserving recipient of a special grace. Cardano thus explained to himself the discoveries he had made despite his constant disregard for standard methodology. His belief in a transcendent intuition, somehow provided by a daemonic *famulus*, is clearly related to magic and the Neoplatonic ideology of his time (derived from Ficino and Pico, it is related to the Cabala). If Cardano's self-portrait is somewhat disappointing as an account of actual cognitive procedures, it is nonetheless an invaluable insight into the bewilderment experienced by a scientist who realized that the standard dialectical procedures left his discoveries unexplainable. Meanwhile, such procedures retained some value as a mnemonic and expository tool, precisely because they implied a stable world picture and a relatively closed *speculum* or encyclopedia. Cardano's adoption of a Neoplatonic "black box" (under the guise of a prompting *daimon*) makes him somewhat less interesting than we should like (as an epistemologist, if not as a man), simply because so many Renaissance thinkers resorted to the same ideological device in order to paper over the epistemological chasm gaping at their feet.

In many respects, Cardano's self-portrait is quite different from Montaigne's *Essays*. The most significant difference—both for our epistemological purpose and for a generic study of self-portrayal—lies in the *Essays*' all-inclusiveness, while *De Vita Propria* reflects (in all senses of the word) on the scientific accomplishments of a lifetime, which are consigned to Cardano's many other works, obsessively listed and glossed in his *Vita*. We do not actually see Cardano at work as a scientist, except insofar as the *Vita* also is a scientific examination of the very subject who had come upon the remarkable findings that prompted so much jealousy and admiration among his contemporaries. On the other hand, Montaigne consigned to one book his introspective findings and a methodological gloss that, in turn, became an object-discourse in subsequent rewritings, thus producing an open-ended commentary on the heuristic procedures of the subject. Such unity was possible only because Montaigne's field of scientific exploration was the knowing subject himself. Thus Montaigne could, and in a sense, was forced to, conflate in one book the various subdivisions of the humanistic encyclopedia. Practice and theory often are inextricably connected in the *Essays*. Besides, one hesitates to call Montaigne a theoretician. One certainly ought to refrain from calling him a philosopher (in any meaningful sense of the word), even with charitable intent. For there is no science (or philosophy) of the singular. It is evident that his method must be found faulty and his findings trivial according to any coherent set of epistemological criteria. Idiosyncrasy and endless scribbling about oneself will never produce a falsifiable hypothesis. In a sense, then, Montaigne must remain a case, like Freud's Dora or his President Schreber, eagerly waiting to become grist for the scientific mill of a proper theoretician.

But such an unphilosophical lapse from the impersonal logos of theory, such a deliberate dwelling in mere opinion, may, under certain circumstances, become a powerful challenge to the validity of what generally passes for sound method and argument. Having reduced the objects of scientific enquiry to the subject himself, Montaigne freed his description of cognitive procedures from the constraints of methods inherited from the Aristotelian and scholastic tradition. He was thus enabled to focus on the actual workings of his self and text, which cannot be confused with the formalized figures of apodeictic argument. None of his descriptive notations could be considered ill formed, aberrant, or beside the point. Montaigne did not punctually assert *cogito* (or *dubito*). All his doubt is *doubting*, a process, and so is his tentative *asserting*. Montaigne did not simply recycle the dialectical procedures of rhetorical invention. It is true that many of his chapters deal with virtues and vices, their genera, species, and differentiae. This cogitation often resembles the procedures of the rhetorical art of memory. His early, weak misreaders were therefore not too wrong in believing that his book was a treasury of ethical discourses, something akin to a *speculum* or a commonplace book. But it is more accurate to observe that each chapter is—to some degree—a deliberate transgression of Aristotelian method and memory procedures, a test of how far from traditional topics ordinary discourse can wander without breaking altogether. Transcending the topical limitations of each chapter or essay, the book as a whole becomes a complex heuristic device geared to the unveiling or constructing of a self and book. Montaigne's undertaking was—awkwardly but productively—caught between two divergent conceptions of representation: imitating and making. He sometimes meant his book to imitate a pre-existing and already constituted entity: "It is not my deeds that I write down; it is myself, it is my essence" (II, 6, "Of Practice"). Such an imitation sometimes suggested a virtual universality of the findings, since "each man bears the entire form of man's estate" (III, 2, "Of Repentance"). The Aristotelian echo in this sentence hints that the *Essays* might after all be read as anthropology, or at least as a modern version of Aristotle's *Ethics*. Yet, in other places, the *Essays* define themselves as an invention (in the modern sense) rather than a faithful recollection or imitation. A well-known passage of III, 3, "Of Experience," observes that the *Essays* have become a self-productive, self-mirroring, and virtually infinite process:

> How often and perhaps how stupidly I have extended my book to make it speak of itself! Stupidly, if only for this reason, that I should have remembered what I say of others who do the same: that these frequent sheeps' eyes at their own work testify that their heart thrills with love for it, and that even the rough, disdainful blows with which they beat it are only love taps and affectations of maternal fondness; in keeping with Aristotle, to whom self-appreciation and self-depreciation often

spring from the same sort of arrogance. For as my excuse, that I ought to have more liberty in this than others because I write of myself and my writings as of my other actions, because my theme turns upon itself, I do not know if everyone will accept it. (III, 13, "Of Experience," pp. 818–19, trans. Donald M. Frame)

This apologetic defense of self-commentary and self-study is subtly laced with an allusion to Aristotle's *Nichomachean Ethics* (Book IV, 1123B–1125a), and particularly to his discussion of the Greek cardinal virtue, *megalopsychia* (magnanimitas, high-mindedness). This allusion is particularly significant because Aristotle also used *megalopsychia* as an example in his *Posterior Analytics* (II, xiii), when he dealt with *definition* in the context of scientific methodology. By drawing the reader's attention to two well-known Aristotelian *loci*, Montaigne implicitly underscored the deviation of his own self-mirroring procedures from the impersonal, logical, and universal method of Aristotelian science, which he considered a verbal game, a systematic progress through linguistic networks that failed to map the world, and were not likely to lead to new empirical findings:

Our disputes are purely verbal. I ask what is "nature," "pleasure," "circle," "substitution." The question is one of words, and is answered in the same way. "A stone is a body." But if you pressed on: "And what is a body?"—"Substance."—"And what is substance?" and so on, you would finally drive the respondent to the end of his lexicon. We exchange one word for another word, often more unknown. I know better what is *man* than I know what is animal, or mortal, or rational. To satisfy one doubt they give me three; it is Hydra's head. (III, 13, 818–19)

Claiming to know (better) what man is, Montaigne seems to be proposing some sort of intuitive mode of cognition, which might be suggested by such a formula as *I am—a man*. Montaigne's dismissal of philosophical technicalities places him in the camp of the humanists, who, by and large, thought that politics, ethics, and rhetoric were worthier subjects than physics and metaphysics. Yet, in Montaigne, this commonsense attitude is not unexamined: it is coupled with a rather systematic doubting of man's ability to achieve any valid truth whatsoever. Montaigne's decision to settle for self-study is epistemologically significant because it shows the subject engaged in the very process of falsifying widely held beliefs or hypotheses. The subject himself is not a stable bunch of predicates. Montaigne's introspection as an activity, an ongoing process, is inscribed in the endless commentary of the text upon itself, its own building and undoing.[4]

Inventing the subject in Montaigne's *Essays* is a cognitive undertaking that anticipates Bacon's attempt to build a new *organon*. The first-person text, however, does not presume to be didactic, nor its description of mental process to be universally applicable. It is a micro-*organon* to Bacon's macro-*organon*. Only with Descartes's *Discourse* and *Meditations* will a first-person epistemological discourse openly claim universal exemplarity. But the "I" in Descartes is very different from Montaigne's "I" in the *Essays*. So different, in fact, that the *Discourse on Method* was published anonymously.

On the other hand, Montaigne's *Essays* are, like Bacon's work in general, a typically Renaissance attempt to pervert rhetoric, and particularly the procedures of dialectical invention, in order to turn it into a tool of discovery. Like so many of his contemporaries, Montaigne took up again (however reluctantly and ironically) the old encyclopedia of virtues and vices inherited from Aristotle and Cicero through an endless succession of rhetors, both pagan and Christian. The ethical and "psychological" commonplaces borrowed from rhetorical textbooks by medieval allegories and *specula* are still recognizable in the *Essays*, which echo at times the traditional *encomia* of virtue and vituperation of vice. In this respect, Montaigne differs little from Bacon, whose *Colours of Good and Evil* are, in a sense, one more commentary on Aristotle's *Ethics*. And, of course, Descartes's *Traité des passions* can be read as an attempt to write a *speculum* in the new key, or a Cartesian version of Aristotelian ethics.

In the Renaissance, all efforts to overthrow traditional epistemology and to build a more reliable method were forced to assimilate the dialectics of invention, in their attempt to undermine the scientific hegemony of syllogistic argument and apodeictic reasoning.

Less evidently, perhaps, rhetoric's traditional emphasis on *ethos*, the orator's projection of a persuasive *persona*, played a crucial role in this epistemological crisis. Cardano's display of self-righteousness is *ethos*, and so is Montaigne's low profile. Natural judgment (which is being tested in the *Essays*) derives its authority solely from the subject's credibility. The writer will be deemed reliable only insofar as he is seen examining himself and testing his own beliefs, displaying himself in the act of clearing the deck. Ethos, then, is an intrinsic component of Descartes' exemplary progress. Ethos confers authority and persuasiveness upon the Cartesian *cogito* and method.

Between *speculum* and method, self-portrayal appears to be a guarantee of epistemological reliability, just as much as it is a record of actual cognitive procedures. The ethos of the self-portraitist was offered as a methodological touchstone by those Renaissance philosophers who, like Descartes himself, meant to bury Aristotle, and presumed to start science from scratch. This is implicit in the somewhat overconfident lines of Descartes' preface to his *Treatise on Passions*, with which I shall conclude:

Nothing makes more apparent the extent to which the sciences we received from the Ancients are faulty, than what they wrote about the passions; for although this is a subject the knowledge of which has always been greatly desired, and which does not seem to be among the most difficult, because, as each person experiences them, one does not need to reach outside for observation in order to discover their nature, nevertheless, what the Ancients have taught about them is so little, and mostly so unbelievable, that I can have no hope of approaching truth except by steering clear of the paths they have followed. I shall therefore be forced to write here as if I were dealing with a subject no one would have touched before me.

Juan Bautista Avalle-Arce

Novelas ejemplares
Reality, Realism, Literary Tradition

In the year 1613 Miguel de Cervantes Saavedra brought out in Madrid a collection of twelve short stories, which he entitled collectively *Exemplary Novels*. After a slow and dubious start in the literary world, Cervantes was then at the height of his fame. His years in the Spanish army were far behind him in time, and so were his years of captivity in Algiers. His first published novel had come out more than a quarter of a century earlier. That book, *Galatea*, a highly experimental pastoral novel, had met with an all too modest success, although Cervantes clung to the pastoral theme to his, literally, dying days. He had written an unspecified number of plays, which he chose not to publish until a few years after the *Exemplary Novels*. But the competition with Lope de Vega, the Monster of Nature, had proved too strenuous, and Cervantes had given up writing for the theater. In 1605 he had published the most successful novel in literary history: the first part of *Don Quixote*. Its success had been immediate and immense, and Cervantes had left the reading public dangling with the written promise of a second part, whose very sketchy outline appeared at the end of *Don Quixote* of 1605.

It is interesting to reconsider the fact that Cervantes deliberately chose not to follow up the success of *Don Quixote*. He decided not to publish the promised continuation, to postpone it, and this decision had the gravest consequences. The continuation was destined to come out all right—not written by Cervantes but by an imitator who called himself Alonso Fernández de Avellaneda, whose real identity will remain unknown forever, short of a literary miracle. But Avellaneda's continuation would not appear until the year after the publication of the *Exemplary Novels*. It was a strange and fateful decision for Cervantes to postpone the obvious and imminent success of the second part of *Don Quixote* in favor of publishing these short stories. His decision underscores the special place that the *Exemplary Novels* had in the literary estimation of their author.

He had been at work on them since before the publication of *Don Quixote* in 1605. We know this because "Rinconete y Cortadillo," the third of the *Exemplary Novels*, is mentioned in chapter 47 of the *Don Quixote* of 1605. Furthermore, we have a different manuscript version of "Rinconete y Cortadillo" from the one Cervantes chose to publish in 1613. And we have a very different version of "El celoso extremeño" as well, thanks to the literary curiosity of a priest from Sevilla named Francisco Porras de la Cámara, who, no later than 1605, collected in a manuscript the two above-mentioned short stories. I cite some of these facts to bring into perspective the artful and deliberate care with which Cervantes treated his collection of short stories. He was at work on two of them before 1605, and when he published these same two stories in 1613 the revisions were more than considerable.

In the preface to the *Exemplary Novels* Cervantes goes out of his way to call the reader's attention to the literary revolution he is about to start. As he writes in the preface (I should point out that I use throughout this paper Harriet de Onís's translation): "I am the first to essay novels in the Castilian tongue, for the many which go about in print in Spanish are all translated from foreign languages, while these are my own, neither imitated nor stolen. My genius begat them, and my pen gave them birth." This, far from being a show of literary arrogance, is nothing but the naked truth, as the slightest consideration of the Italianate short stories of Juan de Timoneda (d. 1583) makes very evident. I mention Timoneda's name because he was the most successful of Cervantes's predecessors in this genre. In other words, Cervantes set out in the *Exemplary Novels* to invent a new literary genre in

Spanish. He was fully aware of the novelty of the experiment, and he wanted his reader to be equally aware.

Let me briefly consider the first and the last of the *Exemplary Novels* to emphasize my point. The first one is "La gitanilla" ("The Gypsy Maid"), and it should be obvious that Cervantes set a very special store by it, since he chose to give it the place of honor in the collection. Why? It should be clear that the first story in a collection must successfully ensnare the reader and not let him wander. Which qualities contributed to making "La gitanilla" a successful reader-trap? I think that the most successful single quality is the literary typology contained in that short story. Gypsies had arrived in Spain by the early fifteenth century, and they had been officially outlawed by the state as early as the reign of the Catholic kings. Officially condemned as vagrant and thieves, gypsies had no room in literary history, save for a few bit parts in the earliest Spanish theater. Cervantes broke with this literary condemnation, bringing gypsies into full focus in the first of his *Exemplary Novels*. The success of this experiment would be attested to by Victor Hugo in *Notre Dame de Paris*, whose female protagonist is the gypsy girl Esmeralda, and in our century by Federico García Lorca in his *Primer romancero gitano*, where the second *romance* is precisely called "Preciosa y el aire," Preciosa being the name of Cervantes's protagonist in "La gitanilla." To this day the gypsy remains a social outcast, but he has been saved from literary oblivion by the magic art of Cervantes.

But there is more to it than that. "The Gypsy Maid" begins with these words: "It would seem that gypsies, men and women alike, came into the world for the sole purpose of thieving." By 1613, the date of publication of the *Exemplary Novels*, Spanish literary history knew a canonical literary form dedicated to thieves and thieving—the *novela picaresca*, the romance of roguery, adumbrated by *Lazarillo de Tormes*, that anonymous novel published in 1554, and brought to full fruition by Mateo Alemán in his two-part *Guzmán de Alfarache* of 1599 and 1604. So "The Gypsy Maid" begins with the clear insinuation that the reader is about to enter a picaresque world sui generis. But the world we enter is one of romantic love and travel. If we look at Spanish literary history again, we will see that the literary genre dedicated to narrating travels and studying romantic love was the Byzantine novel, which I prefer to call the novel of adventures, which would constitute, precisely, the subject of the posthumous novel of Cervantes, his *Persiles y Sigismunda*. So "The Gypsy Maid" offers the reader kaleidoscopic literary possibilities, incarnated in a group of social pariahs, redeemed by love. I think that Cervantes was quite right in thinking that "The Gypsy Maid" would be the successful snare to keep the reader glued to the pages of the *Exemplary Novels*.

Now let us turn to the last piece in the collection, "El coloquio de los perros" ("The Dialogue of the Dogs"). This "novel" has two immediate and distinctly unique qualities, which I want to emphasize now, although I will return later to the narrative as a whole. First, let us consider that this text is exactly what its title implies: the dialogue between two dogs, Cipión and Berganza, outside the hospital in Valladolid. The subject of their dialogue is, mainly, the autobiographical reminiscences of Berganza, interspersed with philosophical comments by Cipión. Talking animals, of course, will take us to the opposite extreme of literary realism and, for that matter, completely outside the realm of reality. We are in a world of fantasy and satire that had been previously explored, many centuries earlier, by the Greek satirist Lucian. But it is highly unlikely that Cervantes could have known Lucian, because the very few works of Lucian that circulated in Spanish had been printed outside Spain, in Lyon and in Strasburg. Cervantes could have known, however, *The Golden Ass* of Apuleius, translated into Spanish by Diego López de Cortegana in 1513, with various reprintings. The golden ass, however, is a former human being now devoid of the faculty of speech, and he does not come into contact with any other animal of similar characteristics. The possible model for talking animals in the medieval, Aesopic fables was too elementary in its conception and functions to be of effective use to the Cervantine imagination.[1] In other words, when reading "The Dialogue of the Dogs" we are confronted with the imagination of its author completely untrammeled and in absolute freedom, abandoning the norms of realism and from the outlines of reality. These have been the boundaries of the other eleven *Exemplary Novels*, but upon reaching the last one, the one that will act as a golden brooch to close the collection so auspiciously opened by "The Gypsy Maid," Cervantes will abandon reality as a literary nourishment, and with the most graceful of intellectual pirouettes will openly embrace fantasy. Plato never dreamed of putting one of his philosophic dialogues to the use that this one is being put to by these two Cynic philosophers, and when I say Cynic I am referring to all possible meanings of the word.[2]

The second unique characteristic of *The Dialogue of the Dogs* is that it literally has no beginning, an extraordinary occurrence in the annals of literary history. The way that Cervantes has manipulated things for this remarkable occurrence to take place has to do with the characteristics and plot of the eleventh of the *Exemplary Novels:* "El casamiento engañoso" ("The Deceitful Marriage"). The protagonist of this novel is a soldier, Alférez Campuzano, who illustrates in his life and artistic development the folkloric tale of the deceiver deceived. On the streets of Valladolid, Campuzano meets an old friend of his, Licenciado Peralta, who asks him about his dejected and sickly appearance. The gist of the story told by Campuzano concerns his plan to deceive a woman, who in turn tricks and dupes him, leaving him with a most embarrassing social disease. To cure himself of this, Campuzano repairs to the local hospital. The treatment he undergoes there puts him in a feverish state, and in the ensuing delirium he thinks or imagines that he hears two guard dogs, under his window, exchanging in human voices their life stories. When he comes out of his delirium Campuzano jots down the conversation he thinks he has heard, and at the moment of the narrative he brings forth his jottings and places them in front of his friend, Licenciado Peralta. Peralta sits down comfortably, takes the sheaf of papers, and tells his friend that he will read the notes, out of curiosity if for no other reason. And he begins his reading. So, *sensu stricto,* "The Dialogue of the Dogs" is nothing but the act of reading on the part of the Licenciado Peralta. This process of reading has already begun in "The Deceitful Marriage," which ends with the following words: "The Alférez leaned back, the Licenciado opened the notebook, and at the very top he read the following title." Thus "The Dialogue of the Dogs" begins with no formal beginning.

But this is not the only structural innovation that Cervantes makes in "The Dialogue of the Dogs." He engages in structural telescoping carried to dizzying extremes. Let me try to explain myself. As I said before, the subject matter of the dialogue is mainly the autobiographical reminiscences of Berganza. At one point in his narrative Berganza recalls how he got to the Andalusian village of Montilla, famous at that time for its witches. There he ran into a witch named Cañizares, who recognizes him, in his canine form, as the long-lost son of another witch named La Montiela. At this point we are told that Berganza's real name is Montiel, and we get an outline of the life of La Montiela. Now the story of La Montiela is a function of the story being told of his life by Berganza, which functions as only part of "The Dialogue of the Dogs," which, as we have seen, is the product of the reading of Licenciado Peralta, a secondary character in "The Deceitful Marriage," which is in turn the product of the retelling of his own recent past by Alférez Campuzano to Licenciado Peralta. So we have this dizzying structural telescoping: a story (that of La Montiela) within a story (that of Cañizares) within a story (the life of Berganza) within a story (the dialogue of the dogs) within a story (the reading of Licenciado Peralta) within a story (the artful deceit played on the sickly Alférez Campuzano). At this point we can say that we are light-years away from the elementary structure of the folk motif of the deceiver deceived, or of the Aesopic fable, which is where it all began.

Now I wish to turn to some of the other uses to which Cervantes put literary tradition in his *Exemplary Novels*. I will try to be very specific, and to that end I will concern myself with only one literary tradition and the imaginative uses Cervantes made of it. The literary tradition I have in mind is that of *la novela picaresca*, the rogue's story, which I have mentioned earlier. As I said before, this tradition was set into motion in the Spanish peninsula by the anonymous author of *Lazarillo de Tormes* in the year 1554. Three editions came out in that year, in Alcalá, Burgos, and Antwerp. This little masterpiece was immediately continued by various authors, but in the climate of new moral and religious strictures during the reign of Philip II (1556–98), it lost its popularity, was thoroughly censured and refurbished, and reappeared as *El Lazarillo castigado* ("Lazarillo Punished"), attributed to the pen of the royal officer Juan López de Velasco. Nowadays there is a raging polemic as to whether *Lazarillo* is a picaresque novel or not. I will not take sides, at least not here. I will only point out that Cervantes recognized it as such (more about this later), which allows me to consider it as such for my purposes. Whatever its dominant genre, *Lazarillo* effectively outlined the standard form of the picaresque novel, which was brought to its perfection in the *Guzmán de Alfarache* of Mateo Alemán.

The narrative form of the picaresque novel became conventionalized and canonized in a hieratic form from the first moment. Its subject matter was intended to seem autobiographical. The picaro, the rogue, told his life from birth to a time that usually did not coincide with the actual moment of writing. For example, *Lazarillo* ends at a time considerably prior to the time of writing. As Lázaro is made to say: "At that time I was at the height of my good fortune"; these are the last words of his autobiography. *Guzmán de Alfarache*, with its illusion of autobiography, ends with the repentance of the picaro, that is to say, his metaphorical death; the repentant Guzmán will write his life to set an example for others.

In dealing with his first moments in life the picaro dwells especially on his ancestry. Lázaro tells us that his father was a thieving miller, captured, tried, condemned, and sentenced, while his mother quickly became the concubine of a Negro slave. It is at this point that Lázaro sets out into the world. Guzmán de Alfarache, for his part, was the son of a Jewish, Genoese merchant, with the very serious consequences that such a background had in Golden Age Spain, given the national, suicidal obsession with *limpieza de sangre*, blood purity. As if these factors were not sufficiently alienating, the Genoese, Jewish merchant becomes a convert to Islam, marries a rich Moorish woman, steals all her money, escapes to Spain, and reconverts to Christianity. At this point he meets the woman who is to become Guzmán's mother. She is the concubine of a very rich and very old nobleman. Although her ancestry, as far as it can be traced, consists of whores, she deceives her old paramour with Guzmán's father, and Guzmán is, naturally, born out of wedlock.

The elements that the picaro wants to stress about his ancestry are those that will accentuate the sense of infamy *a nativitate*. But, as can also be seen, the infamy of Lázaro is only social, whereas the infamy of Guzmán is social, racial, and religious. This gradual stress on the all-pervading infamy of the protagonist will become a characteristic of the genre as it unfolds in time, as has been richly demonstrated by the fine study of the late Marcel Bataillon.

The autobiography of someone who is an infamous scoundrel from birth cannot but have a very jaundiced outlook on society. The point of view of the picaro, as Francisco Rico has suggested, is exclusive and completely negative. This is of paramount importance to the texture of the picaresque novel as a genre, for the point of view of the picaro is the only functional one in his autobiography. This last characteristic is, of course, proper to all autobiographies as a literary genre. Furthermore, the autobiography of the picaro will be highly selective, another characteristic of the genre. In the case of Lázaro, for example, the speaker selects from his life only those elements that in his own opinion, will serve to explain his success in life. For Lázaro success in life consists of the fact that he no longer has to work for a living, because his wife is the concubine of a priest from Toledo.

That Cervantes knew well the models of the picaresque genre is a foregone conclusion. Although he paid no compliments to Mateo Alemán and his *Guzmán de Alfarache* (not even in his all-embracing literary catalogue of Spanish men of letters, which he entitled *Viaje del Parnaso*), this was due to the fact that *Guzmán* had preceded his *Don Quixote* and was its main competitor in the novelistic field. But Cervantes did mention and praise *Lazarillo de Tormes*, in a passage to which I shall return.

In the works of Cervantes we can collect a rich gallery of roguish types. Leaving aside the *Exemplary Novels*, two of his literary characters are very particular prototypes of the picaro as interpreted by his creative mind. The first one is Pedro de Urdemalas, the protagonist of a play of the same title, who winds up his life of roguish antics as the head of a tribe of gypsies, which should draw our minds subtly back to "La gitanilla" ("The Gypsy Maid"). The other wonderful picaro created by Cervantes is Ginés de Pasamonte, a character in both parts of *Don Quixote*, a special and distinguishing characteristic since he is one of the very few characters, other than the two protagonists, to appear in both parts. In *Don Quixote* of 1605 Ginés de Pasamonte is a galley-slave, and his antics in that part will lead to a tremendous textual confusion that should not concern us today. Because of his many crimes Ginés has been sentenced to the galleys, but while in jail he has been writing his autobiography, which, as he says, will enter into direct competition with *Lazarillo de Tormes*. He is then asked if his autobiography is finished. He laughs this off, asking how he could have finished it when he is still alive.

This last observation is worth considering from a few different viewpoints. In the first place, Ginés alludes to his autobiography, but we never see it, it is unfinished. In point of fact, Cervantes never wrote any kind of autobiography, fictional or nonfictional, a point I will have to return to later on. In the second place, Ginés appears in the novel in midlife, as a full-fledged picaro, a tried and sentenced criminal; we do not follow his education in crime but rather see its consequences. And in the last place, the novel focuses on Ginés de Pasamonte at a time in his life when he is totally unrepentant—he is almost proud of being a galley slave—a fact which places him at the opposite extreme from Guzmán de Alfarache, who had by then become the picaro par excellence. In the second part of *Don Quixote* Ginés de Pasamonte continues to be completely unrepentant. In 1615 Ginés makes his reappearance as Maese Pedro *el titerero*, Master Peter the Puppeteer, and in this guise he hoodwinks his audience, most particularly Don Quixote and Sancho Panza, his main victims in the first part.

I said that Cervantes had an obvious dislike for autobiography as a literary genre, since he never wrote one. The closest he came was in the first part of *Don Quixote*, in the story of the captive captain, and even then his story, told in the first person by the captain himself, centers on the episode of his captivity in Algiers and his escape. Before passing on to the analysis of the picaros in the *Exemplary Novels*, I want to approach briefly this Cervantine dislike for autobiography. As I said before, and this is by way of insisting on a basic truth, autobiography presents us with but one viewpoint, that of the author of the autobiography. In the course of the narrative other viewpoints might be presented, but they are always subordinated to the teller's point of view, because of narrative exigencies if for no other reasons. That is to say, autobiography constitutes an extreme form of literary dogmatism, because it presents one point of view to the exclusion of all others.

José Ortega y Gasset, the famous twentieth-century Spanish philosopher, once said that truth is but a point of view. And if that point of view remains motionless, truth will inevitably be distorted, with parts of it out of focus; it will suffer. A conjunction of points of view, on the other hand, will enhance truth, will help to clear up its outline. In an intuitive and artistic way Cervantes knew this long before Ortega y Gasset; multiple points of view constitute the fundamental tenet of his narrative art. This is why he spurned autobiography, which is the presentation of truth and reality from a single point of view, without the possibility of a challenge. On the contrary, he favored dialogue, explicit or implicit dialogue, because dialogue, as Plato had so admirably demonstrated, is the presentation of two or more different points of view. If Cervantes had but known it, he would have enthusiastically subscribed to Plato's statement in the *Republic*: "Dialogue is the coping stone of the sciences" (VII, 534).

This is why *Don Quixote* as a novel really gets under way only after the creation of Sancho Panza, who becomes immediately a verbal sparring partner for his master. From now on, nature, reality, and truth will be seen from at least two different points of view. This, of course, is enhanced by the hallucinatory nature of Don Quixote's mind, which distorts reality while in the process of apprehending it, whereas Sancho's prosaic nature refuses any distortion whatsoever. This is why *Don Quixote* has become the greatest novel-dialogue ever written. The novel is conceived and executed as an exchange of viewpoints, as an immense dialogue, which can take place even at a great distance, as when Sancho, in the second part, goes to govern the famous island of Barataria. While discharging this illustrious duty Sancho is aided and abetted by the ever-present advice and letters of his master, which is a way of maintaining alive an implicit dialogue. There is no point in illustrating the almost eternal, explicit dialogue that occurs between master and servant at other points in the book, so full of merry verbal pranks and most serious intellectual queries.

This is another way of saying that Cervantes's mind had an intellectual thirst for dualities, dualities at minimum, because he considered the presentation of a single viewpoint a pauperization of reality. This was the great discovery of *Don Quixote*, and Cervantes would remain faithful to it throughout his creative career. This is why he could never bring himself to write a picaresque novel, which in its autobiographic, canonical form represented precisely that pauperization of reality that inhibited his creative imagination. The intellectual necessity for multiple viewpoints very likely explains Cervantes's love for the theater, an early love that he still avowed very late in life, when he published a selection of plays in 1615, the year before he died. In the prologue he wrote for this selection, *Ocho comedias y ocho entremeses nunca representados*, he confirms much of what has just been said.

There is no point in going any further into Cervantes's dual intellectual necessities or his demand for multiple viewpoints. It can be seen even in the titles of so many of his texts. I will choose but a few, taken exclusively from his *Exemplary Novels*—"The Two Damsels," for instance, or "Rinconete y Cortadillo," or "The Dialogue of the Dogs." The last one, to be sure, appears in explicit dialogue form. All this should explain why Cervantes had an actual abhorrence to writing a truly picaresque novel.

This is not to say that Cervantes restrained himself from experimenting with the picaresque genre. I have already mentioned some of the wonderful picaresque types he created. The creation of these types was bound to lead him to experiment with the genre, to see if it could yield the possibility of multiple viewpoints. One thing to remember, at this juncture, is the fact that from the start of his literary career Cervantes demonstrated a wonderfully fertile, experimental turn of mind. One must only look back to *Galatea*, his first published novel, a pastoral, which at the opening of its idyllic, bucolic world presents a brutal murder of one shepherd by another shepherd.

The frustrated autobiography of Ginés de Pasamonte could be considered one such experiment with the picaresque genre. But in the *Exemplary Novels* we have two such full-scale experiments, which it is time to consider. I am referring to "Rinconete y Cortadillo" and to "The Dialogue of the Dogs." I have mentioned the fact that "Rinconete y Cortadillo" is known to us in two different versions, one printed in 1613 and one before 1605, both contained in the manuscript of Francisco Porras de la Cámara. I repeat this because it demonstrates the early intellectual need that Cervantes felt to experiment with the picaresque genre. And also because it demonstrates the artful care that Cervantes took with his literary experiments.

"Rinconete y Cortadillo" tells the story of two teenagers who meet by happenstance at an inn in La Mancha and decide to make their way together to Sevilla. There they perform some minor thefts in San Salvador Square. But they are detected by Ganchuelo, a member of the fraternity of thieves and criminals presided over by Monipodio; Ganchuelo decides to take them to the house of Monipodio to be examined, pay their dues, and join the fraternity. This is precisely what happens. The last two-thirds of the novel are dedicated to the description of the kind of human beings who attend a soirée in the patio of Monipodio's house. That is to say, we are dragged into the heart of the criminal life of Sevilla, which is an extension of the kind of life into which Guzmán de Alfarache was born. But the presentation of this world could not be more diametrically opposed to the technique adopted by Mateo Alemán. The consideration of these differences will serve to emphasize the dimensions and scope of Cervantes's experiment with the picaresque genre.

From the very first words of Cervantes's tale we can detect a veritable gulf between his concept of the picaresque and that of his predecessors: "One of these hot days of summer two lads chanced to find themselves in the Molinillo Inn." This is to say, the fate of these two boys is going to be molded by chance ("acaso," in the original). But the action, the intervention, of chance, fortune, or whatever you want to call it is unthinkable in the picaresque genre. The life of the picaro is governed exclusively by predetermination, indeed by predestination, as is made only too clear by the morose care with which the speaker describes his criminal ancestry. The picaro is a criminal because he cannot be any other way; he faces a destiny of crime because he was predestined to it by his ancestry. To a certain extent this literary predestination can be seen as a result of the original conception of the picaresque novel as an antichivalric novel. Amadís de Gaula, the greatest chivalric hero produced in Spain, was predestined to be such, for he was the son of the heroic king Perión de Gaula and of the most beautiful princess Elisena. Similarly, Lazarillo de Tormes was predestined to be a petty criminal, because his father was a thieving miller and his mother something just this side of being a prostitute. Chance cannot play any part whatsoever in any picaresque novel; if it did, then by chance the picaro might turn out to be good—in other words, he might cease to be a picaro. Hence the novel would lose its raison d'être. The conversion of the picaro, Guzmán, for example, has nothing to do with chance; it is, instead, allied with the contemporary theological polemic *de auxiliis*. But from its first line "Rinconete y Cortadillo" opens its doors widely to the action of chance, because Cervantes, as I have demonstrated repeatedly, had an almost religious respect for human free will in its literary representation. The life of Don Quixote richly demonstrates this: on account of physiological reasons he becomes mad, and after he is mad he chooses to call himself Don Quixote—but much later, on his deathbed, he chooses freely to abdicate, to give up, his freely chosen identity of Don Quixote.

The role of chance in the first line of "Rinconete y Cortadillo" serves a purpose analogous to free will in the world of Don Quixote. But it also serves its own very definite and subtle literary purpose. At the end of the novel Rinconete "made up his mind to advise his comrade that they should not linger in that vicious and evil life." In other words, Cervantes's picaros are free to abandon their evil way of life at any time they feel like it; the entrance into, and the exist from, the picaresque life of Sevilla is an exercise of the will for Rinconete and Cortadillo. Neither Lázaro nor Guzmán were given, or could have been given, that option, for the reasons already mentioned.

The criminal life into which Lázaro and Guzmán were born is described only from their viewpoint, since each is writing his own autobiography, as is the case in the canonical picaresque novel. But, obviously, such is not the case with "Rinconete y Cortadillo," which spurns the simplistic approach to literary reality by having a double protagonist and, consequently, a double perspective on literary reality. For example, upon their entrance into Sevilla each youth enters the life of crime in his separate way, and the narrative thread will at first follow one and then the other. During the long episode on the patio of Monipodio's house, the literary viewpoint will alternate between youthful protagonists. And at the end of the novel the literary point of view will rest squarely with Rinconete. The last paragraph begins: "Although nothing but a boy, Rinconete had a good head on his shoulders, and was decent by nature." Toward the end of the same paragraph the author intervenes to tell us that "we must leave for some other occasion the account of his life and adventures," with the implied promise of a future unicity of literary viewpoint. Let us note in passing that this personal intervention of the author in the novel, this sort of narrative distance and control, is impossible by definition in the picaresque novel, where the distance is permanently fixed by the autobiographer's point of view

Another significant divergence from the canonical picaresque lies in the fact that the *novela picaresca* is eminently an urban novel, because to practice his tricks the picaro needs the city mobs. By contrast, "Rinconete y Cortadillo" begins with a completely rural setting: "One of those hot days of summer two lads chanced to find themselves in the Molinillo Inn, which stands on the outskirts of the famed plains of Alcudia on the way from Castiel to Andalusia." Only after this significant start does the novel move leisurely to its urban setting of Sevilla.

For the sake of brevity I will point out one last divergence, this time between Cervantes's tale and *Guzmán de Alfarache*. Upon leaving his house, Guzmán's first adventure is his encounter with a mule driver who victimizes him and steals from him. Guzmán asks for the help of justice, but gets no redress, which demonstrates his complete impotence before the world. He has to learn and practise deceit in order to defend himself in the world. The first adventure of Cervantes's youthful protagonists also involves a mule driver at the Molinillo Inn, but here it is the boys who trick the mule driver, steal his money, and when attacked by the mule driver defend themselves successfully against him. The importance of the different dénouement to identical adventures is considerable. The young boys do not need to learn deceit in order to defend themselves successfully against the world; they fall back upon their combined strength and succeed; they are self-sufficient. At the bottom of this significant difference lies the fact that on account of Guzmán's early impotence and defeat, the tone of his tale is pessimistic, melancholy, and bleak. But the early show of self-sufficiency and victory makes the tone of the lives of Cervantes's characters happy, gay, graceful.

Now to "The Dialogue of the Dogs," which I consider to be Cervantes's other experiment with the form of the canonical picaresque tale in the *Exemplary Novels*—and by far the most ingenious and artful. The audacity of this experiment is extraordinary. To point out just some of the most obvious differences with the canonical picaresque, one need only recall that the protagonists are not human beings but rather two dogs, a most original and unique development of an Aesopic fable. The lonely protagonist of the *novela picaresca* is replaced by two, and its autobiographical form by a dialogue, with its consequent alternation of viewpoints.

But Cervantes has left enough characteristics of the picaresque genre in "The Dialogue of the Dogs" to make it easily identifiable as his most audacious and daring experiment with that genre. I will go one step farther and state that "The Dialogue of the Dogs" is Cervantes's travesty, ironization, and reworking of Mateo Alemán's *Guzmán de Alfarache*. Some other points of comparison will emerge later, but for the moment I want to stress only one. A major criticism addressed to the *Guzmán de Alfarache* is that each adventure is followed by lengthy passages of moralizing and philosophizing, passages invariably longer than the adventure itself. To be sure, this characteristic makes the reading of *Guzmán de Alfarache* quite an arduous experience. Of course, adventure and moral are all related from the same first-person viewpoint, with its categorical denial of any possible variation in the narrative tone. But in "The Dialogue of the Dogs" Berganza tells his own life from the moment of birth, with a passing reference to his ancestry ("this would lead me to believe . . . that my parents must have been mastiffs"), but his main role is to attend to the narrative of his life. He does not usually stop to philosophize or moralize about himself or his adventures. Such philosophical commentaries are usually supplied by Cipión. Such alternating viewpoints and functions give variety and spice to the sum total of the narrative, solving in the most dexterous and innovative way the enormous artistic problem that Alemán had created for himself in adopting the single point of view of an autobiographer's narrative.

As I have just mentioned, as in any picaresque novel Berganza begins the story of his life with a reference to his ancestry. He tells us, also, that he was born in Sevilla, like Guzmán; like Guzmán he was born into a life of crime. Berganza was born in the slaughterhouse of Sevilla, which he describes in the following terms: "All who work there, from the lowest to the highest, are persons of elastic conscience, cruel, fearing neither man nor devil; most of them are married without benefit of the clergy; they are birds of prey, and they and their doxies live on what they steal."

In a way analogous to Guzmán de Alfarache, the first adventure of Berganza consists of being tricked and duped, not by a muledriver, but by a beautiful girl, in a way somewhat reminiscent of *La Celestina*. The deceit into which he has fallen brings about the wrath of his first master, and gets him into deep trouble with the master, a butcher from Sevilla. Berganza runs away to save his skin and goes into the service of some shepherds, safely removed from the city. This suggests two characteristics of "The Dialogue of the Dogs," each worthy of comment. First, with each new master he serves, Berganza changes his name. At various times he is known as Gavilán, Barcino, Montiel, or Berganza, the name under which he is known in Valladolid. I have discussed at length this characteristic in relation to *Don Quixote*, and my conclusions will remain the same. Cervantes gives his protagonist various names, or, better still, the protagonist gives himself various names, to identify some deep-set, vital change. From the semianonymity of the beginning (what was his real name after all? Quijada? Quesada? Quejana?), the protagonist proceeds to call himself Don Quijote de la Mancha, and at various times in his life he will be known as The Knight of the Sad Countenance, The Knight of the Lions, Shepherd Quijotiz, and finally, on his deathbed, he will identify himself forever as Alonso Quijano the Good. This *polionomasia*, this changing of personal names, has its roots in the Judaeo-Christian tradition, and we know that Israel is the name given in the Old Testament to Jacob after he wrestled the angel of the Lord. In the New Testament, Saul of Tarsus was a bitter Christian-hater, but after the vision on the road to Damascus and his conversion, he came to call himself Paul. The use to which Cervantes puts this form of *polionomasia* is analogous, in the sense that the change of personal name differentiates the various stages of a man's life, or of a dog's life, for that matter. This, of course, goes against the grain of the picaresque, because the life of the picaro is one continuous reality, that of the life of crime.

The second characteristic that I want to point out is that in telling his autobiography we see Berganza serving various masters. Beside the two already mentioned, Berganza serves, to mention just a few, a rich merchant in Sevilla, a constable, a soldier, and a dramatist. This characteristic of the picaro serving a chain of masters became canonical in the picaresque genre as early as *Lazarillo de Tormes*, where we see the protagonist first serving a blind beggar, then the stingy priest of Maqueda, then the hungry and miserable nobleman of Toledo, then a friar of dubious reputation. In fact, each of the seven chapters of *Lazarillo de Tormes* presents the protagonist serving a different master. This characteristic became so ingrained in the picaresque genre that it was to serve as the title of a late Spanish picaresque novel: *Alonso, mozo de muchos amos* ("Alonso, servant of many masters"), by Jerónimo de Alcalá, who published the first part in 1626 with such great success that he quickly had to publish a second one later the same year. To this extent, Cervantes is quite willing to go along with classical features of the canonical picaresque. This one feature he found most useful to air his views on literature, narrative technique, contemporary society, and even the burning issue of the day, the expulsion of converted Moors, which was going on at the very time of the publication of the *Exemplary Novels*.

There is no question, having read "The Dialogue of the Dogs" with the picaresque structure in mind, that Cervantes utilizes the *novela picaresca* with the same overwhelming irony as he utilizes in *Don Quixote* the romances of chivalry. There were standard situations and human types in both genres that he could use, imitate, parody, ironize. He did all of these things to the canonical picaresque in his minor masterpiece of "The Dialogue of the Dogs." Maybe the most valuable lesson that this tale can present to us lies in the demonstration that Cervantes could put to some remarkable uses the autobiographical form of the picaresque. The truth of the matter is that in "The Dialogue of the Dogs" he invented a new literary genre of such extraordinary novelty that it has had no followers: the autobiography in dialogue form.

Timothy J. Reiss

Power, Poetry, and the Resemblance of Nature

The following essay has to do with the relation of political theory to literature and mimesis. It concerns the relation of political theory and activity in the seventeenth century's formulation and creation of a new kind of nation-state—and literature as it becomes a political act, arguing and asserting the stable power relations of such a state. Acting together, political theory and literature produce a concept of representation as they invent a particular concept of universal reason and nature, of reason in nature and of nature in reason, essential to that new ordering of power.

It seems to me that the form taken by these relationships reveals something quite new and relatively unfamiliar ("relatively," because some aspects of such relationships may have been important in antiquity). By and large, we will be able to see how very different in impulse the notion of text, of reading, and of writing was prior to the seventeenth century from what came after. Such dates, of course, are only approximate, and the generalization should perhaps not be quite so absolute. Yet the fact remains, to take an example of principal importance for the Middle Ages, that Augustine's turning inward through memory and *sermo* to grasp some transcendence is one kind of conception of meaning indicative of a very different idea of merely human language (*lingua*) from what was subsequently to be the case. And the Augustinian texts tend to form a kind of constant background reference throughout the period between at least Scottus Eriugena and Juan Ruiz (not to mention Erasmus, or even Descartes). To be sure, they form a sort of stable sounding board within an ongoing development, rather than any fixed and unchanging motif; but that an Augustinian point of reference remains fundamental to medieval concepts of meaning seems beyond doubt, at least as far as practice is concerned.

In Augustine, the certainty of some ultimate meaning would have been guaranteed by the imprint of a divine "text" upon the human soul. Later, the attempt to attain meaning will increasingly be undertaken through other authoritatively meaningful texts, whether the paradigm text be Augustine himself, some secular text endowed with quite special value (such as those of Vergil, Ovid, and Dante), or even some more abstract process of interpretation referred to an ideal reader. Robert Hollander, in his essay, is able to show how Dante's *Commedia* forms the text underlying the *Decameron*, and suggests that it was, as all these paradigm texts, "not only a revered text," a text being "gingerly scrutinized for its moral validity and its poetic truthfulness," but at the same time one "not always to be trusted." Such ambiguity seems always to lead to a multiplication of meanings, of which the many viewpoints and hallucinatory perspective of *Don Quijote* or the Chinese boxes of the *Novelas ejemplares* may well be as exemplary as the title of the latter works.

Earlier essays in this volume have shown how extremely common this kind of textual relationship was, from the *Libro de buen amor* to Petrarch, from the *Roman de la rose* to Erasmus and Cervantes. Together they show us a progressive secularization of what happens in Augustine: a replacement of the authoritative text imprinted upon the soul by the repetition of a more and more simply human text. Another example of this development toward an eventually quite different kind of conceptual process is no less telling. Among other things, I will be trying to show how important was a conflation during the seventeenth century of author and king to a new concept of meaningfulness, of human action in general, and of literature in particular. Now, it is certainly the case that a superficially similar conflation is to be found already in Dante. Nonetheless, the difference is quite vast.

By the end of the seventeenth century, such a conflation will have created a purely human identity whose essence is its self-possession and rational will, and whose action aims to fulfill simply human goals. In Dante the writer's *auctoritas* and the princely *auctoritas* are merely a stage in the passage toward the divine *Auctor*, much as, for Augustine (as the *De Trinitate*, no less than the *Confessions*, reveals) the exploration of "self" is but a reaching through appearance to its own effacement in the Divinity. Of such a process, once again, the *Commedia* is exemplary, and there, too, one can see how a paradigm authoritative text (in this case Vergil), far from acting (as later) as an ambiguous source of guidance and misguidance, gradually effaces itself before the ultimate glory whose presence fills the *Paradiso*, and in so doing emphasizes, precisely, its own trustworthiness.

Still, in Dante, between the dual human *auctoritates* and the single unique *Auctor* a certain polarity is set up at least potentially, creating a space within which will eventually occur a multiplication of levels of meaning that is (once again) potentially infinite. Such a multiplication will itself create an ever-increasing distance from any such "place" as that of an originating Meaning, *Auctor*, *Logos*, or whatever. Such a multiplying of levels appears to become ever more dizzying as we come into the sixteenth century, as is particularly revealed in such poetics and grammars as those of Pierre Fabri and John Palsgrave. During the second half of the same century, this would have led first to attempts at grasping a fugitive self as a meaningful locus, such as can be seen in Cardano, Montaigne, or Erasmus, in whose writing new texts and new meanings generated from a given paradigm text seem to be precariously gathered together by an equally precarious subject. Thomas Greene explores something rather similar to this when, taking a phrase from Erasmus through Terence Cave's work on that author, he discusses the endless "cornucopia" of the *Adagia*, whose interpretation and whose possible meaning he views as open to a "literally interminable" reading, a copious fountain of writing whose possibility is nevertheless always referred to the small *ur*-phrase that anchors all potential readings in something like an originating intention, however precarious.

The unlimited expansion of such "dissemination" remains therefore faithful to an origin, and Greene underscores—as do others—the seeming secularization of earlier conceptualizations of meaning and representation that this seems to indicate, when he speaks of the "something theurgic" in Erasmus's elucubrations. For, finally, an originating self does not yet exist, and such efforts lead to a dissolution of any idea of representation. They lead to such endless transformations of merely potential reference as can be seen in Ralegh or Fulke Greville, in Shakespeare or Sidney. Any claim of control over the transforming and transfiguring power of language, or of ability to effect knowledge or make anything, indeed, but mere fiction, is always undermined by massive ambiguities—just precisely what the *Arts poétiques* of the late seventeenth century would reject (albeit with the notable, and significantly forgotten, exception of Emanuale Tesauro's great baroque poetic, *Il cannocchiale aristotelico*). By that time it may well be possible that perspective, whether in writing or in painting, whether in the *Princesse de Clèves* or the popular art of anamorphosis, could have offered something like a focal point for universal meaning, a way through surface indefiniteness to the underlying order of the clear and distinct. Yet it remains the case, certainly through at least the late seventeenth century, that such perspective continues to emphasize the uniqueness of *one* view or reader, to underscore, as I have put it elsewhere, the enunciator's *responsibility* for the composition of meaning. The universalization of a new concept of representation and meaning will therefore depend upon what one might term an "objectivizing" of the subject, an effort to leave the subject's ordering power intact while making it appear to be a property of ordinary language itself, a property of the community of speakers. This relation of private to public will take on a variety of names: that of "taste" in the area of aesthetics, of "contract" in that of political and economic theory, of "concept" in epistemology, and so on.

The following essay examines, therefore, one moment in an

ongoing but historically situated and socially conditioned process of displacement of the making of sense, a displacement of the concepts of origin and intention, of signification and reference. Such a process is perhaps the fundamental mark of the period between, say, Ockham and Bacon, during which occurred a transformation from the transcendent meaningfulness of Augustine toward something else, whose inception could be signaled by the name Descartes. My essay will be concerned with that inception. I will argue that the fluid and ambiguous concept of meaning characteristic of the Renaissance gives way to a fixed concept and practice of signification—that representation, however complex, becomes fundamentally monolithic. Responsibility and intention pass from reader to writer, before such responsibility and intention are both occulted, subsumed in the objectivity of a universal reason whose eventual model will be the scientific order of mathematical experimentalism. The denial of that sense of "vulnerability" Greene ascribes to Erasmus and his contemporaries (whose sense is no doubt akin to that of my term "responsibility," maintaining the implications of risk but lacking the ethical overtones) is then absolute. I will argue that this transformation is the consequence of a fundamentally *political* activity.

By the second half of the sixteenth century, it had become commonplace to consider the concurrent corruption of language and decay of civil society. Reference to the Hydra-head of civil broils intermingles, in Shakespeare as in Montaigne, with the use of the same cliché to refer to the deceitful or overly artful misuse of language. Thucydides' text on the simultaneous dissolution of language and the state becomes a hackneyed triviality.[1] A play such as the anonymous *Tragédie du sac de Cabrières*, probably written between 1566 and 1568, concerns as much the power and misuse of language as it does the Catholic massacre of Cabrières.[2] This concurrence is as practical as it is theoretical. In August 1570, Louis Le Roy signed the dedication to his *Exhortation aux François pour vivre en concorde, et iouir du bien de la paix*. In the same month and place, Saint-Germain-en-Laye, Charles IX (to whom Le Roy's text is dedicated) signed the text of the so-called Peace of Saint-Germain, bringing to an "end" the second religious war: two well-written texts intended to bring stability to civil confusion. Le Roy, though not the treaty, quotes at very considerable length Thucydides' text, and his *Exhortation* centers on the relation between linguistic and civil confusion.

One could give dozens of similar examples. I mention this text chiefly, however, because it can serve to underline an interesting aspect of what I have just called the "commonplace" that associates linguistic and social disturbance. With one or two exceptions, it is above all to be found in writers one would call "political." Among them, it is especially prevalent in the writings of the *Politiques*, the mediators between the Huguenot and Ligue extremes. To be sure, and as all the papers presented at this conference have profusely emphasized, others speak constantly of the need to consider linguistic problems and to improve the vernacular languages. Humanists such as Dolet, Peletier, or Sebillet in the 1540s, a poet such as Du Bellay at the end of the same decade, "grammarians" such as Vauquelin in the 1570s or Laudun in the 1590s, philosophers and jurists, all concentrate on the same theme. For the most part, only writers oriented toward essentially political matters tend to insist upon the aforesaid equation. Grammarians, poets, humanist teachers, although they note often enough the potential for linguistic corruption, are restrained as to its possible effects. Typical of such is the view expressed by Roger Ascham, reminding us how in antiquity, "whan apte and good wordes began to be neglected," then "began, ill deedes to spring." Yet Ascham considers this to occur "first in Philosophie: and after in Religion." There is an end to it. Not for him is there any question of the body politic.[3] Doubtless the England of 1570 was less unstable than the France of the same period, but that is not the point I wish to emphasize here. The fact of the matter is that for writers like Ascham, the improvement of linguistic usage is a relatively unhurried matter of time and education, however fundamental a question it may be. For more politically oriented writers, the question is primary, critical, and immediate. (An affirmation of this kind certainly needs to be qualified in regard to the theater and a poem like d'Aubigné's *Les*

Tragiques, but in these cases it is more a matter of reader interpretation than direct statement.)

It is in this context, therefore, that one should consider the significance of Bacon's argument situating writing and what he calls "experientia literata" at the very foundation of all "right" and "legitimate" knowledge, whether in the sphere of natural-philosophical or political thinking. Indeed, even when he is speaking of the former case, the Chancellor frequently draws his metaphors either from his own experience in political and legal life or from written histories of such experience—Machiavelli's *Discorsi* being a favorite resource in this second case. For Bacon, ordered writing is at the basis of all and any right method; and method is at the basis of all legitimate knowledge of nature and of all stability and increase in a healthy political society. Galileo says little else when he speaks of the necessary alliance between the language of mathematics and the language of the world. In his well-known letter to Mersenne of November 20, 1629, Descartes speaks of the possibility of discovering a natural and universal philosophical language whose basic words and the letters composing them would correspond to the natural order that thinking establishes among concepts. He remarks that such a language depends upon the ordering of "all men's thoughts" according to "the true philosophy." Descartes is clearly referring here to what he would publish eight years later as his *Method*. For him, as for Bacon and Galileo, right language and right method are one and the same: both are essential to human knowledge and action.[4]

We can go further. We need not be reminded, perhaps, that the context of Bacon's writing was that of a career as lawyer, politician, and statesman, concerned all his life with the stability of government and civil society. It is hardly surprising that, like Jean Bodin's earlier *Method* of history, Bacon's concern with language and discourse should have been to seek a new logic (as he always referred to it) capable of revealing the general law underlying all particular customs of peoples and transformations of states.[5] From the date of his publication of the *Sidereus Nuncius* (1610) until the end of his life, Galileo, for his part, dramatically confronted the political dimension of his search for a new language and method. What of Descartes? Here, too, the question of power forms an integral component.

As he recorded it in the *Olympics*, Descartes' illumination concerning his "marvellous science" occurred on November 10, 1619. In the *Discours de la méthode*, he tells us that this was in Germany, as he was returning from the Emperor Ferdinand's coronation to the army, participating in the beginning of what the future would know as the Thirty Years War. Such a context is of fundamental importance to the *Discours*, and the implicit goals of an ostensibly "mere" philosophical method are immediately politicized, through the use of an architectural metaphor:

> It is true that we do not see anyone throw to the ground all the houses in a city, with the sole intention of rebuilding them differently, and of making its streets more beautiful. But you certainly do see lots of people knocking down their own houses to rebuild them, and sometimes they are even forced to do so, if they are in danger of collapsing by themselves and if their foundations are not quite solid. In the light of that, I came to feel that it was doubtless unreasonable for a private individual to undertake to reform a state, by changing everything from the foundations up, and knocking it down to stand it up again; and to reform the body of the sciences, or the order established in the schools for teaching them.[6]

Thus, he asserts, he wishes only to correct his own thinking, and not at all those "things that concern the public," even though these do reveal certain "imperfections." He assures us that any stable situation is better than a change, even though, as he had written just a little before, the best ordered states are certainly those that have, from the beginning, "maintained the constitutions of some prudent legislator."

This remark, in its turn, had followed upon the assertion that a building constructed by a single architect is in general incomparably better ordered than one put together pell-mell by many hands—an argument that Descartes had then immediately applied to the construction of entire cities, to the only true religion founded by God, and to the excellence of the Spartan constitution supposedly "invented . . . by one man." We may perhaps be forgiven for doubting the limits Descartes claims to be placing upon the potential use of his new method, all the more when we see him return at the beginning of the next section to his architectural image. By its means he is able to compare his "morale par provision" to a temporary dwelling, useful while he is erecting the new one, and he is able to situate the superiority of the laws he will follow while doing so only to the fact that he is accustomed to them: for the Persians and the Chinese may well be just as "sensible" (*sensés*).

Such relativity suggests another commonplace, and one we have already seen implied by Bodin: the idea that it should be possible to discover the elements of universal law, the fundamental nomothetical rules of all human societies. Hobbes so describes his object at the beginning of the *De Cive*: "not," he writes, "to point which are the laws of any country, but to declare what the laws of all countries are."[7] Such an idea will find a counterpart of fundamental importance to literary and aesthetic theory in the constant opposition drawn between the universal laws of poetry common to great writing at all times and in all places, and the matters specific to a precise cultural context—the first equated with the permanent laws of nature, the second with the actions of humans and the elements of nature in so far as they relate to such actions. (Descartes' distinction between the universal rationality of the *Method* and the relative nature of the laws to be obeyed according to the injunction of the *morale provisoire* is therefore utterly typical.)

In Hobbes, as elsewhere, the achievement of such a goal is possible only on the assumption that all humanity is fundamentally alike, whenever and wherever it has been, is, and will be found, and that humans are alike chiefly in their voluntarism (willful rationalism), their fear of death and therefore mutual divisiveness, their desire for power, and their right to (self) possession. Like Descartes' common sense and universal reason, these assumptions form the fundamental axioms of a right method. Bacon, too, in a text dating from 1608, formulates his method of right reason in terms of clearing the ground and laying the foundations of a new building. And he, too, is quite specific that he is talking as much of civil society as of science, that he is talking of the "rules of argument," of the "first principles" of a logical method, of new "forms of proof" and a fresh "basis of discussion," of new ways of "understanding," and of reformed "minds," of language and discourse.[8]

The political writers of the late sixteenth century had viewed the improvement of language and the stabilizing of civil society as a single problem. The tetrad of Bacon, Galileo, Hobbes, and Descartes likewise saw method, language, natural philosophy, and political order as forming a single network. The new concept of poetical representation becomes the focal point organizing this network of relations. It is perhaps this that will be behind Diderot's assertion, a century later, to the effect that in situating "the *beautiful* within the perception of relationships . . . you will have the history of its progress from the birth of the world right up till today." "The perception of relationships," he insists, "is therefore the foundation of the *beautiful*," while the ability so to perceive them is "taste, in general."[9]

By the fourth decade of the seventeenth century, it will be assumed that the right use of language accompanies the methodical use of reason, that the stable ordering of political power is concomitant with the rational (and still divinely created) order of nature. Language, correctly used, corresponds through its grammar with the universal rational order of methodical common sense. Such common sense, the general reason of mankind, is found to be at the very least adequate to the order of nature (the *mathesis universalis*) and at best fully conversant with its equally rational processes. Bouhours selects his own tongue as alone having achieved this: "It alone, in my opinion, is able to paint well according to nature, and to express things exactly as they are" ("Il n'y a qu'elle à mon gré qui sçache bien peindre d'après nature, & qui exprime les choses precisément comme elles sont"). Thomas Sprat, with an equally nationalistic sense of excellence, chooses rather to praise the Royal Society's improvement of language: "They have exacted from all their members a close, naked, natural way of speaking, positive expressions, clear senses, a native easiness, bringing all things as near the Mathematical plainness as they can, and preferring the language of Artizans, Countrymen, and Merchants, before that of Wits and Scholars." Such a view comes close to Bouhours's requirement of linguistic "transparence": "fine (*beau*) language resembles a pure, clean water without any taste." And a century later, Dr. Johnson will be able to generalize further the same conception in his discussion of Dryden's critical precepts: tragedy, he says, provides us with a poetical order that achieves its rational legitimacy and correctness to the truth of things because that order corresponds to "the nature of things and the structure of the human mind."[10]

I have taken these later examples—Bouhours, Sprat, Diderot, and Johnson—in order to indicate the installation of a mode of conceptualization that endures up to the beginning of the nineteenth century at least, and, I would argue, with some slight variation, up to our own time. Time is lacking to make the argument here, though it will be a leitmotiv accompanying what I have to say.[11] The axiomatic assumption of these coherences of discourse, mind, and nature is in place by the mid-seventeenth century. It means that the syntax of a properly ordered language (its "precellence," as it had been termed certainly since the late sixteenth century) automatically provides us with an analysis of the order of reason *and* of the order of the material world—the coherence theory of truth. At the same time, ways are found to argue that grammatical predicates are precise representations of mental concepts, while these latter are at least adequate representations of material phenomena—the correspondence theory of truth.[12] These are the fundamental assumptions of what I call "analytico-referential" discourse. The mediatory role of a stable language is quite apparent, and one is immediately drawn to ask what permits such faith in its coherence with method in the accuracy of its mediatory role, and in its necessary stability and universality.

Like Descartes, Hobbes ascribes such faith at least partly to the certainty of method—whose exemplar is geometry: "whatever things they are in which this present age doth differ from the rude simpleness of antiquity, we must acknowledge to be a debt which we owe merely to geometry. . . . Were the nature of human actions as distinctly known as the nature of *quantity* in geometrical figures . . . mankind should enjoy . . . an immortal peace." Or again: "Geometry therefore is demonstrable, for the lines and figures from which we reason are drawn and described by ourselves; and civil philosophy is demonstrable, because we make the commonwealth ourselves." The same may be taken as applying in matters of art, while it cannot apply to the material world "because of natural bodies we know not the construction."[13] Vico was later to express the same sentiment. Method here, then, refers simply to a knowledge of the mutual coherence of all matters. It does not, alone, seem to be enough.

For Hobbes also writes, in the very same place as the earlier of the two passages just quoted: "wisdom, properly so called, is nothing else but this: *the perfect knowledge of the truth in all matters whatsoever*. Which being derived from the registers and records of *things*; and that as it were through the conduit of certain definite appellations" cannot but be the consequence "of a well-balanced reason; which by the compendium of a word, we call *philosophy*."[14] But such a view implies not simply the mutual coherence we have just seen. It also requires some kind of correspondence: to know "the registers and records of *things*." Here, Hobbes does not require any formal proof of such a possibility; he merely appeals to a practical evidence. After Copernicus, he writes:

> the doctrine of the motion of the earth being now received, and a difficult question thereupon arising concerning the descent of heavy bodies, Galileus in our time, striving with that difficulty, was the first that opened to us the gate of natural philosophy universal, which is the knowledge of the nature of *motion*. So that neither can the age of natural philosophy be reckoned higher than to him.

I have already mentioned Galileo's requirement concerning the coincidence of the language of mathematics and that of nature. Hobbes's point is that Galileo's equations really provide us with an analysis of concrete material substances in motion, and that in so far as they work, therefore, the figures that compose them can genuinely be said to correspond to the moving objects composing the natural event to which they refer. The combination of geometry and Galilean mathematical experimentalism, therefore, provides us with a method coherent with the order of nature and the mind, and at the same time correspondent with concepts on the one hand and discrete objects in nature on the other. It is of this that Hobbes speaks when he asserts that "Civil Philosophy" is "no older . . . than my own book *De Cive*," and when he comments that he is going to put "into a clear method the true foundations of natural philosophy."[15] I would suggest that when Rapin speaks of Aristotle's *Poetics* as being the only necessary rule for forming "wit" ("l'esprit"), he is thinking as much of this Hobbesian method as he is of the Cartesian, with which he is usually credited: "Indeed, properly speaking, his *Poetics* are only nature put into method, and good sense reduced to principles" ("la nature mise en méthode, & le bon sens reduit en principes").[16] Such a statement corresponds quite precisely to Hobbes's Galilean experimentalism and geometrical method.

In addition to the arguments of the philosophers concerning the faith one might have in the mediatory role of a stable language and a certain method (and we will return to Hobbes and others in a moment), the other chief argument—if one can call it that—seems to be one of power. My choice of Hobbes was not entirely indifferent. The linking of power, of accurate knowledge of nature through a methodical representation that analyzes and imitates at the same time, of the ordering of a stable civil society, and of the notion of a steady "progress" and expansion within that stability, strike me as fundamentally Hobbesian in its impulse. If one adds Hobbes's concern with matters literary from the beginning to the end of his life, then his almost emblematic role is the more deeply underscored. But let me return more exactly to the matter of the use of power as a foundation for these diverse relationships, and most particularly as it concerns the domain of literature and of language.

In 1640, La Mesnardière in his *Poétique* had already made a distinction between those who could enjoy great tragedy and those who clearly could never hope to do so. The distinction is made in terms of order and disorder, and with the aid of the principal metaphor we have already seen used to this end in the sixteenth century. But this time it is used to insist upon what is almost a class distinction (if the anachronism may be forgiven) between the polite and the vulgar, the useful and the superfluous, the delightful and the indifferent. La Mesnardière is writing of great theater, especially of tragedy:

> Now, if we want to pass from the consideration of Utility to that of Delight, matters which are inseparable in the judgment of Philosophers, it is easy to infer that the vulgar masses (*multitude grossière*) cannot obtain any pleasure from a serious, solemn, chaste, and truly tragic discourse; and that this many-headed Monster can at best only understand the superficial ornaments of the Theater.[17]

In 1660, Arnauld and Lancelot addressed their *Grammaire générale et raisonnée* to one whose education will permit him, they say, a "scientific" access to linguistic usage and reason, others achieving it only through "habit." In his *Nouvelle méthode* of 1656, a text on the "purity" of the French language, Claude Irson had already distinguished on just these grounds between "l'homme raisonnable" and "le vulgaire" who operate only "par hazard." In 1647, Vaugelas, dedicating his *Remarques sur la langue française* to the chancellor Séguier, remarks that the latter is the absolute master of language, as well as being a genuine "souverain Magistrat" who represents the will of the prince. Indeed, this last was accurate enough, since the chancellor held the Great Seal and since this was during the Regency. So far as the administration of justice was concerned, Séguier was indeed supreme. In 1668, Gérard de Cordemoy dedicated his *Discours physique de la parole* to Louis XIV, by this time firmly on his throne, identifying right language with the king himself, who uses it perfectly and from whom proceeds language in its perfection.[18] Such assertions reach their paroxism with Bouhours, who is worth quoting at length on the subject:

> Our great Monarch occupies the first rank among these fortunate geniuses, and . . . there is no-one in the kingdom who knows French as he knows it. Those who receive the honor of approaching him, are astonished by the clarity (*netteté*) and the precision (*justesse*) with which

he expresses himself. That free and easy manner (*cét air libre & facile*) of which we have spoken so much, enters all he says: all his terms are right and well-chosen (*propres, & bien choisis*), though they are not at all affected (*point recherchez*), all his expressions are simple and natural (*simples, & naturelles*): but the turn he gives them is the most delicate and the noblest in the world. In his most intimate talk, there never escapes a word unworthy of him, or that is not marked by the majesty which accompanies him everywhere. He always acts and speaks like a king, but like a wise and enlightened king, who on all occasions maintains the proprieties required in each matter. Not even the tone of his voice lacks dignity, and that indescribable majestic something that conveys respect and veneration. Because good sense is the principal rule he follows when he speaks, he never says anything but what is reasonable; he says nothing useless; he somehow says more things than words: that can be seen every day in those so judicious and precise answers he gives without pause to the ambassadors of princes and to his subjects. In short, he speaks so well, that his manner of speaking (*langage*) can provide a true idea of the perfection of our language (*langue*). Kings must learn from him how to rule; but peoples must learn from him how to speak.[19]

It will soon become clear that the place where language is displayed at its finest is poetry (literature), as poetry is also responsible for bringing both language and power to their summit.[20] In a word, then, the king is both the principal poet of his country and the unique sovereign. He brings political and linguistic stability. Only a year later, Dryden in England voices similar sentiments, albeit rather more subdued. The recent refinement in "conversation" in England, writes the Poet Laureate, is due to the court "and, in it, particularly to the King, whose example gives a law to it." Fortunate (says Dryden, somewhat ironically) in having been able to acquire an acquaintance with "the most polished courts of Europe," Charles II has been able to reform both the "barbarism" and the "rebellion" of the nation to which he has returned. A century and a half later, Hegel will still assert that human experience from which art is lacking is barbaric. Poets, Dryden now remarks, should be those who can most benefit from the king's twofold "excellency," his bestowal of political stability and his gift of eloquence and the art that will necessarily follow.

Here we have the precise response to the problem posed at the end of the sixteenth century, and still discussed in socio-political terms. "There would be no society among men," asserts Bernard Lamy, "if they could not give one another perceptible signs for what they think and what they want." No doubt such a sentiment could be found in antiquity with no difficulty, and almost everywhere in the Middle Ages. But now it exists in a context to which Thomas Sprat can serve to give added precision: "the purity of Speech and greatness of Empire have in all Countries still met together. The *Greeks* spoke best when they were in their glory of conquest. The *Romans* made those times the Standard of their Wit, when they subdu'd and gave Laws to the World."[21] In one way, then, the king, with his possession of, and power over, language, can guide all its other users in social action and in natural knowledge. Poets, the most exquisite users of a language, can learn from him. In another way, however, it is poets who are the legislators, poets who show the way to action and representation, poets who hold the ultimate power, because it is they who, in spite of everything, show the way to, and control the right and proper use of, language. After the mid-seventeenth century, literature and literary criticism acquire the task of ordering the diverse claims and assumptions of which I have been speaking up till now.

In 1650, Sir William Davenant addressed the preface to *Gondibert*, his epic poem, "To his much Honour'd Friend Mr Hobs."[22] The text is a quite remarkable one, making a constant equation between reason and political action, between great poetry and power, between the rousing of Machiavellian *virtù* ("Ambition" and "Vertue," as Davenant calls it) and the creation of "this new Building" that all great poetry must be. One immediately recalls the new building of which both Bacon and Descartes (not to mention Hobbes) spoke of constructing, referring to the methodical ordering of reason and common sense. Poetry, says Davenant, must be aimed first at "Divines," chief among men, because it can help them carry out the task to which they are ordained: "to temper the rage of humane power by spirituall menaces, as by suddain and strange threatnings madness is frighted into Reason" (*PG*, p. 33). Such rage of human power is akin to Hobbes's conception of the state of nature as being the condition of humankind where all give free reign to their "desire for power after power." Hobbes, of course, puts an end to it through the consent of the contract, not by poetry. However, we may have reason to pause a moment if we think that the two are utterly unconnected.

In the *Rudiments* Hobbes relates how he sought for the fundamental "material" of human relations that could be considered equivalent to the axioms of geometry and that would permit him, as we saw, to elaborate a demonstrable civil philosophy on a parity with geometry:

> When I applied my thoughts to the investigation of natural justice, I was presently advertised from the very word *justice*, (which signifies a steady will of giving every one his *own*), that my first enquiry was to be, from whence it proceeded that any man should call anything rather his *own*, than *another man's*. And when I found that this proceeded not from nature, but consent; (for what nature at first laid forth in common, men did afterwards distribute into several *impropriations*).

For Hobbes, then, this "justice," confirming the consented-to distribution of personal property and avoiding the otherwise necessary "contention," marks the moment when "all quit that right they have to all things."[23] It is, that is to say, the moment of the "covenant" discussed in the *Leviathan*. In the *Rudiments* the founding axiom of that moment—the inception of stable civil society—is the concept of justice. I would ask, simply, that this be kept in mind, for we will see that the concept of "poetical justice" will come to be considered fundamental both to the way in which poetry can be at once a revelation of the true order of things and a representation of specifically local realities, and to the way in which it presents as permanently legitimate the ethical and political assumptions of a particular ideology.

After "Divines," Davenant continues, the next in importance to whom poetry must be addressed are the "Leaders of Armies" (*PG*, p. 35). For generals are to be esteemed

> as the painfull Protectors and enlargers of Empire, by whom it actively moves; and such active motion of Empire is as necessary as the motion

of the Sea, where all things would putrifie and infect one another if the Element were quiet: so it is with men's minds on shore, when that Element of greatness and honor, *Empire*, stands still, of which the largeness is likewise as needfull as the vastness of the Sea; For God ordain'd not huge Empire as proportionable to the Bodies but to the Mindes of Men, and the Mindes of Men are more monstrous and require more space for agitation and the hunting of others than the Bodies of Whales. (*PG*, p. 36)

Let us not forget here, should we read such sentences with some slight feeling of surprise, that this is the preface to a poem in which we are being presented the concept of *Leviathan* before the event. The leaders of armies, then, have always been "oblig'd to Poets," both for the record of their deeds and for "that their Counsels have bin made wise and their Courages warm by" poetry, as those of the "Grecian Captains" were by Homer (*PG*, p. 37). Lack of attention paid to poets means to "be content with a narrow space of Dominion; and narrow Dominion breeds evil, peevish, and vexatious mindes and a Nationall self-opinion" (*PG*, p. 37). Finally, after the generals come the "*Statesmen* and Makers of *Laws*," equally in need of poetry: none of these four categories of leaders should believe "they could perform their work without [poetry]" (*PG*, p. 38).

Government, he goes on, "resembles a Ship, where though *Divines*, *Leaders* of *Armies*, *Statesmen*, and *Judges* are the trusted Pilots, yet it moves by the means of winds as uncertain as the breath of Opinion." And how could it be otherwise, he asks, when these pilots "are often divided at the Helm?" (*PG*, p. 40). Having then discussed such divisions at some length (*PG*, pp. 40–44), Davenant concludes: "Thus we have first observ'd the Four chief aids of Government, *Religion*, *Armes*, *Policy*, and *Law*, defectively apply'd, and then we have found them weak by an emulous war amongst themselves: it follows next we should introduce to strengthen those principal aids (still making the people our direct object) some collateral help, which I will safely presume to consist in Poesy" (*PG*, p. 44). For poetry, he adds, "like contracted *Essences* seems the utmost strength and activity of Nature" (*PG*, p. 48). It can therefore guide all other activities.

Davenant, not being an overly modest man, no doubt considered himself ideally suited to fill such a role. Raised in court circles (he had been page to that Fulke Greville, Lord Brooke, whose poetry has already received some scrutiny here), he was the author of many successful plays between 1629 and the closing of the theaters, and had become Poet Laureate on the death of Ben Jonson in 1638 (John Dryden was to succeed Davenant upon his death in 1668). During the civil wars he was Lieutenant-General of the Ordnance under the Duke of Newcastle, so that he could well assert his knowledge of "Courts and Camps," as well as of poetry, to be entire—and not always safe: in the very year of the preface to *Gondibert*, while trying to lead a French colony to Virginia, his ship was captured by the English and Davenant was imprisoned on the Isle of Wight (where he wrote the third book of *Gondibert*). In October 1650, he was put on trial in London, and only the intervention of John Milton is credited with having saved his life (a favor he was later to repay after the Restoration, when Milton was threatened with exclusion from the benefit of the Act of Indemnity, a situation that could easily have led to his own trial and execution).

However that may be, and whatever Davenant's opinion on the role of poetry and the poet as it referred to himself, so exalted a view of the aims and capacities of poetry (and of literature, in the broad sense) is not restricted to exiled Cavaliers nor to the age of the Frondes. In 1712, John Dennis will speak of "the most noble and exalted of all Arts," as he notes how poetry (in both the narrow and the broad sense) was written and appreciated by "all the great Statesmen who have best succeeded in Affairs of Government"; and he provides us with a list that runs from Moses to Maecenas, from Solon to Scipio and Caesar, from Lycurgus, Plato, and Aristotle to Machiavelli and Harrington, from Alexander and Tacitus to Richelieu: "who laid the Foundation of the *French* Greatness, wrote more than one Dramatick Poem, with that very right Hand which dictated to the Cabinets of so many Sovereign Princes, and directed the successful Motions of so many conquering Commanders"—a greatness, he adds, that was to be "sapp'd and undermin'd and overturn'd by a

British Poetick Ministry." In 1787, we find Marmontel making the same kind of assertion, commenting upon "the political and moral objectives (*l'objet politique et moral*) of heroic poetry, and above all of tragedy" in Greek antiquity, and noting "the lyric poet's role, or rather ministry, in councils, armies, the special games, and at royal courts . . . and in the same way . . . the orator's function at the parliamentary assembly: he was counsel, guide, and censor to the republic; he attacked, he protected the chief men of State."[24]

In Marmontel's case, one could perhaps argue that such a view at least partly reflects the political unease that will bring the Revolution only two years later, but this conception of the literary man is already widespread in the seventeenth century. Usually, no doubt, it is rather more toned down. Thus, Rapin remarks mildly: "Poetry, being an Art, must be useful by the quality of its nature, and by the essentially subordinate position that all Art must maintain in relation to Politics (*la subordination essentielle, que tout Art doit avoir à la Politique*), whose general goal is the public good." He is not, however, suggesting that literature is secondary to politics; rather that its purpose is political through and through. He would agree with Rymer, writing twenty years later, that "in the days of *Aristophanes*, it was on all hands agreed, that the best *Poet* was he who had done the most to make men vertuous and serviceable to the Publick."[25] The purpose of poetry, Davenant had remarked, is to "conduce more to explicable vertue, to plaine demonstrative justice, and even to Honor" (*PG*, p. 9). That is why on the one hand the great poets of antiquity were "men whose intellectuals were of so great a making . . . as perhaps they will in worldly memory outlast even Makers of Laws and Founders of Empires" (*PG*, pp. 5–6), and why on the other they should refer to "the most effectual schools of Morality [which] are Courts and Camps" (*PG*, p. 12). Here, at last (you may say), we are coming back as promised to the matter of justice. For courts, says Davenant, (meaning "all abstracts of the multitude, either by King or Assemblies") are par excellence places of justice (*PG*, p. 13), while armies themselves are like judges, these last being "avengers of private men against private

Robbers," the first being "avengers of the publique against publique Invaders, either civill or forraign, and Invaders are Robbers." The parallel continues with a comparison of siege armies to circuit judges (PG, p. 13).

Like armies and like judges, literature fortifies us against the wolves: "If any man can yet doubt of the necessary use of Armies, let him study that which was anciently call'd a Monster, the Multitude,—for Wolves are commonly harmlesse when they are met alone, but very uncivill in Herds." If any one doubt this, let him ask "why Fortification hath been practic'd so long till it is grown an Art?" (PG, p. 13). This, of course, is straight out of Hobbes who, at the beginning of the *Rudiments*, makes precisely this comparison of nations with wolves to individuals as tamed animals, and likewise asks why "we see all countries, though they be at peace with their neighbours, yet guarding their frontiers with armed men, their towns with walls and ports, and keeping constant watches."[26] Justice, as it appears in Hobbes, is essentially a way of creating and maintaining an equilibrium between wolfish men. Davenant underscores the fundamental relation between such a notion of justice and ethical poetry, power politics and the nature of man, between a concept of the elite few and the common "Herd," as he writes:

I may now beleeve I have usefully taken from Courts and Camps the patterns of such as will be fit to be imitated by the most necessary men; and the most necessary men are those who become principall by prerogative of blood, which is seldom unassisted with education, or by greatnesse of minde, which in exact definition is Vertue. The common Crowde, of whom we are hopelesse, we desert, being rather to be corrected by laws, where precept is accompanied with punishment, then to be taught by Poesy. (PG, p. 14).

Poetry—literature—then teaches "patterns" that must be "fit to be imitated by the most necessary men." Quite clearly, these most necessary men are those who, by birth, education, virtue, and a proper sense of their own place and value (what the ancients called "magnanimity"), are alone fitted to lead the multitude and to fulfill what Davenant might refer to as the utmost possibilities of human action and achievement. One may perhaps recall once again that such a view is very close to the Hegelian. The German philosopher will also argue that the greatest art depicts ideal actions (moral and free ones within situations involving fundamental issues of life and death, of right and wrong, good and bad, and so on) and requires an audience capable of recognizing and asserting their own similar freedom: "such people, Hegel believes, are usually to be discovered in the upper classes of society, specifically in the nobility."[27]

In order to achieve such communication, poetry needs to teach, not simply patterns, but at the same time the events and actions that complete them and fill them out, as variables do a set of logical constants. The purpose of the "Heroick Poem" is as "in a perfect glass of Nature to give us a familiar and easie view of our selves" (PG, p. 1). Literature, Davenant adds, "should represent the worlds true image often to our view" (PG, p. 3). It must provide the "truth operative, and by effects continually alive, [which] is the Mistris of Poets, who hath not her existence in matter but in reason" (PG, p. 11); it is a contemplation of "the general History of Nature," rather than a "selected Diary of Fortune" (PG, p. 3). The poet, Rymer will write, must know all things, but he must "by a particular Chymistry extract the essence of things."[28] We have already seen Davenant use just this expression. Poetry, then, for Rymer as for writers two centuries later still, teaches both the patterns from which the most powerful ("necessary" or "noble") men can learn and the discrete events that fill out these patterns. It shows the rationality of the natural order, congruent, as I earlier suggested, with that of the mind and that of correctly used language, at the same time as it reflects (by "correspondence") the elements that concretize that rational structure.

Literature is "of all Arts the most perfect," adds Rapin, because it achieves both a coherence with the order of nature and a representation of the discrete phenomena constituting events in the world: "for the perfection of the other Arts is limited, that of Poetry is not at all: to succeed in it one must know almost everything." Hegel, too, will claim that because only the poetic art, which includes both theater and literature, can provide us with all the aspects of "the action as a process complete in itself," manifesting both the discrete events that compose the action and the dialectical laws of its government by idea, it is the most considerable of the arts.[29] For his part, Davenant had concluded that literature does not only show the universality of the rational order of things, it is "the best Expositor of Nature, Nature being misterious to such as use not to consider, [and] Nature is the best interpreter of God" (*PG*, p. 48). Not to accept such a concept and use of literature (for the term "poetry" is always used in a broad sense) is therefore to "give a sentence against the Law of Nature: For Nature performs all things by correspondent aids and harmony" (*PG*, p. 49).

Literature, Davenant argued, not only expounds nature by providing a knowledge of events and phenomena, but also functions *like* nature. For "Nature (which is Gods first Law to Man, though by Man least study'd)" and "Reason" are fundamentally one: reason "is Nature, and made art by Experience" (*PG*, p. 51). On the one hand, then, we have a concept of literature as in a referential relationship with what is here called "nature": a concept that responds to Thomas Sprat's praise of the Royal Society on the grounds that, among other things, its achievements would be useful "in furnishing to wits and writers an inexhaustible supply of images from nature and works of art."[30] This itself reflects an order of human endeavor giving the advantage to literature. On the other hand, we have a concept of literature that sees it, not as a representation of things, but as a methodical presentation of the underlying order: Johnson's equation of nature, mind, and literary discourse. Here, too, it is perhaps worthwhile to take a forward glance at Hegel. For him, as Kaminsky once again summarizes the position, the human spirit seeks to achieve its full self-consciousness by attaining a "knowledge of the rational structure that permeates the world; that is, he tries to organize sensuous data in such a way that the presence of the Idea is recognizable. Out of this endeavor arises Art."[31] The similarities hardly need emphasizing, and I will return to them at least once more before drawing more concluding implications from them.

Earlier on, we saw Rapin assure us, through his commentary on Aristotle, that when we speak "properly" of literature we are speaking "only of nature put into method, and good sense reduced to principles." Such a sentiment is echoed exactly by Dennis, when he tells us that "the Rules of Aristotle are nothing but Nature and Good Sense reduc'd to a Method." Rapin speaks of the rules as reducing "nature to a method" but only "so as to follow it step by step." By these rules, he goes on, "everything becomes just, proportionate, and natural, just because they are founded upon good sense and upon reason."[32] Davenant had long before echoed Hobbes's desire for a methodical treatment of matters human, by asserting, as Rapin and Dennis were to do, that Aristotle simply "labours to make Poesy universally current by giving Lawes to the Science" (*PG*, p. 52). Rymer takes it yet further:

The truth is, what Aristotle writes on this subject, are not the dictates of his own magisterial will, or dry deductions of his Metaphysicks: But the Poets were his Masters, and what was their practice, he reduced to principles. Nor would the *modern Poets* blindly resign to this practice of the *Ancients*, were not the Reasons convincing and clear as any demonstration in *Mathematicks*. 'Tis only needful that we understand them, for our consent to the truth of them.[33]

That is precisely why Dryden argues that the fundamental rules of tragedy should always be copied from the ancients: for these are the rules of reason and the rules of nature—"those things only excepted," he goes on, "which religion, customs of countries, idioms of language, etc., have altered in the superstructures." It is these superstructures that provide us with what Dryden had earlier called "a just and lively image of human nature, representing its passions and humours, and the changes of fortune to which it is subject; for the delight and instruction of mankind."[34] Kaminsky's summary of Hegel's view is again revealing here: "The artistic experience, Hegel will argue, however, is not divorced from its temporal and environmental setting. The Idea . . . is the force that permeates all living things and makes them evolve spiritually as well as physically. Each successive age produces a little more consciousness of how the Idea manifests itself in spirit and in nature."[35] The "lively image" of which Dryden spoke is thus also achieved through a knowledge of law; modern tragedy, he says as an example, is superior to that of antiquity because "natural causes are more known now," and therefore the order of tragedy can better "fulfill that law" that is fundamental both to thinking and to the world. This idea is perhaps not so very far different from Hegel's later evolutionary concept of art and spirit.

What is absolutely clear, in any case, is that a good deal of the "pleasure" of poetry (of literary and dramatic art, that is to say), a pleasure so widely and universally asserted as essential to all significant literary activity throughout the neoclassical era, comes precisely from this combination of law and superstructure, brought together and given focus (as we have seen and will soon see further) by a particular concept of "justice." For pleasure is, one might say, as pleasure does. It is certainly the case, as Domna Stanton observed, that in 1668 La Fontaine appears to insist upon the idea that "in France, only what gives pleasure is given consideration; that is the great rule, and, so to speak, the only one." So he writes. But La Fontaine has just that moment completed a distinction between the body and soul of literature, informing his reader that the first is plot (*Fable*), while the second is moral teaching (*la Moralité*), and observing that while the substance of the story as such may fluctuate and change, there is no way of dispensing with the moral or changing its burden. For the moral in question is bound up in all essential ways with the ethical laws of nature of which we will shortly see Dryden speak. And Corneille, too, will invoke assumptions entirely parallel. Such an idea of *moralité* (Dryden's "ethics" and Rymer's or Davenant's "justice") is then a fundamental ingredient of such pleasure.[36]

A similar view is quite clearly that of an equally celebrated contemporary of the fabulist, all too often taken as divorcing the idea of pleasure from those lawful assumptions whose development I have been tracing. Apparently speaking for Molière in the *Critique de l'Ecole des femmes*, played before the king on June 1 1663, Dorante does not hesitate to ask forcefully whether "the great rule of all rules is not that of pleasing?" Again, yes, no doubt. Yet the pleasure he has in mind is no simple-minded hedonist's orgiastic dream of anarchic delight. It relies on the assumption with which Descartes began the *Discours de la méthode*, to the effect that "good sense is the most widely shared capacity in the world." Dorante presupposes that the groundlings ("le parterre") combine "common sense" with a suitably competent knowledge of the most necessary "rules," and of the "good way of judging" according to the ordinary discernment of the sensible theatergoer. Like Descartes, he emphasizes the universality of common sense—but by no means does he confine it to the groundlings. Like so many of his other contemporaries, he emphasizes the reliability of "the Court's judgment," composed as is that place of privilege, he remarks, of a cross section of tasteful courtiers, of "gens savants," of people of "simple good sense" and of that good "conversation" to which we already saw Dryden refer, and all of quite expert judgment. The rules themselves, he concludes, proceed from a "relaxed observation," and from general good sense. They are necessary, although not alone sufficient, since they must needs be allied with modern habit and taste, and contemporary awareness (the exactly equivalent combination in the spectator and reader, one notes, to the law-superstructure combination in the artistic work itself).[37]

The late seventeenth century, therefore, no longer sees the pleasurable and the useful as a paradoxical association of ideas, much less a contradictory one. They have become united as the aesthetic manifestation of political, rational, linguistic, artistic, and natural stability. The associating of fundamental rational law and cultural superstructures, of the permanent stability of methodical reason and the transitory instability of local phenomena, is the double truth whose presence is the privilege of literature and whose perfect expression is the criterion of beauty and the only true source of aesthetic pleasure. This is what Rymer means when he writes that the authors of tragedy "like good Painters must design their Images like the Life, but yet better and more beautiful than the Life"; or Pope when he remarks that great literature "Gives us Nature still, but Nature methodiz'd"; or

Hume when he speaks of "the original structure of the internal fabric"; or Marmontel when he writes that "art does not consist in going against nature, but in improving it, in embellishing it through imitation, in doing better than it, while doing the same as it," and as he more or less paraphrases Dryden's opposition: "nature has only one road, custom has a thousand twisted and broken pathways." Only some thirty years later, Hegel's view will remain very similar: "Art . . . is superior to nature. It tries to indicate the goals at which nature is aiming. In art man tries to succeed where nature often fails."[38]

Fundamentally, this had long since been the distinction made by Corneille in the *Au Lecteur* to *Héraclius* (1647), when he asserted that the concept of verisimilitude is only "a condition necessary to the organization (*disposition*) and not to the choice of subject, nor to the incidents that are supported by the story." Verisimilitude, what Davenant calls "likelyhood" and Rymer refers to as a "general probability," refers entirely to the laws of nature and of common sense. Provided that probability holds at the level of these laws—what Rymer refers to as the "accuracy" of literature, and what Henry Reynolds referred to around 1633 as following "the perfect and strait line" rather than the "oblique one"—then the subject itself may, indeed must (says Corneille), be unlikely—at least in so far as tragedy is concerned, which depicts human affairs and events taken to an extraordinary degree.[39] The clear parallel here is La Fontaine's body-soul distinction.

There is, then, a kind of tension between making sense (a matter of the coherence of law) and imaging the real—between *poiesis* and *mimesis*. As in the case of the epistemological difficulty confronted by Hobbes, this tension is resolved by an appeal to "justice," by a concept of nature as ethical, by the technical term of "poetical justice." The term itself seems to have been used first by Rymer in 1677, but we have already seen its presence, at least implicitly, in Davenant and Hobbes, where the concept of justice as an equilibrium in nature and in human affairs provides the fundamental axiom for the elaboration of a methodical theory of civil society in the one and of an ethical poetry directing the affairs of men in the other. "Poesy," writes

Dryden, "must resemble natural truth, but it must *be* ethical. Indeed the poet dresses truth, and adorns nature, but does not alter them."[40] This ethical truth of the natural order, corresponding to reason and good sense, and allowing the poet not simply to show but indeed to rely upon the justice of superstructural phenomena, is precisely what "poetical justice" is all about.

In *The Spectator* Joseph Addison chose to write an article mocking both the term and the concept. Dennis took up the cudgels immediately, asserting that such objections were quite unreasonable: "For as *Hobbes* has observ'd, that as often as Reason is against a Man, a Man will be against Reason; so as often as the Rules are against an Author, an Author will be against the Rules." In this case the rules are those known by the phrase "poetical justice," and Dennis, saying that he is defending Aristotle as much as he is Rymer, asks the author of the *Spectator* paper whether he cannot see that the

> Doctrine of poetical Justice is not only founded in Reason and Nature, but is itself the Foundation of all Rules, and ev'n of Tragedy itself? For what Tragedy can there be without a Fable? or what Fable without a Moral? or what Moral without poetical Justice? What Moral, where the Good and the Bad are confounded by Destiny, and perish alike promiscuously. Thus we see that this Doctrine of poetical Justice is more founded in Reason and Nature than all the rest of the poetical Rules together.

It is, Addison avers, the "fundamental Rule."[41] Shades, once again, of La Fontaine's remarks on pleasure.

Justice, in this sense, is the fundamental link between the rational order of nature and the natural order of reason; but it is also axiomatic in the well-ordered state, because such a society is necessarily ordered in accordance with the same common sense. All alike concur in the affirmation that literature is aimed at the rational elite that leads such a society: the poet and the critic always address what Addison calls "the politer part" of society. And this "politer part" is really nothing but a generalization of the superiority of the prince and leaders of the government to which I referred earlier, principally through Davenant. These are the qualified readers who will understand that the superiority accorded to great literature is due to its double truth: to the fundamental and universal laws of all things, and to the superstructural realities of particular cultures. When literature achieves a proper expression of this double truth, it attains to beauty.

Already, in 1701, in the preface to his works Boileau links together inextricably such beauty and such truth. A little later, Addison, discussing what constitutes true wit, suggests tentatively (quoting Dryden with some unease) that it may not be so very different from "good writing in general," which, he remarks, would make Euclid the greatest wit of all. But he then goes on with increasing confidence to refer to Bouhours and Boileau:

> Bouhours, whom I look upon to be the most penetrating of all the French critics, has taken pains to show that it is impossible for any thought to be beautiful which is not just, and has not its foundation in the nature of things: that the basis of all wit is truth; and that no thought can be valuable, of which good sense is not the groundwork. Boileau has endeavoured to inculcate the same notion in several parts of his writings, both in prose and verse.[42]

"Beauty is truth, truth beauty," Keats was to muse a century later, uttering essentially the same sentiments. Nor is Hegel's view of aesthetic verity so very different. But Keats could easily have found his idea in Shaftesbury's affirmation that beauty and good are "one and the same," because the beauty and good in question, like Keats's or Addison's truth, refer to that natural ethical harmony that allows Shaftesbury's Philocles to ally "Nature, reason, and humanity," and his Theocles to apostrophize: "O glorious nature! supremely fair and sovereignly good!" One thinks, too, of Leibniz. But in fact Keats's claim is to be found almost verbatim in Shaftesbury (1711). As Dryden, Rymer, Dennis, Boileau, Bouhours, and Rapin all agree, the world is ethical in its essence. Shaftesbury concurs: "the most natural beauty in the world is honesty and moral truth. For all beauty is truth. . . . In poetry, which is all fable, truth still is the perfection."[43]

The perception of this combination is restricted to the polite elite of wits, to the *honnête homme* who alone has access to such literary production. "Taste" is the name given to such perception, and it, too, partakes of the double truth. We saw that when Molière, through Dorante, was speaking of pleasure and the rules, he relied on precisely the spectator's sensitiveness to the combination in question: whether the spectator was of the groundlings or of the court. A century later, confronting similar assumptions, Marmontel can thus admit that there are many different particular tastes, varying according to time, place, and culture, but such tastes are only *correct* when conjoined with the one fundamental taste: "Thus there is only one supreme judge, one judge alone from which, in matters of *taste* there is no appeal: and that is nature." Rational nature, of course.[44]

Writing somewhat earlier than Marmontel, Hume says much the same when he adds to the perception of "the original structure of the internal fabric" those "general observations, concerning what has been universally found to please in all countries and in all ages," and when he asserts that these two are "drawn from established models, and from the observation of what pleases or displeases." Thus the critic who "will be acknowledged by universal sentiment to have a preference among others" is he who can judge at once by particular "experience" and by the universal "models and principles." We recall Hobbes's combination of geometrical law and Galilean mathematical experimentalism as it was found, for example, in Davenant or Rapin. The judgment of truth and beauty takes into account general rational law, "the different humors of particular men," and "the particular manners and opinions of our age and country."[45] Once again, the underlay of Rapin and Dryden, of Bouhours and Dennis, is clear enough, not to mention its apparent culmination fifty years after Hume in Hegel. But the Scottish philosopher, like the others, also insists upon the *necessary* nature of the ethical dimension of the general law. Beauty, truth, and justice are one, and the ability so to see them is also essential to the true critic, who must also realize that the laws ruling their association provide the regularities of all moral human action (and therefore, potentially, the science of such action):

And with what pretense could we employ our *criticism* upon any poet or polite author, if we could not pronounce the conduct and sentiments of his actors either natural or unnatural to such characters, and in such circumstances? It seems almost impossible, therefore, to engage in science or action of any kind without acknowledging the doctrine of necessity, and this *inference* from motions to voluntary actions, from characters to conduct.[46]

As so often, these last lines are immediately reminiscent of Hobbes's argument relating to the founding fiat of civil society as Leviathan, to the idea of contract as founded in some kind of natural justice.

The combination of a concept of universal rational law and one of natural justice as the foundation both of that law and of all right action leads, then, to a concept of ethical necessity following the same kind of laws (if not the very same ones) as direct physical or material causal relations. In the same way, and as a direct consequence of *the very same set of arguments*, the aesthetic pleasure provoked by beauty in poetry (and its "truthful" double relation to an "ethical" nature) is therefore *essentially* rational (and, as such, may be opposed to the "sublime," which is, rather, irrational).[47] I started out with the political writers of the religious wars and with Hobbes. Perhaps I may conclude with Locke, the philosopher of the Glorious Revolution and of Whig liberalism.

Hume, as we have seen, calls for a taste capable of picking out the necessary laws of truth and beauty. Forty years earlier, thinking of the intimate connection between the nature of things and right thinking (not to mention correct writing), Addison had called for the critic's acquaintance with the great poets of antiquity and, perhaps recalling Euclid, for his possession of a "clear and logical head." Perhaps also recalling Rymer's comment to a similar effect, Addison goes on to say that "Aristotle, who was the best critic, was also one of the best logicians that ever appeared in the world." Logic, control of the right use of language, and knowledge of nature and of the affairs of humanity are the essence of the great critic as they are also of the great writer of literature:

Mr Locke's *Essay on Human Understanding* would be thought a very odd book for man to make himself master of, who would get a reputation by critical writings; though at the same time it is very certain, that an author who has not learned the art of distinguishing between words and things, and of ranging his thoughts, and setting them in proper lights, whatever notions he may have will lose himself in confusion and obscurity. I might further observe, that there is not a Greek or Latin critic who has not shown, even in the style of his criticisms, that he was master of all the elegance and delicacy of his native tongue.

"The truth of it is," he adds with obvious zest, "there is nothing more absurd, than for a man to set up for a critic, without a good insight into all the parts of learning." The true critic knows the standard of taste and the real beauties of a written work, as well as its coherence with natural, rational law and the exactness of its correspondent image of superstructural phenomena, for he possesses "a relish for polite learning."[48] And the completeness of such learning provides access to the double truth and to the pleasure derived from its perception.

We have come a long way indeed from the concern with the instability of the state and the concomitant confusion of language from which I set out on these tortuous pathways. A fundamentally *political* preoccupation has led to the establishment of a new epistemology based on a concept of natural reason, of methodical common sense; it has produced an acceptable (if distinctly complex) claim for the objective referentiality of language, of discourse, of thinking, and it has produced the liberal concept of "possessive individualism," making possible the forging of a new idea of civil society. Within this conjuncture literature has been created, with a very particular and privileged role of leadership to perform. Addison's linking of the author of the *Two Treatises of Government* to the ideal of the true critic of such literature is therefore a fitting conclusion, one not in the least fortuitous. The modern meaning of the word "literature" is not timeless: it is attached to a particular political order, whose ideology it comes to express. By and large it remains our own.

And with that, I was going to conclude; but in view of the preceding efforts to show how what was forged in the seventeenth century remained largely unbent and entirely unbroken certainly into the nineteenth century, I cannot forbear adding one further comment about the extent to which this literary ideology is still our own. Hegel, whom I have been increasingly mentioning, presents his concept of Idea as the underlying rational law of all phenomenal events: Idea, he argues, is what art gets at. But only during a specifiable stage of human development, for when humanity becomes sufficiently developed, then art itself is replaced by philosophy, which tells formally what art can only show performatively, "as in a mirror, darkly." Indeed, like Saint Paul, Hegel presents his philosophy as a passage to clarity and ultimately complete knowledge—complete knowledge of Idea, which is the underlying oneness of the state as it is of reason and of nature—uniting all three. Art, or literature (including drama) as the fullest form of art, is the penultimate stage in achieving such knowledge.

When Marx erases the Hegelian Idea and replaces its epistemological function with that of concrete relations of economic production as the true infrastructure, he has qualitatively changed the relation of Dryden's, Hume's, or Hegel's model to the superstructure: the model is no longer a fixed model, law, or rational idea. It is an ongoing and self-transforming process. This cannot but change the whole concept of what art and all other human activities are all about. I would submit that it has not yet done so, not even (if we stick with matters of art for the present) in the case of so-called Marxist critics. We still emphasize either the nomothetic value of the text (viewed nowadays as a self-realizing rhetorical impulse) or the moral, didactic, or conceptual significance of the literary artifact—the only difference being that we now tend to see them as opposed, rather than complementary, aspects. I would suggest that, with this development, the mirror has become even darker, if indeed it has not cracked from side to side.

Contributors

Juan-Bautista Avalle-Arce is Kenan Professor of Spanish at the University of North Carolina. He has published extensively on Cervantes. His latest book is *Dintorno de una época dorada*.

Michel Beaujour is Professor of French at New York University. His most recent study of French Renaissance literature is *Miroirs d'Encre*.

Kevin Brownlee, Assistant Professor of French and Italian at Dartmouth College, is currently working on a study of the *Roman de la Rose*. His book, *The Dynamics of First-Person Discourse in the Late Middle Ages: Guillaume de Machaut and His Self-Presentation as Poet*, is now in press.

Marina Scordilis Brownlee is Assistant Professor of Spanish and Portuguese at Dartmouth College. She has published *The Poetics of Literary Theory: Lope de Vega's Novelas a Marcia Leonarda and Their Cervantine Context*. She is now finishing a book on the *Libro de Buen Amor*.

Terence Cave is a Fellow and Tutor in Modern Languages, St. John's College, Oxford. His study of imitation theory in the Renaissance, *The Cornucopian Text*, has received wide acclaim.

Thomas M. Greene is Professor of English and Comparative Literature at Yale University. His books include *The Descent from Heaven*, *Rabelais: A Study in Comic Courage*, and *The Light from Troy*.

Robert Hollander, Professor of Comparative Literature at Princeton University and President of the Dante Society of America, is the author of numerous widely respected studies of Dante. His most recent work, *Il Virgilio Dantesco* is in press. He is now preparing a study of Dante and Boccaccio. He has been Montgomery Visiting Professor at Dartmouth.

Murray Krieger is University Professor of the University of California. The most recent of his books is *Theory of Criticism: A Tradition and Its System*. He is a Fellow of the School of Criticism and Theory, which he founded in 1975 and directed until 1981.

Contributors

John D. Lyons, Professor of French and Italian and Chair of Comparative Literature at Dartmouth College, writes frequently on Madame de Lafayette. His most recent book is *The Listening Voice: An Essay on the Rhetoric of Saint-Amant*.

Stephen G. Nichols, Jr., is Chair of French and Italian and Professor of Comparative Literature at Dartmouth College. His most recent book is *Romanesque Signs: Early Medieval Narrative and Iconography*.

Timothy J. Reiss is Professor of Comparative Literature at the University of Montreal. He is the author of two influential studies of seventeenth-century French tragedy. His latest book is *The Discourse of Modernism*.

Eugene Vance is Professor of Comparative Literature at the University of Montreal. He has written widely on Saint Augustine and is the author of *Reading the Song of Roland*. He has recently completed a book on sign theory and poetics in the Middle Ages.

Nancy J. Vickers, Associate Professor of French and Italian at Dartmouth College, has recently completed a book on the Renaissance *blasons du corps féminin*. She is currently at work on a study of Dante and Petrarch.

Notes

Introduction

1. Erich Auerbach, *Mimesis: The Representation of Reality in Western Literature*, trans. Willard Trask (Princeton: Princeton University Press, 1971), p. 6.
2. René Wellek, *Concepts of Criticism*, ed. Stephen C. Nichols, Jr. (New Haven: Yale University Press, 1963), p. 351.
3. Ibid., p. 351.
4. *Mimesis*, p. 102.
5. Ernst Robert Curtius, *European Literature and The Latin Middle Ages*, trans. Willard Trask (New York: Pantheon Books, 1961), p. 15.
6. Ibid., p. 15.

Saint Augustine: Language as Temporality

1. For a general assessment of Augustine's place in Western sign theory, see Marcia L. Colish, *The Mirror of Language* (New Haven: Yale University Press, 1968), pp. 8–81; also pp. 342–48.
2. For a rich appreciation of Humanist doctrines of language see Marjorie O'Rourke Boyle, *Erasmus on Language and Method in Theology* (Toronto: University of Toronto Press, 1977).
3. Augustine's theories of time have been criticized by logicians, for example, Hugh M. Lacey, "Empiricism and Augustine's Problems about Time," *Review of Metaphysics*, 22 (1968), pp. 219–45; reprinted in *Augustine, A Collection of Critical Essays*, ed. R. A. Markus (New York: Doubleday, 1972), pp. 280–308. This same volume contains two excellent essays on Augustinian sign theory: R. A. Markus, "St. Augustine on Signs," pp. 61–91, and B. Darrell Jackson, "The Theory of Signs in St. Augustine's *De doctrina christiana*," pp. 93–147.
4. St. Augustine, *The Confessions* 11. xxvii.35. References to the Latin text are to the Skutella edition as published by A. Solignac, *Les confessions* (Paris: Désclée de Brouwer, 1962), Bibliothèque augustinienne, 2 vols.; English translations are by John K. Ryan, *The Confessions of St. Augustine* (New York: Doubleday, 1960). Further references to this work will be cited in the text as *Conf.*
5. Let us recall Augustine's definition of "sign": "A sign is a thing which causes us to think of something beyond the impression the thing itself makes upon the senses." *De doctrina christiana* 2.i.1, trans. D. W. Robertson, Jr., *On Christian Doctrine* (New York: Bobbs Merrill, 1958), p. 34, henceforth cited in the text as *DDC*.
6. Cf. Jean Jolivet, *Arts du langage et théologie chez Abélard* (Paris: Vrin, 1969), pp. 14–15.
7. Augustine, *De trinitate* 4. xxi. 30; English translation my own, based on the Latin of the Benedictine edition as translated into French by M. Mellet, O.P., and Thomas Camelot, O.P., *La trinité* (Paris: Desclée de Brouwer, 1955).

8. Lucretius, *De rerum natura*, ed. Martin Ferguson Smith, trans. W. H. D. Rouse (Cambridge: Harvard University Press, 1975), Loeb Classical Library, 2, p. 216 ff.

9. Plato, *Cratylus*, trans. B. Jowett (New York: Random House, 1937), p. 173.

10. R. H. Robins, *Ancient and Medieval Grammatical Theory in Europe with Particular Reference to Modern Linguistic Doctrine* (London: G. Nell and Sons, 1951), ch. 1.

11. Gerda Eilata, "'Seeing Voices': Lisibility and Visibility in the Tora," unpublished paper presented at a colloquium, "Lisibilité/Visibilité," organized by Claude Gandelman, Ben Gurion University, April 30, 1981.

12. *De Genesi ad litteram* I. ix. 15, ed. P. Agaësse, S.J., and J. Moingt, S.J., in *Oeuvres de Saint Augustin* (Paris: Desclée de Brouwer, 1972), p. 48–49.

13. Augustine, *Commentary on Psalm* 76, in *Oeuvres complètes de de Saint Augustin*, trans. M. Raulx (Bar-le-duc: Louis Guérin, 1871), vol. 9, p. 213. English translation my own. Further references to this work are abbreviated as *Comm.* and are included in my text.

14. Augustine, *De catechizandis rudibus*, ed. and trans. G. Combès and M. Farges (Paris: Desclée de Brouwer, 1949), in *Oeuvres de Saint Augustin*, vol. 11., hereafter referred to as *De cat.* in my own text.

15. Augustine, *De Musica* 1. ii, ed. and trans. Guy Finnaert, and F. J. Thonnard (Paris: Desclée de Brouwer, 1947), in *Oeuvres de Saint Augustin*, vol. 7.

16. Augustine, *De ordine* 2. vi. 34, ed. and trans. Robert P. Russell (New York: Cosmopolitan Science and Art Service, 1942), p. 139, henceforth referred to as *De ord.* in my text.

17. Augustine, *The City of God* 2. xxi, trans. Marcus Dodds (New York: Random House, 1950), pp. 60–61, hereafter abbreviated as C.D. in my own text.

18. Augustine, *Of True Religion* xxi. 41, trans. Louis O. Mink (South Bend: Regnery/Gateway, 1959), pp. 37–38, henceforth referred to as *De vera rel.* in my text.

Romanesque Imitation or Imitating the Romans

1. "Je vous ai quelquefois parlé d'architecture romane. C'est un mot de ma façon qui me paraît heureusement inventé pour remplacer les mots insignifiants de *saxone* et de *normande*. Tout le monde convient que cette architecture lourde et grossière, est l'*opus romanorum* dénaturé ou successivement dégradé par nos rudes ancêtres. Alors aussi, de la langue latine, également estropiée, se faisait cette langue romane dont l'origine et la dégradation ont tant d'analogie avec l'origine et le progrès de l'architecture." F. Gidon, "L'Invention de l'expression *architecture romane* par Gerville (1818)," *Bulletin de la Société des Antiquaires de Normandie* 42 (1934), 285–86.

2. J. D. Lyons, "Subjectivity and Imitation in the *Discours de la Methode*," to appear in *Neophilologus*.

3. Ibid.

4. *An Inquiry into the Origin and Influence of Gothic Architecture* (London: Longman, 1819), p. 76, n. 4.

5. Ibid., p. 80, n. 7.

6. Ibid., p. 6.
7. Ibid., p. 82, n. 10.
8. Ibid., p. 50.
9. M. M. Davy, *Initiation à la symbolique romane* (XIIe siècle) (Paris: Flammarion, 1977), p. 17. Cf. also p. 21: "Le latin est la langue universelle, il véhicule les idées indépendamment de leur origine et assure l'unité de l'Europe. On le retrouve dans la poésie, les chroniques, l'hagiographie, la liturgie. Le français sourit dans les chansons. Au XIIe siècle, le goût de l'antiquité est incomparable."
10. M. F. Hearn, *Romanesque Sculpture: The Revival of Monumental Stone Sculpture in the Eleventh and Twelfth Centuries* (Ithaca: Cornell University Press, 1981), pp. 167–68. Cf. also the following statement:

The revival of monumental stone sculpture in Western Europe, begun in the eleventh century and realized in the twelfth, . . . bore some important similarities to the long-lapsed sculptural tradition of Roman Antiquity. As in Imperial Rome, twelfth-century sculpture was grounded in the human figure, often life-size, and it was both plastic and frequently monumental in conception. It was harmoniously related to a setting equally plastic in its articulation, a relationship that obviated any sense of arbitrariness in the composition of the images and guided the viewer's gaze in such a way as to order the significance of the images perceived. Moreover, the sculpture was public in function, giving palpable form to abstract concepts of religion and rulership. (Ibid., p. 17)

11. Terence Cave, *The Cornucopian Text* (Oxford: Clarendon Press, 1979), p. 36.
12. Ibid., p. 29.
13. Ernst G. Grimme, *Der Aachener Domschatz* (Düsseldorf: Verlag L. Schwann, 1973), Catalogue Number 22, pp. 24–28. Grimme includes a bibliography in his notice on the cross.
14. "In der Mitte antiker Kameo mit Bildnes des Kaisers Augustus. . . . Ein karolingischer Siegelschnitt, der am unteren Teil der Kreuzfläche angebracht ist und dem Kreuz seinen Namen gegebenhat, zeigt ein Herrscherbild mit der Umschrift XPE ADIVVA HLOTARIUM REG. Diese Umschrift ist auf Lothar II von Lotharingien (855–869) zu beziehen" (ibid., pp. 24–25).
15. Thomas G. Bergin, *Dante* (New York: The Orion Press, 1965), pp. 24–25.
16. In his book, *Dante and the Idea of Rome* (Oxford: Clarendon Press, 1957), pp. 18–19), Charles Till Davis reminds us that:

The German emperors, who could not claim kinship with the ancient *Romania* on grounds of language or customs, used *Romanus* primarily as a legal term, denoting a life lived under Roman law and imperial authority. But even more inclusive than Justinian's code was another bond which united the peoples that had once belonged to the old Roman world: the Christian faith. Since the Church had her seat in Rome, and western Christendom had spread along the path marked out by older, secular domination, it was natural that the concept of *populus Romanus* should be linked with that of *populus Christianus*. Orosius provided the perfect formulation of this viewpoint when he said:
. . . *ubique patria, ubique ex et religio me est . . . Latitudo orientis, septentrionis copiositas, meridiana diffusio, magnarum insularum largissimae tutissimaeque sedes mei iuris et nominis sunt, quia ad Christianos et Romanos Romanus et Christianus accedo.* [Orosius, *Historiae adversum paganos*, ed. C. Zangemeister, 1882, v, ii, 1, 3]

17. André Grabar, *Christian Iconography: A Study of Its Origins* (Princeton: Princeton University Press, 1980), p. 43.

18. In Book 5 of his *De Divisione Naturae*, Eriugena contrasts the constant motion of humans in the world with the immutable divinity which "moves only immobilely in itself." The relation of Eriugena's philosophy to the Romanesque theophanic portals has been explored by Yves Christe, *Les Grands portails romans: Etudes sur l'iconologie des theophanies romanes* (Geneva: Droz, 1969), and M. F. Hearn, *Romanesque Sculpture*. For a more extensive discussion of the relation of Eriugenean philosophy to Romanesque semiotic systems, see my forthcoming book, *Romanesque Signs: Early Medieval Narrative and Iconography* (New Haven: Yale University Press, 1983). On the importance of Eriugena for the tenth, eleventh, and twelfth centuries, see John Marenbon, *From the Circle of Alcuin to the School of Auxerre: Logic, Theology, and Philosophy in the Early Middle Ages* (Cambridge: University Press, 1981).

19. Gertrud Schiller, *Iconography of Christian Art*, trans. Janet Seligman (Greenwich, Conn.: New York Graphic Society, 1972), 2, p. 5.

20. "The Crucifixion image on the back of the processional cross known as the Cross of Lothar is the earliest known example to include the dove: it stands in the center of the wreath held by the *dextera Domini*. . . . The symbol of the hand of God with the wreath was eliminated during the twelfth century and the image of God the Father with the dove of the Holy Ghost sometimes appears above the Cross" (ibid., 2, p. 108). "On the Cross of Lothar the wreath encircles the dove. This symbol brings a suggestion of the idea of the Trinity into the image of Christ's Death, probably for the first time" (ibid., 2, p. 122).

21. "The dove was added to this delineation of God the Father . . . and it came to represent the Trinity" (ibid., 1, p. 7).

22. Marenbon, *From Alcuin to Auxerre*, Chapters 3 and 4.

23. Brian Stock, "The Philosophical Anthropology of Johannes Scottus Eriugena," *Studi Medievali*, 3rd series, 8 (1967), p. 5. Eriugena derives this concept from Maximus the Confessor:

There is nothing contained in the created universe from the highest to the lowest which is not found in man: therefore he is rightly described as the *officina omnium*, 'the workshop of everything.' Like a well-balanced symphony which is composed of many disparate sounds, man unites in *unam harmoniam* everything which flows from God and which has its origin in him. [Stock, p. 5]

24. "Et his omnibus incomparabiliter altius et mirabilius mihi uidetur quod sancti Dionysii Ariopagitae auctoritate utens asseris, *ipsum uidelicet deum et omnium factorem esse et in omnibus factum*—hoc enim adhuc inauditum et incognitum non solum mihi sed et multis ac paene omnibus. Nam si sic est, quis non confestim erumpat in hanc uocem et proclamet: *Deus itaque omnia est et omnia deus!* . . ." (*De Diuisione Naturae*, III, 10 [MPL 122, 650CD]; *Iohannis Scotti Erivgenae Periphyseon [De Diuisione Naturae], Liber Tertius*, ed. I. P. Sheldon-Williams, with the collaboration of Ludwig Bieler [Dublin: Dublin Institute for Advanced Studies, 1981], p. 98 [Scriptores Latini Hiberniae, 11]). Cf. also: "By theophanies, I mean the aspects of visible and invisible things by whose order and beauty God is known to exist. Through these things we do not discover what He is, but that He alone exists." Ibid., 5, 26 [MPL 122, 919C].

25. Marenbon points out that Eriugena represents a position, vis-à-vis the theory of Universals, that he terms "hyper-realism." This will be important for the question of intersubjective knowledge which we shall discuss later. "There is no difference, [Eriugena] says, between what is *said of a subject* and the subject itself. For example, Cicero, the individual subject, and Man, which is *said of* Cicero and of every other man, are one and the same. The species 'in its numerous members is whole and one in the individual, and these members are one individual in the species' [I, 25, MPL 122, 471A; Sheldon-Williams, I, p. 102, 19–20]. This 'hyper-realism' is made more workable by John's theory of 'analytic' collection and 'diaretic' descent, which preserves a measure of distinction between particulars and Universals, despite their logical identity." *From Alcuin to Auxerre*, pp. 75–76.

26. John the Scot, *Periphyseon, On the Division of Nature*, trans. Myra L. Uhlfelder, with summaries by Jean A. Potter (Indianapolis: Bobbs-Merrill, 1976), p. xxxi.

27. Brian Stock, "*Intelligo me esse*: Eriugena's '*cogito*,'" *Jean Scot et l'histoire de la philosophie* (Paris: Editions du CNRS, 1977), p. 332; *De Divisione Naturae* 4, 9 [MPL 122, 776C].

28. ". . . dialecticae cuius proprietas est rerum omnium quae intelligi possunt naturas diuidere coniungere discernere propriosque locos unicuique distribuere, atque ideo a sapientibus uera rerum contemplatio solet appellari?" (*De Diuisione Naturae* I, 44 [MPL 122, 486B], ed. Sheldon-Williams, *Liber Primus* [Dublin: Dublin Institute for Advanced Studies, 1978], p. 136 [*Scriptores Latini Hiberniae*, 7].

29. *Periphyseon*, trans. Uhlfelder, p. xxxi.

30. Stock, "*Intelligo*," p. 333.

31. Ibid., p. 330.

32. "Nulla natura siue rationalis siue intellectualis est quae ignoret se esse quamuis nesciat quid sit. . . . Dum ergo dico, Intelligo me esse, nonne in hoc uno uerbo quod est Intelligo tria significo a se inseparabilia? nam et me esse, et posse intelligere me esse, et intelligere me esse demonstro. Num uides uno uerbo et meam OYCIAM meamque uirtutem et actionem significari? Non enim intelligerem si non essem neque intelligerem si uirtute intelligentiae carerem nec illa uirtus in me silet sed in operationem intelligendi prorumpit" (*De Diuisione Naturae* I, 48 [MPL 122, 490B], ed. Sheldon-Williams, *Liber Primus*, p. 144. The best discussion of the philosophical implications of Eriugena's *cogito* may be found in Stock's article, "*Intelligo*," quoted above (n. 27). On pages 332–34, Stock takes particular pains to show how Eriugena's *cogito* differs from Augustine's.

33. Stock, "*Intelligo*," p. 330.

34. ". . . actio siquidem diffinitionis ratiocinantis intelligentisque naturae actio est . . . nulla enim natura quae se ipsam non intelligit *esse* aut sui aequalem aut se inferiorem potest diffinire. [Nam quod supra se est quomodo potest cognoscere dum eius notitiam non ualeat superare?] Solius ergo intellectualis naturae quae in homine angeloque constituitur diffinitionis peritia est" *De Divisione Naturae*, I, 43 [MPL 122, 485A], Sheldon-Williams, 1, pp. 132–33).

35. Ibid., 1, 43 [MPL 122, 485B], Sheldon-Williams, 1, pp. 132–34.

36. Ibid., 4, 5–7 [MPL 122, 750C–772B]; Stock, "*Intelligo*," p. 331.

37. "Possumus ergo hominen definire sic: Homo est notio quaedam intellectualis in mente divina aeternaliter facta" (ibid., 4, 7 [MPL 122, 768B]; Stock's translation, "*Intelligo*," p. 331).

38. *De Divisione Naturae*, 4, 7 [MPL 122, 768B–C].

39. "Poenam praevaricationis naturae in hoc manifestari non temere dixerim. Nam si homo non peccaret, in tam profundam sui ignorantiam profecto non caderet; sicut neque ignominiosam generationem ex duplici sexu ad similitudinem irrationabilium animalium non pateretur" (ibid., 4, 9 [MPL 122, 77A–B]; Uhlfelder, p. 251).

40. "Ipse siquidem, qui solus absque peccato natus est in mundo, Redemptor videlicet mundi, nusquam nunquam talem ignorantiam perpessus est, sed confestim, ut conceptus et natus est, et seipsum et omnia intellexit, ac loqui et docere potuit, non solum quia sapientia Patris erat, quam nihil latet, verum etiam quia incontaminatam humanitatem acceperat, ut contaminatam purgaret; non quia aliam accepit praeter eam quam restituit, sed quia ipse solus incontaminatus in ea remansit, et ad medicamentum vulneris vitiatae naturae in secretissimis ipsius rationibus reservatus" (ibid., 4, 9 [MPL 122, 777B–C]; Uhlfelder, p. 251).

41. Stock, "*Intelligo*," p. 332.

42. Ibid., p. 332.

43. Siquidem dum intelligo quod intelligis, intellectus tuus efficior, et ineffabili quodam modo in te factus sum. Similiter quando pure intelligis quod ego plane intelligo, intellectus meus efficeris, ac de duobus intellectibus fit unus, ab eo, quod ambo sincere et incunctanter intelligimus, formatus. Verbi gratia, ut ex numeris exemplum introducamus: senarium numerum suis partibus esse aequalem intelligis; et ego similiter intelligo, et intelligere te intelligo, sicut et me intelligis intelligere. Uterque noster intellectus unus fit senario numero formatus, ac per hoc et ego in te creor, et tu in me crearis" (*De Divisione Naturae*, 4, 9 [MPL 122, 780C]; Stock's translation, "*Intelligo*," p. 332).

44. "In hac autem similiter per decem virgines obviam sponso exeuntes totius humanae numerositatis generalis ad pristinum naturae statum reversio. . . . Species enim humani generis est electorum numerus" (ibid., 5, 38 [MPL 122, 1014D–1015A]; Uhlfelder, p. 350).

45. "Ad quas nemo intromittitur, nisi sapientiae luce refulgens, divinique amoris inflammationibas ardens, quae duo, sapientiam dico et caritatem, pinguedine scientiae et actionis nutriuntur; et ad eas nuptias nullus scientiae et actionis expers, quamvis naturalibus bonis integerrime et pulcherrime floruerit, sinitur ascendere, sed omnino ab eis secluditur. Non enim illuc natura humanam mentem sublevat, sed gratia, et mandatis Dei obedientiae, purissimaeque quantum in hac vita datur, Dei per literam et creaturam cognitionis meritum subvehit" (ibid., 5, 38 [MPL 122, 1014C–D]; Uhlfelder, p. 350).

46. The following passage, *inter alia*, demonstrates the impossibility, within the framework of Romanesque language theory, of a radically subjective "I," a truly Cartesian *cogito*. As this passage illustrates, all assertions of a knowing subject reflect the divine *cogito*: "I" do not speak alone, but rather "It"—the Trinity—speaks through me (*De Diuisione Naturae* 1, 76 [MPL 122, 522B–C]).

And this is the prudent and catholic and salutary profession that is to be predicated of God: that first by the Cataphatic, that is by affirmation, we predicate all things of Him, whether by nouns or by verbs, though not properly but in a metaphorical sense; then we deny by the Apophatic, that is by negation, that He is any of the things which by the Cataphatic are predicated of Him, only (this time) not metaphorically but properly—for there is more truth in saying that God is not any of the things that are predicated of Him than in saying that He is; then, above everything that is predicated of Him, His superessential Nature which creates all things and is not created must be superessentially Morethan-praised. *Therefore that which the Word made Flesh says to His disciples, "It is not you who speak but the Spirit of your Father that speaks in you,"* true reason compels us to believe, and say, and understand in the same way with reference to other like things: *it is not you who love, who see, who move, but the Spirit of the Father, Who speaks in you the truth about Me and My Father and Himself, He it is Who loves Me and sees Me and My Father and Himself in you, and moves Himself in you that you may desire Me and My Father.* If then the Holy Trinity loves and sees and moves Itself in us and in Itself, surely It is loved and seen and moved by Itself after a most excellent mode known to no creature, by which It both loves and sees and moves Itself, and is loved and seen and moved by Itself in Itself and in Its creatures. [*De Diuisione Naturae*, ed. Sheldon-Williams, I, pp. 217, 219]

47. "This process of conversion and the constitution of grace . . . is enacted not only in humanity in general but in every individual who reflects the Trinity in three 'motions' of the soul—intellect, reason, and sense. In the return, sense is absorbed into intellect which is both the first motion of the soul and her perfection, in which once unified she is caught up by the deity in theosis" (I. P. Sheldon-Williams, "Eriugena's Greek Sources," in *The Mind of Eriugena*, ed. J. J. O'Maera and Ludwig Bieler [Dublin: Irish University Press, 1973], p. 12).

48. The example of scripture as the paradigmatic language by which the divinity at once revealed and concealed meaning occurs frequently in Eriugena. The following provides an enlightening example for our inquiry:

The fabric of divine Scripture is intricately woven and entwined with turns and obliquities. The Holy Spirit did not desire to make it so because it grudged our understanding, a possibility about which we should not even think, but because it was eager to exercise our intelligence and to reward hard toil and discovery. [*De Diuisione Naturae* V, 38 (MPL 122, 1010B); Uhlfelder, p. 345]

49. An interesting passage in this respect—but too long to quote here—appears in *De Diuisione Naturae* I, 39 [MPL 122, 481A–483B], ed. Sheldon-Williams, *Liber Primus*, pp. 124–28.

50. I am indebted to Professor Eugene Vance for pointing out the correlation between extrusion/incision and spiritual expression. His appreciative and cogent questions at the Dartmouth Colloquium were most helpful when I revised the paper for publication. I would also like to thank him for inviting me to present it at the Classical and Medieval Foundations of Semiotics Colloquium which he organized under the auspices of the Toronto Semiotic Circle at the Third International Summer Institute for Semiotic and Structural Studies in June 1982.

Reflections in the *Miroër aus Amoreus*

1. All quotations are from the edition of Félix Lecoy (Paris: Champion, 1970–73). The translations are from Charles Dahlberg, *The Romance of the Rose* (Princeton: Princeton University Press, 1971) with selective emendations.

2. "The Lovers' Glass: Nature's Discourse on Optics and the Optical Design of the *Romance of the Rose*," *University of Toronto Quarterly* 46 (1977), 241–62.

3. Cf. in this context the first two books, as opposed to the third, of Andreas Capellanus's *De arte honeste amandi*.

4. I borrow this terminology, with certain modifications, from John D. Lyons, "Subjectivity and Imitation in the *Discours de la Méthode*," *Neophilologus* (forthcoming).

5. As cited in Eric Hicks, *Le Débat sur le "Roman de la Rose"* (Paris: Champion, 1977), p. 110.

6. For Jean's programmatic undoing of the text/gloss opposition, see Nancy Regalado's important article, "'Des contraires choses': La fonction poétique de la citation et des *exempla* dans le *Roman de la Rose* de Jean de Meun," *Littérature* 41 (1981), 62–81 (especially 69–71).

7. Jean thus necessarily includes the only category of female reader addressed by Guillaume, who utilizes a "formule de fabliau" (Paul Zumthor, "Récit et anti-récit: Le *Roman de la Rose*," *Medioevo Romanzo* 1 [1974], 6) to introduce the moral he affixes to the story of Narcissus: "Dames, cest essample aprenez, / qui vers vos amis mesprenes; / car se vos les lessiez morir, / Dex le vos savra bien merir" [1,505–08]). This category of female reader would at the same time (and not without irony) include Guillaume's own beloved, "cele por qui je l'" (= the *Roman de la Rose*) ai empris: / c'est cele qui tant a de pris / et tant est digne d'estre amee / qu'el doit estre Rose clamee" (vv. 41–44). It is of course significant that this kind of singularly privileged addressee no longer functions as a component of Jean's inscribed audience.

8. The same is true of Jean's use of the vocative *dames honorables* (15,185).

9. The irony of the locution *quelque parole* ("a few words [or speeches]") is immediately evident in the context of Jean's systematic use of *amplificatio* throughout his part of the poem.

10. For the importance of the *De periculis* in Faux Semblant's speech see Lecoy, ed., v. 2, pp. 282–90. See also Ernest Langlois, ed., *Roman de la Rose*, notes to 11, 488 ff., and Jean Batany, *Approches du "Roman de la Rose"* (Paris: Bordas, 1973), pp. 99–112.

11. Lecoy, ed., v. 2, p. 297 adduces this passage in the *De periculis* as the subtext for the entire final segment of Jean's apologia, adding that "le développement est, en réalité, un lieu commun."

Autobiography as Self-(Re)presentation

1. Félix Lecoy, *Recherches sur le 'Libro de buen amor' de Juan Ruiz*, ed. A. D. Deyermond (Westmead, England: Gregg International, 1974), especially p. 352 ff.

2. Leo Spitzer, *Lingüística e historia literaria* (Madrid: Gredos, 1955), pp. 103–60, especially 129 ff.; María Rosa Lida, *Two Spanish Masterpieces: The 'Book of Good Love' and 'La Celestina'*, Illinois Studies in Language and Literature 49 (Urbana: University of Illinois Press, 1961), pp. 1–50; Roger M. Walker, "Towards an Interpretation of the *Libro de buen amor*," *Bulletin of Hispanic Studies* 43, 1 (1966), pp. 1–10.

3. Ramón Menéndez Pidal, *Poesía juglaresca y orígenes de las literturas románicas* (Madrid: Instituto de Estudios Políticos, 1957), p. 209; Anthony Zahareas, *The Art of Juan Ruiz Archpriest of Hita* (Madrid: Estudios de Literatura Española, 1965), p. 217.

4. André Michalski, "La parodia hagiográfica y el dualismo eros-thanatos en el *Libro de buen amor*," in *Actas del I Congreso Internacional sobre el Arcipreste de Hita* (Barcelona: S.E.R.E.S.A., 1973), pp. 57–77; Colbert Nepaulsingh, "The Structure of the *Libro de buen amor*," *Neophilologus* 61 (1977), pp. 58–72.

5. Raymond S. Willis, ed. and trans., *Libro de buen amor* (Princeton: Princeton University Press, 1972), p. 10.

6. Pierre Ullman, "Juan Ruiz's Prologue," *Modern Language Notes* 82 (1967), p. 161.

7. Recalling, for example, his reaction upon reading the Holy Scriptures for the first time, Augustine explains: "To me they seemed quite unworthy of comparison with the stately prose of Cicero, because I had too much conceit to accept their simplicity and not enough insight to penetrate their depths" (*Confessions*, trans. R. S. Pine-Coffin (London: Penguin, 1961), p. 60.

8. For a discussion of the paradoxical assumptions at the heart of Augustine's autobiographical enterprise, see Eugene Vance's important articles, "Augustine's *Confessions* and the Grammar of Selfhood," *Genre* VI (1973), pp. 1–28, and "Le moi comme langage: Saint Augustin et l'autobiographie," *Poétique* 14 (1973), pp. 163–78.

9. Book 10, xvi, p. 223.

10. "It was not the pears that my unhappy soul desired. I had plenty of my own, better than those, and I only picked them so that I might steal. For no sooner had I picked them than I threw them away, and tasted nothing in them but my own sin, which I relished" (p. 49).

11. The fact that Juan Ruiz does not see his readers as being reducible to a common denominator is echoed throughout the text by his address to various types of readers within his text. He speaks of *dueñas* (st. 114), the *abogado de rromance* (353), the *clerigo synple* (1154), *amigos* (1632), *varones* (1628), *señores* (1633), and so on. And, as Diego Catalán points out, "En todos estos casos, el autor concibe a su público como escuchando su doctrina y entiéndola según su particular 'seso'" ("'Aunque omne non goste la pera del peral . . . [Sobre la 'sentencia' de Juan Ruiz y la de su 'buen amor')," *Hispanic Review* 38, 5 (November 1970), p. 79.

12. "The Fig Tree and the Laurel: Petrarch's Poetics," *Diacritics* 5 (1975), p. 36.

13. Marcia L. Colish, *The Mirror of Language: A Study in the Medieval Theory of Knowledge* (New Haven: Yale University Press, 1968), p. 28.

14. Books 1, xiii, p. 34 ff., and 2, vii, p. 64 ff.

15. "In combining two of the standard types of medieval erotic literature— the didactic allegory and the *roman*—Juan Ruiz was inevitably led to choose the first person for his narrative." (G. B. Gybbon-Monypenny, "Autobiography in the *Libro de buen amor* in the Light of Some Literary Comparisons," *Bulletin of Hispanic Studies* 34 (1957), p. 67.)

16. Romance is, strictly speaking, self-referential. However, as Northrop

Frye points out, "In every period of history certain ascendant values are accepted and embodied in its literature. Usually this process includes some form of kidnapped romance, that is, romance formulas used to reflect certain ascendent religious or social ideals" (*The Secular Scripture: A Study of the Structure of Romance* [Cambridge: Harvard University Press, 1976], pp. 29–30.)

17. See Colish, *Mirror*, pp. 22–38.

18. Lida, *Two Spanish Masterpieces*, p. 26: "The most salient structural characteristic is the repetition of parallel episodes. The thirteen amorous adventures of the autobiographical novel, very similar to one another in their details and identical in their outcome, each frustrating the poet's desire, illustrate through their repeated failure the didactic thesis which Juan Ruiz explicitly sets forth when he muses on his first defeat."

19. Juan Ruiz begins his four mountain adventures by recalling St. Paul's advice in his *Epistle to the Thessalonians* I, 5: 21, "Omnia autem probate: quod bonum est tenete." Similarly, he ends this sequence with a reference to the *Epistle of St. James* 1: 17, "Omne datum optimum et omne donum perfectum desursum est, descendens a Patre luminum, apud quem non est transmutatio nec vicissitudinis obumbratio." (Sts. 950a and 1043a of the *Libro*)

20. For further discussion, see my note entitled "Permutations of the Narrator-Protagonist: The *Serrana* Episodes of the *Libro de buen amor* in Light of the Doña Endrina Sequence," *Romance Notes* 22, 1 (1981), pp. 98–101.

21. See Gybbon-Monypenny, "Autobiography," p. 69, and his "The Two Versions of the *Libro de buen amor*: The Extent and Nature of the Author's Revision," *Bulletin of Hispanic Studies* 39 (1962), p. 217.

22. The digression on confession (sts. 1128–61) similarly serves to present man (emblematized here by Lord Meatseason) as fundamentally un-self-reflexive, as incapable of internalizing the tenets of his faith, incapable thus of true conversion.

23. Michalski, "Parodia," p. 77.

24. Michalski, p. 66.

25. As Michalski observes, "se trata de una representación alegórica de la guerra que en el alma del Arcipreste se hacen respectivamente la carnalidad y el ascetismo" (p. 66).

26. See also Eduardo Forastieri Braschi, "La descripción de los meses en el *Libro de buen amor*," *Revista de Filología Española* 55 (1982), pp. 213–32.

27. See especially A. D. Deyermond, "The Greeks, the Romans, the Astrologers and the Meaning of the *Libro de buen amor*," *Romance Notes* 10 (1963–64), pp. 88–91.

28. See Brian Dutton, "'Con Dios en buen amor': A Semantic Analysis of the Title of the *Libro de buen amor*," *Bulletin of Hispanic Studies* 43 (1966), pp. 161–76.

29. "It is a very big doctrinal book about a great deal of holiness, but it is a small breviary of fun and jokes (1632a–b). . . . This book was finished, for many evils and wrongs that many men and women do to others with their deceits, and to display to simple people exemplary tales and ingenious verses" (1634b–d).

30. Acutely aware of his innovation, Juan Ruiz juxtaposes his "new book"

(pp. 8, 10) with the traditional, overtly exemplary media of "painting, writing and sculpture [which] were first discovered because man's memory is feeble" (p. 8). Whereas they seek to impose only one interpretation, he acknowledges the failure of this enterprise.

Imitative Distance: Boccaccio and Dante

1. This paper is printed here as it was presented at the colloquium. For a more elaborate consideration of this topic, including a review of previous scholarship, see "Boccaccio's Dante: Imitative Distance," to appear in *Studi sul Boccaccio* 13 (1982). All translations are my own.

Petrarchan Lyric and the Strategies of Description

1. *Rime sparse* 309, 5–8 in *Petrarch's Lyric Poems: The "Rime sparse" and Other Lyrics*, trans. and ed. Robert M. Durling (Cambridge, Mass.: Harvard University Press, 1976), p. 488. All subsequent references to the *Rime sparse* (RS) will be to this edition and translation and will be indicated in the text.

2. Portions of the following appear in my "Diana Described: Scattered Woman and Scattered Rhyme," *Critical Inquiry*, 8 (1981), 265–79.

3. On the notion of describing parts "one by one," see RS 127, 85–91 and RS 273, 6.

4. On this dialectic as fundamental to the *Rime sparse*, see Durling's introduction to *Petrarch's Lyric Poems*, p. 24.

5. See Durling's introduction to *Petrarch's Lyric Poems*; John Freccero, "The Fig Tree and the Laurel: Petrarch's Poetics," *Diacritics*, 5 (Spring 1975); and Giuseppe Mazzotta, "The *Canzoniere* and the Language of the Self," *Studies in Philology*, 75 (1978). The phrase "poetics of fragmentation" is Mazzotta's, p. 274.

6. Cf. Josette Féral, "Antigone or *The Irony of the Tribe*," trans. Alice Jardine and Tom Gora, *Diacritics*, 8 (Fall 1978), 7.

7. By "gothic top-to-toe enumeration" I refer to that descriptive method outlined by Matthieu de Vendôme in his *Ars Versificatoria*, and by Geoffroi de Vinsauf in his *Poetria Nova*, both in Edmond Faral, *Les Arts poétiques du XIIe et du XIIIe siècle* (Paris: E. Champion, 1923). Villon's description of the lost beauties of "La Belle heaulmière" incorporates an excellent example: "Qu'est devenu ce front poly, / Ces cheveulx blonds, sourcilz voultyz, / Grand entr'oeil, le regard joly, / Dont prenoye les plus subtilz; / Ce beau nez droit, grant ne petiz; / Ces petites joinctes oreilles, / Menton fourchu, cler vis traictis / Et ces belles lèvres vermeilles?" In *Oeuvres complètes*, ed. P. Jannet (Paris: Bibliothèque Charpentier, n.d.), p. 107.

8. For lengthy discussion of these qualities of Petrarchan description see Durling, "Petrarch's 'Giovene donna sotto un verde lauro,'" *MLN*, 86 (1971); and Freccero.

9. On Petrarch's role in the popularization of these *topoi*, see James V. Mirollo, "In Praise of 'La Bella mano': Aspects of Late Renaissance Lyricism," *Comparative Literature Studies*, 9 (1972), 31–43; and James Villas, "The Pe-

trarchan Topos 'Bel piede': Generative Footsteps," *Romance Notes*, 11 (1969), 167–73.

10. For examples of the use of these metaphoric codes, see *RS* 71–73.

11. See *RS* 71, 57–60, and *RS* 146, 4–6.

12. Mazzotta, pp. 282–84.

13. Mazzotta, pp. 282–84; see also Durling's introduction to *Petrarch's Lyric Poems*, pp. 31–32.

14. "Some Paradoxes of Description," *Yale French Studies*, No. 61 (1981), p. 44.

15. Beaujour, p. 37.

16. Mazzotta, p. 277.

17. See Leonard Barkan, "Diana and Actaeon: The Myth as Synthesis," *English Literary Renaissance*, 10 (1980), pp. 320–22; and Norman O. Brown, "Metamorphoses II: Actaeon," *American Poetry Review*, 1 (Nov./Dec. 1972), p. 40.

18. See Dennis Dutschke, *Francesco Petrarca: Canzone XXIII from First to Final Version* (Ravenna: Longo, 1977), pp. 196–98.

The Net of Words and the Escape of the Gods

1. See *A Window to Criticism: Shakespeare's Sonnets and Modern Poetics* (Princeton: Princeton University Press, 1964), Parts 2 and 3, and "The Innocent Insinuations of Wit: The Strategy of Language in Shakespeare's *Sonnets*," *The Play and Place of Criticism* (Baltimore: The Johns Hopkins Press, 1967), pp. 19–36.

2. In *Poetic Presence and Illusion* (Baltimore: The Johns Hopkins Press, 1979), pp. 16–17.

3. See *Theory of Criticism: A Tradition and Its System* (Baltimore: The Johns Hopkins Press, 1976), pp. 234–37.

4. I remind the reader also of Ralegh's similar use of "fold" in the concluding line of "Like truthless dreams": "Whom care forewarns, ere age and winter cold, / To haste me hence to find my fortune's fold."

Vulnerabilities of the Humanist Text

1. English translations of passages from the *Adagia* are taken from *The "Adages" of Erasmus*, trans. M. M. Phillips (Cambridge: Cambridge University Press, 1964). The passage quoted above appears on p. 180. Future references will be indicated parenthetically after each quotation. On the one or two occasions where I have not followed Phillips's translation, no parenthetical reference is supplied. Comments by Phillips quoted below are taken from her long introduction to her translations. For the Latin text of the *Festina lente* essay, I have used Erasmus von Rotterdam, *Ausgewählte Schriften*, VII, edited with facing German translation by Theresia Payr (Darmstadt: Wissenschaftliche Buchgesellschaft, 1972). Payr's text follows the Leyden edition of 1703. I have also consulted several editions of the *Adagia* published during Erasmus's lifetime.

2. *Parallels* (*Parabolae sive similia*), trans. R. A. B. Mynors, vol. XXIII of the

Collected Works of Erasmus (Toronto: University of Toronto Press, 1978), p. 131, p. 130.

3. *The Enchiridion of Erasmus*, trans. Raymond Himelick (Bloomington: Indiana University Press, 1963), p. 49, p. 54.

4. "Quid sit paroemia," *Adagiorum Chiliades* (Venice: Aldus Manutius, 1508), p. 1r.

5. This expression is not an adage cited by Erasmus. Its author was one Furius Antias, a Roman poet who appears to have flourished ca. 100 B.C. The phrase happens to be extant because it was quoted by Aulus Gellius (*Attic Nights*, XVIII, 11, 4).

6. Terence Cave, *The Cornucopian Text: Problems of Writing in the French Renaissance* (Oxford: Clarendon Press, 1979), p. 111.

The Mimesis of Reading in the Renaissance

1. I am concerned here primarily with Latin humanism and the French vernacular. An argument similar to mine has already been advanced, with particular reference to Montaigne, by Cathleen M. Bauschatz in her essay "Montaigne's Conception of Reading in the Context of Renaissance Poetics and Modern Criticism," *The Reader in the Text*, ed. Susan R. Suleiman and Inge Crosman (Princeton: Princeton University Press, 1980), pp. 264–91. I should like to take this opportunity to apologize to Professor Bauschatz for failing to read her essay before writing this paper, and for consequently failing to acknowledge her important contribution publicly at the Dartmouth colloquium. Cf. also Michel Charles, *Rhétorique de la lecture* (Paris: Éditions du Seuil, 1977).

2. This example is discussed at greater length in my article "Panurge and Odysseus," to be published in *Myth and Legend in French Literature*, ed. K. R. Apsley, D. M. Bellos, and P. Sharratt (details of publication not yet available). See also Gérard Defaux, "Une rencontre homérique: Panurge noble, pérégrin, et curieux," *French Forum* 6 (1981), pp. 109–22, which corroborates my conclusions with regard to the Homeric paradigm.

3. It is necessary to point out, however, as I failed to do in *The Cornucopian Text*, that Erasmus at many points exploits material derived from his Italian predecessors in the debate. In particular, the notion of "self-expression" occurs in a letter by Politian published before the end of the fifteenth century: see Marc Fumaroli, *L'Âge de l'Éloquence: Rhétorique et "res literaria" de la Renaissance au seuil de l'époque classique* (Geneva: Droz, 1980), pp. 81–83; cf. *The Cornucopian Text: Problems of Writing in the French Renaissance* (Oxford: The Clarendon Press, 1979), pp. 42–43.

4. Antoine Compagnon, *La Seconde Main, ou le travail de la citation* (Paris: Éditions du Seuil, 1979), pp. 235–327; Fumaroli, *L'Âge de l'Éloquence*, especially pp. 464–66.

5. Lino Pertile, "Paper and Ink: the Structure of Unpredictability," in *"O un amy!" Essays on Montaigne in Honor of Donald M. Frame*, ed. Raymond C. La Charité (Lexington, Ky.: French Forum Monographs, 1977), pp. 190–218; Mary B. McKinley, *Words in a Corner: Studies in Montaigne's Latin Quotations*

(Lexington, Ky.: French Forum Monographs, 1981). My remarks on Montaigne in this paper present in condensed form some of the issues covered in my essay "Problems of Reading in the *Essais*," in *Montaigne: Essays in Memory of Richard Sayce*, ed. I. W. F. Maclean and I. D. McFarlane (Oxford: The Clarendon Press, publication expected in 1982).

6. Montaigne, *Œuvres complètes*, ed. Albert Thibaudet and Maurice Rat (Paris: Gallimard, 1962), I.xxxv, p. 220. The page numbers given below for the *Essais* refer to this edition. Translations of all texts are my own.

7. Frederick G. Hodgson, *Pascal's Conversion of Montaigne's "Essais"* (dissertation submitted to the University of California, Santa Barbara, in 1979).

8. Michel Beaujour's *Miroirs d'encre: Rhétorique de l'autoportrait* (Paris: Éditions du Seuil, 1980) has some excellent things to say on this topic.

9. I would not want to suggest, of course, that this *cas-limite* characterizes the whole of Pascal's theory of reading, much of which has a more practical orientation. It remains true that Pascal rejoins Augustine here in exploding that sinfully inflated reader of whom Montaigne has become the paradigm.

10. See Dorothy Gabe Coleman, *The Gallo-Roman Muse: Aspects of Roman Literary Tradition in Sixteenth-Century France* (Cambridge, England: Cambridge University Press, 1979), *passim*.

11. Timothy J. Reiss, *Toward Dramatic Illusion: Theatrical Technique and Meaning from Hardy to "Horace"* (New Haven and London: Yale University Press, 1971); cf. also Reiss's *Tragedy and Truth: Studies in the Development of a Renaissance and Neoclassical Discourse* (New Haven and London: Yale University Press, 1980).

12. Stanley Fish, whose *Self-Consuming Artifacts* (Berkeley: University of California Press, 1972) raises questions similar to those discussed here, would perhaps not agree with me as far as *Pilgrim's Progress* is concerned.

Speaking in Pictures, Speaking of Pictures

1. Leone Battista Alberti, *De pictura*, Book II, section 26. English trans. Cecil Grayson, *On Painting and On Sculpture* (London: Phaidon, 1972), pp. 61–62.

2. Among the works on perspective that I have found useful are Erwin Panofsky, *La Perspective comme "forme symbolique"* (Leipzig, 1927) [French trans. M. Joly (Paris: Minuit, 1975)]; Samuel Y. Edgerton, Jr., *The Renaissance Rediscovery of Linear Perspective* (New York: Basic Books, 1975); Claudio Guillen, "On the Concept and Metaphor of Perspective," in *Comparatists at Work: Studies in Comparative Literature*, ed. S. G. Nichols, Jr., and R. B. Vowles (Waltham, Mass.: 1968) and reprinted in *Literature as System* (Princeton: Princeton University Press, 1971), pp. 283–371; William M. Ivins, Jr., *On the Rationalization of Sight* (New York: The Metropolitan Museum of Art, 1938); Sigfried Giedion, *Space, Time and Architecture* (1941; reprint ed. Cambridge, Mass.: Harvard University Press, 1967); Jean-Louis Schefer, *Scénographie d'un tableau* (Paris: Le Seuil, Coll. "Tel Quel," 1969); and Ernest B. Gilman, *The Curious Perspective* (New Haven: Yale University Press, 1978).

3. Ivins, p. 11.

4. Jurgis Baltrušaitis, *Anamorphic Art*, trans. W. J. Strachan (New York: Harry N. Abrams, 1977). Baltrušaitis suggests numerous historical connections

Notes to pages 168–175   265

between Descartes and the active practitioners and theoreticians of anamorphosis. The Cartesian distinction between resemblance and visual representation is expressed in the treatise *La Dioptrique*, published with the *Discours de la Méthode pour bien conduire sa raison et chercher la vérité dans les sciences* (1637). Descartes notes that

> suivant les règles de la perspective, souvent [les tailles douces] représentent mieux des cercles par des ovales que par d'autres cercles . . . et ainsi de toutes les autres figures: en sorte que souvent, pour être plus parfaites en qualité d'images, et représenter meiux un objet, elles doivent ne lui pas ressembler. Or il faut que nous pensions tout le même des images qui se forment en notre cerveau. [*Oeuvres et lettres* (Pléiade, 1953), p. 204]

5. Rensselaer W. Lee, *Ut Pictura Poesis: The Humanistic Theory of Painting* (New York: Norton, 1967), and D. Dale Cooper, *The Literary Pictorialism of Saint-Amant* (Ph.D. diss., University of Washington, 1973).

6. Marc Fumaroli, *L'Age de l'éloquence: rhétorique et "res literaria" de la Renaissance au seuil de l'époque classique* (Geneva: Droz, 1980), especially p. 677ff. Stephen Orgel's article, "Affecting the Metaphysics," in *Twentieth Century Literature in Retrospect*, ed. Reuben A. Brower (Cambridge, Mass.: Harvard University Press, 1971), pp. 225–45, usefully distinguishes between the twentieth-century conception of images as primarily visual and the Renaissance emphasis on rhetorical use of images to convey nonvisual meaning. Fumaroli's work provides a corrective to Orgel's tendency to assume that the degree of visualization of all rhetorical images was the same.

7. Madeleine V. David, *Le Débat sur les écritures et l'hiéroglyphe aux XVIIe et XVIIIe siècles* (Paris: S.E.V.P.E.N., "Bibliothèque Generale de l'Ecole Pratique des Hautes Etudes, VIe Section, 1965), and Liselotte Dieckmann, *Hieroglyphics: The History of a Literary Symbol* (St. Louis: Washington University Press, 1970).

8. E. Tesauro, *Il Cannochiale Aristotelico* (Turin: 1670; reprint ed. Bad Homburg: Gehlen, 1968).

9. A. Arnauld and P. Nicole, *La Logique ou l'art de penser (1662–1685)*, ed. P. Clair and F. Girbal (Paris: Presses Universitaires de France, 1965). References in the text are to pages in this edition. Translations of this text, and of all other texts quoted hereafter, are my own unless otherwise noted. Except for Latin quotations, all italics are mine.

10. Blaise Pascal, *Pensées*, in *Oeuvres complètes*, ed. Louis Lafuma (Paris: Le Seuil, "L'Intégrale," 1963). References in the text are to the numbers of fragments in this Lafuma edition.

11. Madame de Lafayette, *Romans et Nouvelles*, ed. E. Magne (Paris: Classiques Garnier, 1970).

12. Even if the viewer is also Alphonse, the *agréable* supposes a different function, reception or contemplative enjoyment, on his part.

13. Saint-Amant in *La Solitude* (1620?) celebrates as a *chose agréable* sitting on a cliff and watching a storm at sea in which one can see "Des gens noyez, des Monstres mors, / Des vaisseaux brisez du naufrage, / Des diamans, de l'ambre gris, / Et mille autres choses de pris" (vv. 157–60), *Oeuvres*, ed. J. Bailbé (Paris: Didier, 1971), I, 45.

14. This passage raises a problem that I have not resolved. How does Zayde

read the names that are lettered in a syllabary that is apparently unknown to her?

15. Panofsky, *La Perspective comme forme symbolique*, p. 157.

16. It is worth nothing that in the confession episode of *La Princesse de Clèves* the duke likewise *hears* himself represented within the princess's avowal to her husband that she loves another. In this case as well, the identity of this lover is known only to the two principals and not to the third party (the dauphiness and the husband) within the respective episode.

The *Siège de Metz* is used by the princess largely as if it were a portrait; in contrast to the seascape of *Zayde*, this image of the duke is not described in terms of the relationship of his figure to the rest of the scene. But, as Domna Stanton has suggested to me, the *Siège* serves to present a single aspect of the duke, the "good" military hero and not the mixed character that contains, in the heroine's opinion, the "bad" lover of many women. Thus, unlike a simple portrait, this painting determines or qualifies the "proper noun."

17. *Traité de la connaissance de soi-même*, in *Essais de morale* III (Paris: Desprez, 1723), p. 15, quoted in Louis Marin, *La Critique du discours* (Paris: Minuit, 1975), p. 228.

18. Ibid., p. 21. Also quoted in Marin, *La Critique du discours*. In a passage of Nicole's treatise not quoted by Marin, the anti-Narcissus aspect of the self-image is emphasized: "Qui peut concevoir quel sera le desespoir d'une ame malheureuse, qui après avoir fui toute sa vie de se voir & de se connoître, sera tout d'un coup attachée & colée à cet objet pour toute l'éternité" (p. 41). Having blinded ourselves with the flattering portraits of ourselves, we would be punished by the revelation of our true being. The theme of excessive interest in appearance can thus be turned inside out in the Jansenist use of the metaphor of the image: "il paroît . . . que le monde n'est presque composé que d'aveugles volontaires, qui haïssent & fuient la lumiere, & qui ne travillent à rien davantage qu'à se tromper eux-mêmes, & à s'entretenir dans l'illusion. Où est donc cet amour de la vérité dont on nous flatte?" (p. 30).

19. *La Critique du discours*, p. 226.

20. Baltrušaitis, *Anamorphic Art*, pp. 91–114.

21. Catherine Chevalley de Buzon, in her article "Rationalité de l'anamorphose" (*XVIIe Siècle* XXXI, 3 [1979], pp. 289–96) argues that a viewer's initial reaction to an anamorphic painting is a skeptical one, followed by a moment of optimistic rationalism. Chevalley de Buzon seems entirely correct in her emphasis on the rationality of anamorphosis, but her insistence on initial skepticism fails to take into account the viewer's knowledge that an anamorphic painting is *always* a rationally soluble enigma. Furthermore, her argument that the "skeptical moment" of anamorphosis wakens in the viewer the idea that all is mere illusion fails to take into account that, strictly speaking, the *illusion* is the rational perspective rendering itself. I would argue that all moments of the experience of anamorphic art are characterized by the viewer's consciousness that there is a method that he must acquire in order to understand the phenomenon. This rational method is not incompatible with a *simultaneous* distrust of all that is outside that method. The opposition skepticism/rationality is thus overcome.

22. David, *Le débat sur les écritures*, p. 141, cites a reference in Leibniz to a

catoptric anamorphosis. The further metaphoric importance of perspective in Leibniz is described by H. W. Carr: "In modern phrase we should say that knowledge, of which perception is a mode, is ideal or pictorial; it gives us not the real itself, but a representation of the real. To Leibniz this is the very meaning of individuality because every representation of the universe must be individual. Representation is always from a point of view." *Leibniz* (1929; reprint ed. New York: Dover, 1960), p. 69.

23. Arnauld and Nicole write:

la pureté du langage, le nombre des figures, sont tout au plus dans l'éloquence ce que le coloris est dans la peinture, c'est-à-dire, que ce n'en est que la partie la plus basse & la plus matérielle: mais la principale consiste à concevoir fortement les choses, & à les exprimer en sorte qu'on en porte dans l'esprit des auditeurs une image vive & lumineuse, qui ne présente pas seulement ces choses toutes nues, mais aussi les mouvements avec lesquels on les concoit. [(III, xx), p. 276]

Here again the authors of the *Logic* accentuate the subjective element, the conception of ideas in a mind, as being more worthy of attention than the objective, realistic, or illusionistic representation of the outside world. On the subject of Port-Royal and painting, see Louis Marin, "Philippe de Champaigne et Port-Royal" (1970), in *Etudes sémiologiques* (Paris: Klincksieck, 1971), pp. 127–58.

24. Pascal, who is frequently described as an inductivist, in contrast to Descartes the deductivist, forcefully sets forth the pitfalls of trying to learn from what we see: "Parce, dit on, que vous avez cru . . . dès l'enfance qu'un coffre était vide, lorsque vous n'y voyiez rien, vous avez cru le vide possible. C'est une illusion de vos sens, fortifiée par le coutume, qu'il faut que la science corrige" (*Pensées*, 44). Here *science* is an intellectual activity that corrects the deformations of imagination and perception, for only the enlightened can make proper use of experience. In a similar manner *grace* corrects the spiritual vision of the chosen, for knowledge does not come from the world around us: "Il y a assez de clarté pour éclairer les élus et assez d'obscurité pour les humilier. Il y a assez d'obscurité pour aveugler les réprouvés et assez de clarté pour les condamner et les rendre inexcusables" (*Pensées*, 236).

On the question of inductive knowledge in Lafayette, see my "Narrative, Interpretation and Paradox: *La Princesse de Clèves*," *Romanic Review* LXXII, 4 (November, 1981), pp. 383–400.

The relationship between visualization and induction is treated by Fr. W. J. Ong, who considers the growing emphasis on induction in Renaissance science as part of the visualization of knowledge through "tactics based on 'observation'" ("System, Space, and Intellect in Renaissance Symbolism," in *The Barbarian Within and Other Fugitive Essays and Studies* [New York: Macmillan, 1962], p. 70). Jansenist-Cartesian reservations about induction seem to go hand in hand with a resistance to visualization and thus to be a proof *a contrario* of Ong's description.

Speculum, Method and Self-Portrayal

1. Jean Piaget, "Epistémologie: Nature et méthodes," in *Logique et connaissance scientifique, Encyclopédie de la Pléiade* XXII (1967), p. 11 (my translation).

2. "In *dialectics*, although one system had been known—the Aristotelian—I have divided the system and the practice of it so that individual disciples may make a study of dialectics according to Euclid, Ptolemy, Archimedes, Hippocrates, Galen, and Scotus. In addition I have enlarged upon the classical application of *dilemma*, and, in like manner, of *doctrina crassa*, of the trope, of *amplificatio*; by means of these doctrines very many will strive eagerly to discern the incorporeal form, and separate, as it were, the soul of things from the physical structure; putting thereby experiments in casuistry, which excite amazement, before true scientific knowledge, so that out of a limited field of experience they come to far-reaching conclusions" (*De vita propria*, p. 215).

3. "It is . . . an understanding threefold in nature. First, there is knowledge gained by my senses through the observing of innumerable things. . . . This aspect of my knowledge assumes two questions: What is it? Why is it? In most cases it is sufficient to know what a thing is, because I consider it a misplaced zeal to look into the cause of all these minutiae. Secondly, there is an understanding of higher things obtained through the examination of their beginnings and pursued by conforming to certain principles. This aspect of knowledge is called *proof* because it is derived from the effect based upon the cause. I employ it to pass on to a wider application of the subject under consideration, or to place it in a clearer light, or to give a general application from the particular. However, in this field of understanding I have less rarely arrived at comprehension by a skillful treatment than I have been aided on many occasions by spiritual insight. . . . The third form of my knowledge is that of things intangible and immaterial, and by this I have come wholly as a result of the ministrations of my attendant spirit, through proof in its simplest aspect—that is, a simple statement of its origin, and the fact exists through the most infallible proof." (*De vita propria*, pp. 245–46).

In the context of the *Vita* that describes the physical and temperamental quirks of the author, this idiosyncratic sketch draws attention to an immense gap between those impersonal and universal truths embodied in philosophical *summas* and scientific encyclopedias on the one hand, and on the other, the precarious efforts and mysterious ministrations through which one individual mind achieves a knowledge that is often undistinguishable from crabby opinion or querulous self-affirmation. The self-portrait, as a genre, keeps displaying this difference, which would be erased in an exemplary narrative of progress toward valid method, in other words yielding truth rather than opinion (even attended by "infallible proof" of the visionary kind). Descartes' *Discourse* and *Meditations*, of course, attempt to do away with personal opinion, while retaining the exemplary mode of presentation.

4. Nevertheless, Montaigne's undertaking to know himself might also be seen as a hubristic attempt to achieve divine status. In his *Theologia Platonica*, Ficino wrote: "Propria igitur intelligentia Dei est, ut seipsum intelligat" (II, 9). If God's knowledge is the act of knowing himself, Montaigne's book may be an attempt to go beyond mere self-knowledge, especially in the rather cautionary Delphic sense.

Reality, Realism, Literary Tradition

1. At the end of *The Deceitful Marriage* Cervantes wants to underscore precisely the differences between an Aesopic fable and his own invention, when he has the Licenciado Peralta exclaim: "The times of Maricastaña have come back, when gourds spoke, or those of Aesop, when the cock talked to the fox and other animals to other ones."

2. The same could be said of the Erasmian dialogues, which, as Marcel Bataillon repeatedly demonstrated, in other respects left a deep imprint on the thought of Cervantes.

Power, Poetry, and the Resemblance of Nature

1. See Timothy J. Reiss, "Montaigne et le sujet du politique," to appear.

2. For the larger context of this play, see Reiss, *Tragedy and Truth: Studies in the Development of a Renaissance and Neoclassical Discourse* (New Haven and London: Yale University Press, 1980), pp. 42–49.

3. Roger Ascham, *The Scholemaster*, in *English Works*, ed. William Aldis Wright (1904; reprint ed., Cambridge: Cambridge University Press, 1970), p. 265.

4. The reference to Descartes here is to *Oeuvres philosophiques*, ed. Ferdinand Alquié, 3 vols. (Paris: Garnier, 1963–73), 1, pp. 230–31, henceforth referred to by the initials *OP*. All translations from Descartes and other foreign language texts are my own, as literal as possible. Where italics appear in such texts, they are the author's, not mine. I must beg the reader's indulgence if I refer here again, and later, to writings of my own, but I am trying to provide the theoretical context for what I am discussing here, and such reference seems unavoidable if I am to obtain at least some clarity. Descartes' letter has been discussed at some length, and the Bacon material at even greater, in my *Discourse of Modernism* (Ithaca and London: Cornell University Press, 1982), pp. 279–83, 198–225. On Galileo, see Reiss, "Espaces de la pensée discursive: le cas Galilée et la science classique," *Revue de Synthèse* 85–86 (1977), pp. 5–47.

5. Jean Bodin, *Methodus ad facilem historiarum cognitionem*, in *Oeuvres philosophiques*, ed. Pierre Mesnard (Paris: Presses Universitaires de France, 1951), p. 109. From history, writes Bodin, "we have brought together (*colligimus*) the laws of the ancients, scattered hither and yon, so that we might unite (*conjungamus*) them in this work. And in truth, the best part of universal law (*iuris universi pars optima*) lies hidden in history: and what is of great weight and importance for the best appraisal and evaluation of laws (*ad leges optimè dijudicandas*), the customs of peoples, as well as the beginnings, increase, condition, changes, and end of all commonwealths are derived from it [history]. This forms the chief subject of this method."

6. Descartes, *Discours de la méthode*, in *OP*, 1, p. 581. The earlier reference to the *Olympics* is to *OP*, 1, p. 52.

7. Thomas Hobbes, *Philosophical Rudiments Concerning Government and Society*, in *The English Works* [henceforth *EW*], ed. Sir William Molesworth, 11 vols. (London: Bohn, 1839–45), 2, p. xxiii: "Preface to the Reader." As we

leave Descartes, it is perhaps worth remarking that his attendance at Ferdinand's coronation prefigured other associations. Ferdinand's rival for the empire was Frederick V, Elector Palatine. In 1619 he was elected emperor unilaterally by the Bohemians, who objected to Ferdinand's anti-Protestant stance. Known as the Winter King, because that was the length of his reign, Frederick was defeated at Prague in 1620. This was the winter of Descartes' illumination in Germany, so that as he was writing the *Discours* the instability of the political background could not but be viewed against the intended stability of the method. Especially so, as it concerned persons with whom Descartes was more than simply acquainted: Frederick was married to Elizabeth, eldest daughter of James I of England, from whom he had expected (or at least hoped for) military aid. Frederick was to die in 1632, but two of his sons, Rupert and Maurice, were to fight for their uncle, Charles I, in the English Civil War (Rupert going on to lead his cousin Charles II's navy against the Dutch after the Restoration). His daughter, Sophie, was to become the mother of George I of England, and, during the 1640s, the intermediary in a correspondence between her sister, Elizabeth, and Descartes when that exchange apparently became too risky for direct contact (as Alquié suggests). At Elizabeth's request, and just as ambiguously as in the case of the *morale provisoire*, Descartes sent to her his commentary on Machiavelli's writings (letters of September and October–November 1646, *OP*, 3, pp. 665–71, 680–81). This material is dealt with in my *Poêle et Polis: La Poétique chez Descartes* (to appear).

8. Francis Bacon, *Redargutio philosophiarum*, in *The Works*, ed. James Spedding, Robert Leslie Ellis, and Douglas Denon Heath, 15 vols. (Boston: Taggard and Thompson, 1861–64), 7, pp. 63–64.

9. Denis Diderot, *Recherches philosophiques sur l'origine et la nature du beau*, in *Oeuvres esthétiques*, ed. Paul Vernière (Paris: Garnier, 1965), p. 428. The last passage quoted is from a letter to Mlle. de la Chaux, dated May 1751, cited by Vernière, ibid., p. 388.

10. Samuel Johnson, "Dryden," in *Lives of the Poets: A Selection*, ed. J. P. Hardy (Oxford: Oxford University Press, 1971), p. 162; Dominique Bouhours, *Les Entretiens d'Ariste et d'Eugène* [1671], ed. Ferdinand Brunot (Paris: Colin, 1962), pp. 37, 34; Thomas Sprat, *The History of the Royal-Society of London* [1667], in *Critical Essays of the Seventeenth Century*, ed. J. E. Spingarn, 3 vols. (1908; reprint ed., Oxford: Oxford University Press, 1957), 2, p. 118, henceforth cited as *Spingarn*.

11. And see my "The Environment of Literature and the Imperatives of Criticism," *Europa*, 4, 1 (1981), pp. 29–64.

12. See Reiss, "The *concevoir* Motif in Descartes," in *La Cohérence intérieure. Etudes sur la littérature française du xviie siècle, offertes à J.-D. Hubert*, ed. J. Van Baelen and D. L. Rubin (Paris: Place, 1977), pp. 203–22; and *Discourse of Modernism*, ch. 6. Arguments of the kind I have been rapidly summarizing in the present essay are those that lead to the concept of artificial universal languages. From Dalgarno and Wilkins to Leibniz (where we approach a concept of formal logic), the assumption is, and will remain so for two and a half centuries, that such a language is basically contained *within* natural language, and "merely" needs a kind of purification of syntax and a precise semantics more

exactly correspondent with clear and distinct concepts, in order to be brought into the light of day. Universal languages were supposed to perfect for the scholar and philosopher what the precellence of ordinary language ideally could do for the *honnête homme* and wit.

13. Hobbes, *Rudiments*, in *EW*, 2, p. iv; "Epistle Dedicatory"; and *Six Lessons to the Savilian Professors of the Mathematics*, in *EW*, 7, p. 184.
14. Hobbes, *Rudiments*, in *EW*, 2, p. iii.
15. Hobbes, *Elements of Philosophy. The First Section, Concerning Body*, in *EW*, 1, pp. viii–ix.
16. René Rapin, *Réflexions sur la poétique et sur les ouvrages des poëtes anciens et modernes*, in *Oeuvres*, 2 cols. (Amsterdam: Pierre Mortier, 1709), 2, p. 113.
17. Hyppolite-Jules de La Mesnardière, *La Poétique* (Paris: Anthoine de Sommaville, 1640), p. p.
18. For further discussion of these references, see Reiss, "Du système de la critique classique," *XXIIe Siècle* 116 (1977), pp. 8–9.
19. Bouhours, *Entretiens*, p. 92.
20. Although this relationship between poetry, language, and power will become quite evident in subsequent pages, it is worth quoting here from a later typical, but exemplary, critic, who makes just precisely this equation as it concerns the French:

Your Lordship knows, that it was towards the beginning of the last Century, that the French, a subtle and discerning Nation, began to be sensible of this [overwhelming importance of poetry to the "illustration" of the state and language], and upon it several of their extraordinary Men, both Poets and Philosophers, began to cultivate Criticism. Upon which there follow'd Two very remarkable Things. For, first, the Cultivating of the Poetical Art, advanc'd their Genius's to such a Height as was unknown to *France* before; And, secondly, the appearance of those great Genius's was very instrumental in spreading their Language thro' all the Christian World, and in raising the Esteem of their Nation to that degree, that it naturally prepar'd the Way for their Intrigues of State, and facilitated the Execution of their vast Designs. [John Dennis, *The Advancement and Reformation of Modern Poetry*, 1701, in *The Critical Works*, ed. Edward Niles Hooker, 2 vols. (Baltimore: The Johns Hopkins Press, 1939), 1, p. 203: "The Epistle Dedicatory"]

21. Thomas Sprat, *History*, in *Spingarn*, 2, pp. 112–13; Bernard Lamy, *La Rhetorique ou l'art de parler*, 4th ed. (Paris: Paul Marrey, 1699), p. 1; John Dryden, "Defense of the Epilogue or, An Essay on the Dramatic Poetry of the Last Age," in *Selected Criticism*, ed. James Kinsley and George Parfitt (Oxford: Oxford University Press, 1970), pp. 129–30.
22. Sir William Davenant, "Preface to *Gondibert*," in *Spingarn*, 2, pp. 1–53. Reference to the preface will henceforth be indicated directly in my text by page number preceded by the initials *PG*.
23. Hobbes, *Rudiments*, in *EW*, 2, vi, xvii.
24. John Dennis, "An Essay on the Genius and Writings of Shakespeare (1712)," in *The Critical Works*, 2, pp. 2–3; Jean-François Marmontel, "Essai sur le goût," in *Eléments de littérature*, 3 vols. (Paris: Firmin Didot, 1865), 2, p. 16.
25. Rapin, *Réflexions*, 2, p. 122; Thomas Rymer, *A Short View of Tragedy; Its Original Excellency, and Corruption. With Some Reflections on Shakespeare, and Other Practitioners for the Stage* (1962), in *The Critical Works*, ed. Curt A. Zimansky (New Haven: Yale University Press, 1956), p. 95.

26. Hobbes, *Rudiments*, in *EW*, 2, ii, xv.
27. Jack Kaminsky, *Hegel on Art: An Interpretation of Hegel's Aesthetics* (1962; reprint ed., Albany: State University of New York Press, 1970), p. 33. The reference is to G. W. F. Hegel, *Philosophy of Fine Art*, trans. F. P. B. Osmaston (London: G. Bell and Sons, 1920), 1, p. 263.
28. Rymer, "The Preface of the Translator" [to Rapin's *Reflections on Aristotle's Treatise of Poesie* . . .] (1674), in *Critical Works*, p. 7.
29. Hegel, *Philosophy of Fine Art*, 1, p. 290; Rapin, *Réflexions*, 2, p. 117. Later on Hegel will accentuate yet further this superiority. As Kaminsky paraphrases and cites him:

Poetry, Hegel declared, is capable of unfolding all the conditions of an event, a succession or interchange of emotional states, passions, conceptions, and the exclusive course of human action with more completeness than any other art. Thus poetry, alone among the arts, can give an explicit image of mind and intelligence in action. . . . Its task is artfully to transform images so that the quality of the Idea is best revealed. [Kaminsky, *Hegel on Art*, p. 131; Hegel, *Philosophy of Fine Art*, 4, p. 5].

30. Thomas Sprat, as quoted in Richard Foster Jones, *Ancients and Moderns: A Study of the Rise of the Scientific Movement in Seventeenth-Century England*, 2nd ed. (St. Louis: Washington University Press, 1961), p. 233.
31. Kaminsky, *Hegel on Art*, p. 23.
32. Rapin, *Réflexions*, 2, pp. 113, 126–27; Dennis, *The Impartial Critick: Or Some Observations Upon a Late Book, Entituled, A Short View of Tragedy, Written by Mr. Rymer*, in *Critical Works*, 1, 39.
33. Rymer, "Preface," in *Critical Works*, pp. 2–3.
34. Dryden, *An Essay of Dramatic Poesy* (1668); "The Grounds of Criticism in Tragedy," in *Selected Criticism*, pp. 25, 165.
35. Kaminsky, *Hegel on Art*, p. 29.
36. Jean de la Fontaine, *Fables choisies, mises en vers*, ed. Ferdinand Gohin, 2 vols. (Paris: Belles Lettres, 1934), 1, p. 12.
37. J. B. P. de Molière, *La Critique de l'Ecole de Femmes*, in *Théâtre complet*, ed. Robert Jouanny, 2 vols. (Paris: Garnier, 1962), 1, pp. 494–95, 504–07.
38. Kaminsky, *Hegel on Tragedy*, p. 31; Marmontel, "Essai sur le goût," in *Eléments*, 1, 7, 18; David Hume, "Of the Standard of Taste," in *Of the Standard of Taste and Other Essays*, ed. John W. Lenz (Indianapolis and New York: Bobbs-Merrill, 1965), p. 9; Alexander Pope, *Essay on Criticism*, 1, line 89; Rymer, *The Tragedies of the Last Age Consider'd and Examin'd by the Practice of the Ancients, and by the Common Sense of All Ages, in a Letter to Fleetwood Shepheard, Esq.*, in *Critical Works*, p. 32.
39. Pierre Corneille, "Discours de la tragédie" (1660) and the "Au lecteur" before *Héraclius* (1647), in *Oeuvres complètes*, ed. André Stegmann (Paris: Seuil, 1963), pp. 840, 440; Henry Reynolds, "Preface to *Mythomystes*," in *Spingarn*, 1, p. 149; Rymer, *Tragedies of the Last Age*, in *Critical Works*, p. 23; Davenant, *PG*, p. 2. The comment on *Héraclius* was provoked chiefly by Terence Cave's acceptance at face value of Corneille's remark that people might think the idea here expressed to be a paradox. My reading of the entire epistemic context clearly suggests that, not only is the duality "vraisemblance/invraisemblance" non paradoxical, but that it is in fact strictly in accord with theory. I

refer here to Cave's fine article, "Recognition and the Reader," in *Comparative Criticism: A Yearbook*, vol. 2, ed. E. S. Shaffer (Cambridge: Cambridge University Press, 1980), pp. 49–69; on this matter, see especially pp. 58–62.

40. Dryden, "A Defense of an Essay of Dramatic Poesy" (1668), in *Selected Criticism*, p. 85. A few of these comments and references are drawn from my *Tragedy and Truth*, pp. 6–9, where there is a parallel discussion.

41. Dennis, "To the Spectator, Upon His Paper on the 16th of April 1711" (1712), in *Critical Works*, 2, pp. 18–20.

42. Joseph Addison, *Critical Essays from the Spectator, with Four Essays by Richard Steele*, ed. Donald F. Bond (Oxford: Oxford University Press, 1970), p. 19.

43. Anthony Ashley Cooper, 3rd Earl of Shaftesbury, *Characteristics of Men, Manners, Opinions, Times*, ed. John M. Robertson, 2 vols. (Indianapolis and New York: Bobbs-Merrill, 1964), 2, pp. 128, 37, 98.

44. Marmontel, "Essai sur le goût." The best general discussion of the *honnête homme*, his own self-creation, his place in society and literature, as well as his concept of literature and art, is Domna C. Stanton's *The Aristocrat as Art: A Study of the "Honnête Homme" and the "Dandy" in Seventeenth- and Nineteenth-Century French Literature* (New York: Columbia University Press, 1980). It confirms many of the arguments I have made here, although not without differences. See especially pp. 200–11, 217–24.

45. Hume, "Standard of Taste," pp. 7, 9, 11, 18, 12, 19.

46. Hume, *Enquiries Concerning Human Understanding and Concerning the Principles of Morals*, ed. L. A. Selby-Bigges, 2nd ed. (Oxford: Clarendon Press, 1902), p. 90.

47. One could argue that the concept of the sublime, a naming of the celebrated *je ne sais quoi*, is a kind of reaction to the idea of rational beauty whose elaboration I have been following here—as though the creation of such a system "threw out" as irrational what it could not contain by "explanation," while at the same time seeking to retain it as an essential component of literary specificity—hence both its naming and the assertions of its inexplicability. However, the elaboration of a science of aesthetics during the eighteenth century may well be interpreted as an attempt to explain that inexplicable "sublime" in terms usually psychological. Hegel, of course, will explain it as specific to those great works of literary art where free individuals are placed in fundamentally critical situations and can reveal to the spectator (or reader) the meaning of ideal activity—or rather of activity in the presence of Idea (Sophocles' *Antigone* being exemplary of antiquity, Shakespeare's tragedies of the modern era).

48. Addison, *Critical Essays*, p. 82.

Index

Adage, 12, 133, 135, 140, 141, 147, 154
Adagia (Erasmus), 11–12, 132–48, 156
Addison, Joseph, 242–43, 245
Alberti, L. B., 166–67
Allegory, 13, 149, 151, 153, 160, 164
Anamorphosis, 168, 185
Architecture, 36, 38
Archpriest of Hita. See Ruiz, Juan
Aristotle, 17, 193–94
Arnauld, Antoine, 14–15, 168–69, 174, 179–84, 186, 228
Ascham, Roger, 220
Auerbach, Erich, 2, 251
Autobiography, 71–82, 203–6, 210–11, 214
Avalle-Arce, Juan Bautista, 16, 197–213

Bacon, Francis, 17, 195, 219, 221
Beaujour, Michel, 15, 104, 188–96
Bible, 5, 213
Boccaccio, Niccolò, 8, 83–99
Bodin, Jean, 223
Boileau, Nicolas, 243
Book of Good Love (Juan Ruiz), 7–8, 71–82, 259, 260–61
Bouhours, Dominique, 224–25, 228, 243
Brownlee, Kevin, 6–7, 60–70
Brownlee, Marina Scordilis, 7–8, 71–82

Cardano, Girolamo, 188–96
Cave, Terence, 11–14, 141, 145, 147, 149–65
Cervantes, Miguel de, 16, 197–214
Cicero, 29–30
Colish, Marcia, 75
Commedia (Dante), 83–99, 216–17, 253
Compagnon, Antoine, 155–56
Concepts of Criticism (René Wellek), 251
Confessions (Saint Augustine), 20–27, 33–35, 71–82
Corneille, Pierre, 239, 241
Cratylism, 25
Cross of Lothar, 40–59
Curtius, Ernst Robert, 2–3, 251

Dante, 7, 8, 43, 83–99, 216–17, 253
Davenant, Sir William, 230–37, 242
Davy, M. M., 39
De vita propria (Cardano), 188–96
Decameron (Boccaccio), 83–99
Dennis, John, 233, 242
Derrida, Jacques, 11, 139, 141, 147
Descartes, René, 17, 50–51, 167, 179, 188–96, 221–23, 240, 267, 269–70
Dissemination, 138, 141, 143, 145, 147
Don Quixote (Cervantes, Miguel de) 197–98, 205–10, 213–14
Dryden, John, 229, 239, 241–42

Eberle, Patricia, 61
Ecphrasis, 161–62
Enargeia, 161–62, 168
Encyclopedia, concept of, 159, 163
Epicurus, 24
Erasmus, 11–12, 132–48, 150, 152, 156–57, 263
Eriugena, Scottus, 6, 48–54, 56, 254–55
Essais (Montaigne), 154–59, 161, 188–96

Foucault, Michel, 3
Freccero, John, 74–75
Fumaroli, Marc, 156

Galileo, 221, 226–27
Gerville, Charles de, 36
Giotto, 95–97
Gloss: in humanists, 151, 156; in Jean de Meun, 258n; in Juan Ruiz, 75, 77, 80; in scholastics, 13–14
Greene, Thomas M., 11–12, 132–48
Greville, Fulke, 120
Gunn, William, 37–38

Hearn, M. F., 39
Hegel, G. W. F., 229, 236, 238–39, 247
Hieroglyphic: in Erasmus, 11, 133–34, 136–37, 141; in seventeenth century, 168, 184

History, 45, 47–48, 57, 59, 137, 142–47
Hobbes, Thomas, 223, 225–27, 231, 235, 242
Hollander, Robert, 8–9, 83–99
Horace, 68, 70
Humanism, 17, 20, 90, 220; of Erasmus, 11–12, 132, 134–35, 137–39, 142, 144–46, 148–50; and reading, 155, 160–61, 163
Hume, David, 241, 244

Imitation, 1, 6, 16, 36–59, 61, 76–77, 81, 162

Jansenism, 14–15, 168, 179–85, 266
Jewish thought, 25
Johnson, Dr., 225
Jonson, Ben, 114, 124–25

Krieger, Murray, 10, 110–31

La Fontaine, Jean de, 239
La Mesnardière, J. H. de, 227
Lafayette, Madame de, 14–15, 166–87
Language, 2, 5, 10, 145, 270–71; in Jansenist thought, 180–84; mental, 29; poetic, 64–65, 70, 110–31, 188–96, 224; Saint Augustine and, 20–35; spoken, 27; Stoic theories of, 25, 256
Literature, 1–3, 6–7, 19, 74, 164–65
Locke, John, 245
Lorris, Guillaume de, 60–70, 153
Lucretius, 24
Lyons, John D., 14–15, 166–87

Mann, Thomas, 92
Marcellinus, Ammianus, 43
Marmontel, Jean François, 241, 244
Marx, Karl, 247
Mazzotta, Giuseppe, 104
Metamorphoses (Ovid), 105–8
Method, 15–17, 188–96
Meun, Jean de, 6–7, 60–70
Michalski, André, 78–79
Mimesis: definitions of, 1–4, 18–19; in Humanism, 132, 142–43; of reader, 61, 70; representation of reality, 1–4, 18–19, 55–57, 73, 81, 95–97, 162; romanesque art and, 37, 39–40, 55–57
Mimesis: The Representation of Reality in Western Literature (Erich Auerbach), 2, 251

Molière, 239, 244
Montaigne, Michel de, 13–15, 154–59, 161, 188–96
Music, 32–33

Navarre, Marguerite de, 152
Neoclassicism, 14, 17, 40
Neoplatonism, 6, 12, 48, 150–51
Nichols, Stephen G., 5–6, 36–59
Nominalism, 149, 155, 164
Novel, 16, 170–84, 197–213
Novelas ejemplares (Cervantes), 197–213
Novella, 83–99

Ockham, 219
Ovid, 10, 105–8

Painting, 14–15, 95–97, 166–87; anamorphic, 167, 266
Pantagruel (Rabelais), 153
Pascal, Blaise, 14, 159–60, 167, 169, 186, 267
Perspective, 157, 166–67, 169, 177, 267
Petrarch, 9–10, 100–109
Piaget, Jean, 189
Picaresque, 16, 197–213
Plato, 25
Platonism, 25
Poetry: in Augustine, 29–32; in Boccaccio, 88, 97; in English Renaissance, 10, 110–31; in Jean de Meun, 7, 64–65, 68; in Juan Ruiz, 75; language of, 64–65, 70, 110–31, 188–96, 224; in neoclassicism, 229, 232, 234–36, 241, 271n; in Petrarch, 100–131
Port-Royal Logic (Arnauld), 14–15, 168–69, 174, 179–84, 186, 228
Protestant, 151
Proverb, 133, 135, 146
Psychoanalysis, 147–48

Quotation, 152, 156–57

Rabelais, François, 153–54
Ralegh, Walter, 111–12, 115, 127
Rapin, René, 234, 236, 238
Reader, 16, 54–55, 58; in Hegel, 273; Humanist, 146; inscribed, 12, 60–70, 73, 81; in Renaissance, 14, 149–65; in *Roman de la Rose*, 60–70, 258n
Reading, 7, 10, 12–13, 18, 149, 152–53; act of, 13; theory of, 72, 75–76, 78
Reference, humanist, 144

Reiss, Timothy J., 14, 16–18, 215–47
Renaissance, 6, 10, 40, 177, 219; English poetry of, 110–31; reading in, 13–16, 149–65; science in, 188–96; view of history in, 144–45
Reynolds, Henry, 241
Rhetoric: in Boccaccio, 92–93; Christian, 74; in medieval art, 47; in Renaissance, 15, 150–51, 157, 160–61, 188–96, 256
Rime sparse (Petrarch), 100–109
Roman de la Rose (Jean de Meun), 60–70, 105, 153
Romanesque, 5–6, 36–59
Ruiz, Juan, 7–8, 71–82, 259, 260–61; self-presentation in, 71–82
Rymer, Thomas, 241–42

Saint Augustine, 42, 50, 150, 169, 215–17, 219, 259; definition of sign, 251; language in, 4–5, 20–35; Ruiz, Juan, and, 7–8, 71–82; self-presentation in, 71–82; theories of time in, 20–35, 251
Sallust, 65, 70
Scholasticism, 12–13, 149
Self-portrait, 15, 188–96, 268

Self-presentation, 62, 69, 71–82
Self-referentiality, 48, 141, 259
Shaftesbury, Anthony Ashley Cooper, 3rd earl of, 243
Shakespeare, 112
Sidney, Sir Philip, 116–20
Socrates, 25
Speculum, 15, 76–77, 81, 162–63, 188–96
Sprat, Thomas, 230, 237
Stock, Brian, 51–52, 54
Subject, 10, 159, 163; as painter or viewer, 166

Temporality. *See* Time
Text, 76
Theory, political, 215
Time, 20–35, 145

Vance, Eugene, 4–5, 10–35
Vickers, Nancy J., 9–10, 100–109
Virgil, 98
Voluntarism, 72

Weinberg, Kurt, 178
Wellek, René, 251

LIBRARY OF DAVIDSON COLLEGE